What Color Is Your Parachute?
for Retirement

Planning Now
for the Life You Want

by Richard N. Bolles
and John E. Nelson

TEN SPEED PRESS
Berkeley | Toronto

Copyright © 2007 by Richard N. Bolles and John E. Nelson

Ten Speed Press
P.O. Box 7123
Berkeley, California 94707
www.tenspeed.com

Distributed in Australia by Simon and Schuster Australia, in Canada by Ten Speed Press Canada, in New Zealand by Southern Publishers Group, in South Africa by Real Books, and in the United Kingdom and Europe by Publishers Group UK.

Cover design by Betsy Stromberg
Text design by Linda Davis, Star Type, Berkeley
Illustration composition by Mona Meisami

Library of Congress Cataloging-in-Publication Data

Bolles, Richard Nelson.
   What color is your parachute? for retirement : planning now for the life you want / by Richard N. Bolles and John E. Nelson.
        p. cm.
   Includes index.
   ISBN-13: 978-1-58008-711-7
   ISBN-10: 1-58008-711-6
      1. Retirement income—Planning. 2. Retirement—Planning.
      I. Nelson, John E. II. Title.
HG179.B575 2007
332.024'014—dc22
2007006542

Printed in the United States of America
First printing, 2007

1 2 3 4 5 6 7 8 9 10 — 11 10 09 08 07

To my family.

*This book would not have come into existence
without your love and support.
May it help you in your journeys through the boxes of life.*

—John E. Nelson

Contents

Chapter 6. Discover Your Retirement Strengths 125

Fun is only the beginning: the Three Levels of Retirement Happiness. Discover your strengths and use them for flow and engagement. The difference between strengths, skills, and traits. Who are you to be so happy?

Chapter 7. Who's in Your Social Circle? 155

There is no Automatic Relationship Generator in retirement. Building supportive social networks, in advance. The Three Levels of Relationship Happiness. Your marriage on steroids.

Chapter 8. Where in the World Will You Retire? 173

Retirement increases freedom of place. Exploring the four layers of retirement geography. What's a community? Six ways to use your home. Finding your sense of place for retirement.

Chapter 9. Your Health Is a Matter of Life and Death 203

The difference between biology and medicine, conventional and alternative. The Retirement Medicine Cycle. What's your medical philosophy? Creating your dream body for retirement.

Chapter 10. Retirement Calling! 233

Assembling the picture of your Ideal Retirement. What's beyond Well-Being? Bringing your retirement vision back into the everyday world. Don't wait— live the life of your dreams now.

Preface

This book is part of what we call *The Parachute Library*. Like all books in that Library, it is not intended as a substitute or replacement for its best-selling centerpiece, *What Color Is Your Parachute? A Practical Guide for Job-Hunters and Career-Changers* (nine million copies in print), but as a supplement to it.

Why do we need a supplement? Well, each *time* of Life has special issues and special challenges, where we all could use a little extra guidance. The *time* of Life from age fifty, on, is one of those times. I have a friend named John Nelson, who is an expert on that *time* of Life, and therefore I have asked him to write this book.

My contribution to this book is twofold: (1) To frame some of the questions and challenges during this period, as I have done in my earlier work *The Three Boxes of Life, and How to Get Out of Them: an introduction to life/work planning* (1978). (2) To write this introduction and overview, to get us going.

The *time* of Life that we are talking about here is traditionally called "Retirement." Some people love that word. I'm not one of them. For me, it implies "being put out to pasture"—to borrow an image from a cow. It implies a kind of parole from a thing called *work*, which is assumed to be onerous, and tedious. It implies "disengagement" from both *work* and *Life*, as one patiently—or impatiently—waits to die. It thinks of Life in terms of work.

I prefer instead to think of Life in terms of music. My favorite metaphor is that of a symphony. A symphony, traditionally, has four parts to it—four movements, as they're called. So does Life. There is infancy, then the time of learning, then the time of working, and finally, this time that we are talking about, often called "retirement." But if we discourage the use of the word "retirement," then this might better be called the Fourth Movement.

The Fourth Movement, in the symphonic world, is a kind of blank slate. It was and is up to the composer to decide what to write upon it. Traditionally, the composer writes of triumph, victory, and joy—as in Beethoven's Symphony #3, *the Eroica*. But it may, alternatively, be a kind of anticlimactic, meandering piece of music—as in Tchaikovsky's Symphony #6, *the Pathetique*. There the Third Movement ends with a bombastic, stirring march. The Fourth Movement, immediately following, is subdued, meditative, meandering, and sounds almost like an afterthought.

Well, there are our choices about our own lives: shall the Fourth Movement, the final movement, of our lives be *pathetique* or *eroica*—pathetic or heroic? Your call!

I like this defining of our lives in terms of music, rather than in terms of work.

To carry the metaphor onward, in this Fourth Movement of our lives, we have instruments, which we must treat with care. They are: our **body**, our **mind**, our **spirit**, and what we poetically speak of as our **heart,** which Chinese medicine calls "the Emperor."[1] Body, mind, spirit, heart. Some of these instruments are in shiny, splendid condition. Others are slightly dented. Or greatly dented. But these are the instruments that play the musical notes and themes of this time of our lives.

The traditional notes are: **sleep, water, eating, faith, love, loneliness, survival** (financial and spiritual), **health care, dreams** (fulfilled or unfulfilled), and **triumph**—over all adversities—and even **death.**

Traditionally, the themes for this period of our lives also include **planning.** But I believe the outstanding characteristic of the Fourth Movement in our lives is the increased number of things we call *unexpected.* And that can knock all our plans into a cocked hat. So I prefer to say that one of the notes we strike, is how to handle **interruptions.** Martin Luther King, Jr., perhaps put it best, just before his death:

1. www.itmonline.org/5organs/heart.htm.

"The major problem of life is learning how to handle the costly interruptions—the door that slams shut, the plan that got side-tracked, the marriage that failed, or that lovely poem that didn't get written because someone knocked on the door."

Interruptions, in music, are the pauses between the notes; they are, in fact, what keep the notes from just becoming a jumble. Just listen to the first few bars of Beethoven's Fifth. Thank God for the interruptions, the spaces between the notes.

So, where have we come thus far? Well, I suggested that it is useful to think of Life after fifty as the Fourth Movement in the symphony of our lives—the movement that comes after the first three: Infancy, then The Time of Learning, and then The Time of Working. And it is useful to think that we have instruments, which play certain themes in this movement, as we have seen. That brings us to the $64,000 question: "Toward what end? What is the point of all these notes, all these themes, in the Fourth Movement? What are they intended to produce?"

Ahhh, when I think of the overall impression left with me after I hear the Fourth Movement of any great symphony, such as Schubert's Ninth, one impression sticks out, above all others. And that impression is one of *energy*. I am left with an impression of great energy. And the more the better, say I. Energy is lovely to behold, and even lovelier to possess. That energy belongs in the Fourth Movement because it brings the whole symphony to triumphant resolution.

This, it seems to me, is how people evaluate the Fourth Movement of our lives, as well. Not: did we live triumphantly and die victoriously; but: do we manifest *energy*? Do we manifest enthusiasm? Do we manifest excitement, still?

Ask any employer what they are looking for, when they interview a job candidate who is fifty years or older, and they will tell you: energy. They ask themselves, "Does the candidate (*that's us*) slouch in the chair? Does the candidate look like they're just marking time in Life? Or does the candidate lean slightly forward in the chair as we talk? Does the candidate seem excited about the prospect of working here?"

Energy in people past fifty is exciting to an employer. And to those around us. It suggests the candidate will come in early, and stay late. It suggests that whatever task is given, the task will be done thoroughly and completely, and not just barely or perfunctorily.

All right, then, *energy*. Where shall we find energy, after fifty? When we were young, energy resided in the physical side of our nature. We were "feeling our oats." We could go all day, and go all night. "My, where do you get all your energy," our grandmother would ask us. We were a dynamo of physical energy.

Can't say the same when we reach fifty, and beyond. Oh, some of us still have it. But as we get older the rest of us start to slow down. Physical energy is often harder to come by, despite workouts and exercise and marathons. Increasingly, our energy must more and more come from *within*. It must spring not from our muscles but from our excitement about Life and about what we are doing in this Fourth and final Movement of our Life.

That is why, past fifty, we need to spend more time on the homework of inventorying what in Life we are (still) passionate about. The questions of our youth—**what** *are your favorite skills?* **where** *do you most enjoy using them? and* **how** *do you find such a place and such a job or endeavor?*—become critical when we are past fifty.[2] The nicest compliment any of us can hear as we grow older, is: "What a passion for life she still has! Or, he has! It's thrilling to be around them."

And so, it is time to turn to the body of this book. All of the *frame* that John Nelson proposes, for our looking at this time of our Life, all the *questions* he suggests we must ask ourselves, and all of the *inventory* that he suggests we should do, are essential to finding our *energy* in this Fourth and final Movement of the symphony of our Life. Come with me, as we enter the main body of the book. And we shall make beautiful music, together.

—Richard N. Bolles

2. Detailed instructions for getting at these questions can be found in my book *What Color Is Your Parachute?*, updated annually, and available in any bookstore.

What to Expect from This Book

You may be wondering, *What kind of a retirement planning book is this, exactly?*

That's not easy to answer, because this is a *singular kind* of retirement book. I'm not aware of anything else quite like it. It's not a finance book (although it is about prosperity). It's not a medical book (although it is about health). And it's not a psychology book (although it is about happiness).

You might think of this book as a kind of *retirement buffet,* because it serves up a wide variety of dishes, all in one place. When you're in the mood for steak and only steak, you'll probably go to a steakhouse. But when you want to *cover all the possibilities,* across the board, a buffet is the place to go. This book is like that.

This book may also seem like a seminar. On the one hand, it could serve as an *introductory* seminar, because it doesn't require you to know anything whatsoever in advance; it could be *Retirement Planning 101.* On the other hand, it could be an *advanced* seminar, like the capstone for finishing a certificate or a degree. It helps you take the knowledge you already have from different parts of retirement planning and make connections for *a greater, more integrated understanding*. Because this book can be used as either an introduction or a capstone, it's useful for people at all career stages. Whether you're just starting your career or already retired, you'll find something useful in these pages.

Now, which of those analogies makes more sense to *you*? That's what really counts. The only meaning of this book that really matters is the one *created by you* as you read it. Dick Bolles may be my coauthor, but you, dear reader, are my *cocreator*.

If you're going to take this cocreator job seriously (and I hope that you do), please feel free to write in this book (assuming, of course, that it's your personal copy). For many readers, this is a great way to cocreate meaning with a book. I hereby give you permission to *write all over this one!*

I'll admit, it's still not easy for me to do that. In kindergarten they taught me to show respect for a book by never writing in it, and old habits die hard. If you feel the same way, it's perfectly OK to make photocopies of all the fill-in-the-blank exercises and write on those. But please—be sure to write on *something*.

If permission to write in a book fills you with glee, why not start right now? *Write your name in the front*. After that, just keep a pencil or pen handy whenever you pick up this book. Even before you complete the exercises (most chapters have at least one), *start underlining things* that catch your fancy as you read, and *jot your own thoughts* in the margins. As you personalize this book with your connections and inspirations, you'll make the content more relevant to *you*, and you'll more strongly create the vision of your Ideal Retirement.

Of course, your greatest cocreator role will be doing the actual exercises, whether in the book or on copies. And I hope you scribble all over them.

—John E. Nelson

"I know that someday I will die,
but I will never retire."
—Margaret Mead

CHAPTER ONE

Will You Ever Retire?

W hy are you reading a book about retirement?

Perhaps retirement is a long way off for you, but you're looking ahead, way down the road, and just beginning to imagine what your life might be like. Or perhaps you're far enough along that you're making some general plans and also starting to prepare—because, after all, some retirement preparations take many years. Then again, perhaps for you retirement is just around the corner, and you're making specific plans and wondering if you'll really be ready. Or it could be you've already retired and are planning for all of those years or decades that still stretch out before you.

Whichever of these stages you're in—early career, midcareer, late career, or already retired—you're already at a crossroads. You have a life-changing decision to make: Will you create the retirement that you really want, or will you take the one that just shows up?

If you decide to create the one you really want, the first thing you should know is that retirement is changing. Most of the ideas we've inherited are just plain out-of-date. They're based on the original idea of retirement rather than the way you'll probably want to live your life. Retirement is going to be quite different for you from the way it was for your parents or grandparents.

Traditionally, retirement planning was mostly about financial planning. Don't get me wrong—financial planning is still very, very, important. In fact, *having enough money is essential*. But other things—like nurturing your health—have become important too, because you're probably going to live for a very long time. With today's medical technology, a longer life span is almost a certainty—but a longer *health span* is not. How can you increase your chances of being healthy and vital as you age?

These days, too, you can ask yourself practical questions, in advance, about what will really make you happy in retirement. Financial security helps protect against unhappiness but doesn't directly lead to happiness. If you don't want to leave your happiness to chance, you can design a retirement that makes meaning and fulfillment more likely, too.

So whereas the traditional concept of retirement planning was primarily about money, a more realistic approach now also gives equal weight to health and happiness. You can actually make plans for all three. When you prepare for *prosperity*, *health*, and *happiness*, you're on the road to *Retirement Well-Being*. After all, you wouldn't want to just settle for prosperity when you can have all three!

Retirement planning is changing in another way, too. Our parents and grandparents were mostly focused on how to retire *from something*—their job. For you, though, retirement planning can focus on retiring *to something*—your next stage of life. So much has changed, and will continue to change, that the first step in planning is to let go of any old-fashioned restrictions on what retirement should or shouldn't be. For you, retirement can be anything you want it to be. However, to *make it into what you really want*, you need to *figure out what that is and how to go about getting it*. That's where this book comes in.

Consider this your personal guidebook to creating a complete picture of your own Retirement Well-Being. In each chapter, you'll find information and exercises that will help you fill in a part of that picture. Each chapter focuses on one or two of the key elements of retirement that you should know about, drawn from one of six scientific fields of knowledge:

- Prosperity is at the intersection of finance and geography.
- Health is supported by biology and medicine.
- Happiness is built on the foundation of psychology and sociology.

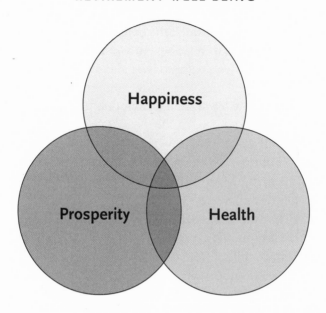

You'll learn more about these six fields in chapter 3. For now, you need to know that as you apply these key elements in each area of your life, the picture of the retirement that you really want will become clear.

You will also be exploring two more areas beyond those six fields. One is at the center of the six fields, because it's at the center of your life: based on your values, it's your preferred *Ways to Live* (see chapter 4). Seeing all of these elements on your One Piece of Paper will help you get a sense of your calling, or life purpose (see chapter 10). A *Retirement Calling* can be a very powerful thing, because you may have more freedom to pursue your calling in retirement than at any other time.

The other area is *not* connected to the six fields. It's what I call *Retirement Hogwash*—a polite term for the persuasive messages that the retirement industry marketers use to lure you into buying their version of retirement. Once you know how to deconstruct these messages (see chapter 4), you'll see that most of what they're selling is not necessarily what you need for your Retirement Well-Being. Only by cutting through, and rising above, these messages can you get to your true self and discover what you want your retirement to be.

As you make your way through the book, gathering your responses to these seven areas, you'll create a picture of your Ideal Retirement— a map for the life that you want to live, and a vision for where your *journey to retirement* will take you. (Never underestimate the power of a positive vision.) Now let's take a look at that journey.

The Journey to Retirement

For most of human history, across many different cultures, life has been thought of as a journey. You set out on the journey of life, following its twists and turns, heading—you hope—in the right direction. You may join in with a group of fellow travelers, trusting that there's safety in numbers. You assume that everyone else knows the way, and they must know where they're headed, and if you just follow the group, you'll arrive at wherever it is that you're supposed to go. There's a path going that way, and it's well-worn from so many travelers, so it's easy to spot.

That type of journey—the safety-in-numbers journey—seems to be the secure path. It's the one most people take. But in reality it's a risky path. Just because it's the path that most people take doesn't necessarily mean that it's *your* path. Even though it's well-worn, you may not like the journey, or the destination either. Here's the unfortunate truth: right now, in Western society, *the well-worn path leads to an outdated, old-fashioned approach to retirement.*

There is, however, another journey you can take: *your own journey.* When you decide to take your own journey, you may need to leave the well-worn path, parting company with some of your fellow travelers. Instead of following the group, you choose your own destination, plan how to get there, and decide what preparations to make.

Taking your own journey may at first seem like a riskier path to take. It isn't the well-worn, safety-in-numbers path that others are taking. *It's an adventure.* But in truth, it's also the safer path. When you follow your own path, it's your own journey and your own destination. Instead of following in the footsteps of the group, you've got your eyes wide open, with a clear view way down the road. Right now, in Western society, this may be the only way to get the retirement that you really want.

When you choose your own path to retirement, you take responsibility for your life's journey. When you heed the *call to adventure*, you feel, in a way, as though you're leaving the conventional world behind and entering a new and different world. You're likely to face tests and challenges along your path, and it's not always easy. You aren't completely alone, though—you'll get advice and support from helpers and companions along the way. And when you choose your own destination and follow through with plans and preparations, you know that you're taking your own authentic journey. You live the life that you're meant to live, rather than the one that just happened to show up. Indeed, for many of us, retirement offers the greatest opportunity we'll ever have to follow our own path and find our own freedom. The journey to retirement can literally be the journey to freedom.

When you're creating your own journey to retirement, this book can be your guide at every point along the way:

- **Early Career.** If it's still early in your career, you may simply want to get a general sense of direction toward your retirement destination. (Are you headed in the right direction and taking some beginning steps?)

- **Midcareer.** If you're further along, in the middle of your career, you can use this guide to get a clearer picture, in more detail, and to check up on your progress. (Do you now know where you want to go and how to get there?)

- **Late Career.** If you're in the later part of your career, well along on your journey, this guide will help you get a crystal-clear, detailed view of your retirement. (Can you see the definite outlines of your destination, and are your preparations almost complete?)

- **Retirement.** If you've arrived at your destination and you're already retired, this book can be a guide for exploring the landscape in a new way—or even to help you select another destination. (Does your retirement look as good from up close as it did from far away?)

Of course, being *on the journey* can be just as important as arriving at the destination. In embarking on your own journey, you have a chance to learn about the world—and learn about yourself, too. When you're following your own path, along the way you grow and develop and *become more authentically yourself.*

How Retirement Was Created

Once upon a time, retirement didn't even exist, at least not the way we think of it today. Most people worked for themselves, as farmers, or fishers, or craftspeople, or traders. They pretty much kept working into their later years, but at a slower pace, relying less and less on their physical strength and stamina—and more and more on their acquired knowledge and skills—as they aged. If they were clever and fortunate, they found ways to do more of the work that they liked (and less of the work that they didn't). But most people couldn't afford to stop working in any case, and so they kept on, as best they could, as long as they needed to. Except in the case of sickness or an accident, withdrawing from work was a *gradual process.* It was a natural transition, and it was like that for thousands of years. Although aging has always been a part of the human life course, retirement has not.

So what happened?

The Industrial Revolution happened, and many of the people who had worked the land or pursued their own cottage crafts went to work in factories for someone else (or rather, for some*thing* else—that new entity that came to be the corporation). In factories, everything became *standardized.* All the machines were in rows. All the nuts and bolts were in standard sizes. All the jobs were standardized, too, so people with the same jobs did the same things in the same way. All the people worked in shifts—each shift's workers starting at the same time, taking a break at the same time, and quitting at the same time.

The work in factories was fast, demanding, standardized. People had always worked hard, but not in such a structured, mechanistic way. As workers aged, they couldn't gradually slow down or focus more on using their knowledge and skills. After all, factories were organized around efficient production, not around the natural life

The One Best Way to Retire?

In the early days of the twentieth century, the Industrial Revolution was getting up to full speed in the United States. The industrial workplace was so different from the old agrarian way of life that experts developed whole new ways of thinking about work, the workplace, workers, and productivity.

The most revolutionary thinker of the day was Frederick Winslow Taylor (1856–1915). Think of him as essentially the very first management consultant.

Taylor's seminal ideas were outlined in his book *The Principles of Scientific Management*. One of them was to expand standardization from *things* (like nuts and bolts) to human *behaviors*. His goal was to discover the "One Best Way" to do a job and then make sure every worker did the job in that exact way. This thinking sparked a new profession—the efficiency expert—which ultimately transformed the industrial workplace. More important, this way of thinking spread to construction, the military, the office, and even schools. Peter Drucker, the famous professor of management, wrote at mid-century that "Taylorism" could be the most important, lasting contribution that the United States had made to Western thought since the Federalist Papers. Taylor's impact was international as well: a translation of *The Principles of Scientific Management* sold one and a half million copies in Japan.

Taylor gave serious attention to the matching of people and jobs—something of a counterpoint to the early vocational guidance movement. We don't know what he might have thought about retirement, as he died at the age of fifty-nine in 1915. However, Taylorism did propel a broad movement toward standardizing human workplace behavior. And it's logical to see the standardized approach to retirement—the One Best Way to retire—as an offspring of that movement. Thus the standard retirement is truly a relic of twentieth-century thinking.

Isn't it time to move on to a twenty-first-century way of thinking about retirement?

course of humans. Workers were seen almost as a part of the machines that they operated. So factory owners decided to get aging workers out of the factory by implementing a new practice: retirement. It was similar to replacing a worn-out part of a machine. After all, with an increasing population, there were plenty of younger, stronger, faster workers ready to fill those jobs.

It was also pretty easy to sell the idea of retirement to workers—especially when it included a retirement pension! Because the Industrial Revolution increased the prosperity of many workers, more and more people could afford to stop working as they got older. As retirement caught on, it fundamentally changed the human life course.

Like everything else in the factory, though, retirement was *standardized*. Everyone was expected to retire at more or less the same age. It didn't matter that one person was as fit as a fiddle and the next one had one foot in the grave. Or that one person loved the work and the next one hated it. None of that was taken into consideration, and for the sake of standardization, retirement was based on age. After all, for employers and employees, age is easy to measure and to specify. How healthy a person is, or how much that person loves the job, may be more relevant to the timing of retirement—but these are also much more difficult to measure.

Nevertheless, the die was cast. This standardized approach to retirement, based on age, meant that instead of the withdrawal from work happening gradually, as it had for most of human history, it became an all-or-nothing deal. When retirement was created, it was created as an *event*—a specific point in time. Before workers reached the retirement event, they went to work full-time, every workday. When they reached the retirement event, they stopped working completely.

This factory-oriented, standardize-everything thinking spread far beyond industrial employers into many other work settings. The idea of a standardized retirement stuck. It stuck with employers, and it stuck with employees. And today, we're still stuck with it. Whether or not it makes sense for employers or employees, in most organizations retirement is still seen as an *event*, and it's still an all-or-nothing deal. (Little by little, that's starting to change. Thank goodness!)

Take a Different Path to Retirement

There's something else that we can sometimes be stuck with. That's the underlying assumption that the employer is in charge of the retirement event. *The employer, remember, gets to make the retirement rules.* The rules may specify that we qualify to receive a certain benefit at a particular age, after so many years of service. (For example, you could be a participant in a pension plan whereby you receive the full benefit at the normal retirement age of sixty-five, with thirty years of service.) But if you accept that the employer is in charge of your retirement event, then you're just following the well-worn path. You're accepting the standardized version of retirement. If you're not careful, that can give you a *countdown mentality* ("Only eleven years, eight months, two weeks, and four days to go—hallelujah!"). A countdown mentality can make you unintentionally put your life on hold! On a more subtle level, it can leave you feeling like you're not in charge of our own retirement. It can make you feel that you need to wait until the normal retirement age to become emancipated—when finally, at last, you'll be set free to do what you really want with your life.

Wait just one darn minute. *Who's retiring who?* It's true that every employer has rules. Usually, lots of them. But just because there's a standard approach to retirement at your organization doesn't mean you have to follow it. At any point in time, if it makes sense for you, you can retire your employer! Yes, you can take charge of your retirement event—but only if you're prepared. (That's what this book is about.) If you decide to retire your *employer*, but you're not ready to retire *yourself*, you'll need to find another job or career. (That's what the original *What Color Is Your Parachute?* is about.)

You can take your own path and make your own plans. You can *de-standardize* your retirement—and instead *customize it to fit the life you want to live.*

Depending on your job and your employer, you may have almost no flexibility in customizing your retirement event, or you may have a great deal. (If you're one of the ever-growing number of the self-employed, or a small business owner, you have carte blanche—so you can get really creative.) In some cases, employers are willing to bend over backwards to accommodate workers, and in other cases they won't bend an inch. If your knowledge or skills are in high demand and low supply, your employer may be eager to entertain your creative ideas about a "flex retirement." But if your employer sees you as just one more cog in the machine and imagines that there are plenty more cogs where you came from, you don't have much bargaining power.

Your flexibility in your job, with your employer, in your industry, is ruled by the particularities of your situation rather than the generalities of the marketplace. You won't know how much you can customize your retirement event—or transition—unless you try. Also, you know best what the culture of your workplace is—and how close to the vest you need to keep your retirement cards. At some organizations, if an employee so much as admits that some day, in the far distant future, he or she might possibly want to retire, the employer will immediately suspect that the worker is starting to slack off and not taking the job seriously. If you know that to be the case at your organization, you don't need me to tell you to be discreet! If, however, your organization is one where you can be up-front about your long-term and short-term plans, that's much better for you and for your employer, too.

Following Your Own Path:
Ten Ways to Customize Your Retirement

If you decide to opt out of the standardized approach to retirement, you can leave the rules and the conventions behind. You get to make your own rules. Or even to create what Carol Anderson, a life planning pioneer, calls a *No Rules Retirement.* For example, you could:

---

1. Change to a career you love, and never retire at all (like Margaret Mead).

2. Start your own business, and never be retired by someone else, because you're the boss.

3. Retire early, because you've made plenty of preparations in advance.

4. Retire early, then start a new career.

5. Renegotiate your job into just what you do well, then retire late because you love it so much.

6. Eliminate the worst parts of your job, then cut back to part-time to do only the best parts.

7. Take a phased retirement, tapering off over months or years.

8. Take a revolving retirement, where you come back for part of each year, or for specific projects.

9. Retire, then work as a consultant under a flexible contract related to your old job, either for your former employer or for a contracting firm.

10. Retire, then go to work for your employer's supplier or customer, or even a competitor.

Note: Look before you leap! Do your research to make sure you optimize the benefits you can receive for when you want to retire. This is a complex area, and although you're the expert on your own life, someone else is probably the expert on your employment contract and your employee benefits. Do yourself a favor and bring those two kinds of expertise together in your planning. If you work for an organization that allows this sort of up-front communication, you can discuss it with your human resources and benefits folks. But if mum's the word, you may need to take all of your information to an outside professional. Either way, unless you happen to be a benefits expert yourself, you need to brainstorm your plans with one!

Retirement Isn't Just an Event—
It's a Stage of Life

Following your own path and customizing your retirement isn't easy. That's because it's not just the employer but society in general that has set up this all-or-nothing approach to work and retirement. Society has more or less divided life into stages. The retirement event has been the doorway from the *life stage* of work into the life stage of retirement. And much earlier, another event—graduation—was the doorway from the life stage of education into the life stage of work. These very definite transitions have divided life into three stages: education, work, and retirement. These stages are so different from one another that you might even think of them as boxes. (For an in-depth exploration of the Three Boxes of Life, see Richard Bolles's book of the same name.) They look like this:

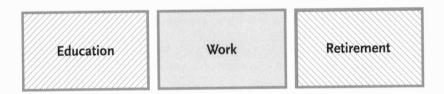

The box of education was created to hold the activities of learning and self-development. The box of work was created to hold the activities of working and being productive. But the retirement box differs from the other two in that it was defined by what retirees *could no longer do*; that is, it was created around the activities of *not learning* and *not working*. This means the contents of the retirement box have been mostly related to *leisure*—the idea being that the retiree was too worn out to either learn anything new or produce anything new.

Society has set things up so that, on your life's journey, you're supposed to first focus mostly on *self-development* (the first box), then mostly on *being productive* (the second box), and finally mostly on *leisure*—that is, on *not* developing and *not* being productive. So the contents of the three boxes look like this:

Development	Productivity	Leisure

One problem with these stages being like boxes is that when we're inside one, it's difficult to see ahead into the next one. When we were in the education box, we knew all about that box—the ground rules, the expectations, and the criteria for success. But we couldn't peek ahead into the next box very well, so we didn't truly know much about work or understand what really goes on there. As a result, when we transitioned from education to work it took us awhile to understand that almost everything was different. We needed to figure out what was happening, how to survive, and how to be effective in that new world. We didn't know it, but most of what we had learned about succeeding in the world of education didn't apply to the world of work. Ouch! Only after some nasty surprises, skinned knees, lessons learned, help from others, and a lot of experimenting did we finally get the hang of it. We learned the new ground rules, expectations, and criteria for success in the world of work. (And, boy, was that ever an education!)

So how about the next transition, the one from work to retirement? That must be a piece of cake. That's a transition from a difficult box into an easy box, right? After all, in the first two boxes, someone else calls the shots. In the third box, *you* call the shots. You get to decide what your retirement is about, don't you?

The answer, of course, is yes. (Aye, and *there's the rub!*)

Although we all have free will, it's also true that when we're in the box of education, our parents, our teachers, and (especially) our peers create an environment that pretty much tells us what we should be doing in that box. We learn not to step out of line. In small ways, we may think we're "doing our own thing." But if we really try to do our own thing—in a well-meaning way—those who are invested in the education box usually straighten us out—in a well-meaning way—or put us back on the well-worn path. After all, there's safety in numbers.

So when it comes down to it, the first box doesn't really allow us all that much freedom. Or maybe it's that we just don't have the ability, yet, to *see* our freedom. One way or the other, though, most of us follow the well-worn path and do what's expected of us.

Likewise, in the box of work, our boss and our coworkers and the Joneses (are we keeping up with them?) are there to keep us in line. We're supposed to keep on the straight and narrow. Again, although we do have free will, the environment pretty much tells us what we should be doing in the second box. But we definitely have a lot more freedom and more choices than we did in the first box—or maybe we just develop a greater ability to *see* our freedom.

Either way, in the second box, many of us begin to consider ways to diverge from the beaten path. For some it may happen little by little, through imagining and carefully executing a plan. For others it may happen all at once, through downsizing, or illness, or the need to relocate. But for still others it may not happen at all, as the responsibilities and opportunities of the second box conspire to keep them on the straight and narrow.

Finally, for the box of retirement, there aren't any parents, or teachers, or bosses, or coworkers to keep us in line. We're left alone, more or less, to do whatever we want. When we're planning our retirement, we're the ones who get to decide what the rest of our life will be about. But unlike the *overabundance* of guidance for the first and second boxes, there's *too little* guidance for the third box in its new twenty-first-century form. That's because (1) the world has changed so much, and (2) most of us don't want an old-fashioned retirement, anyway. So what's the solution?

Time to Break Down the Boxes

When retirement first began and people were retiring from factories or other physically demanding work, they were more or less *worn-out* and in declining health. So retirement was designed around leisure (and *not developing*, and *not being productive*) because that's all most retirees were really up to. A few hardy souls lived to a ripe old age, but most didn't.

Now, however, more and more retirees are living a long time. Instead of retirement lasting a few *years*, it can now last a few *decades*. And not only has the average *life span* gotten longer, but the average *health span* has, too. These days, many people hope to maintain their vitality well into old age, even after they retire, so they can spend the first decade (or two) of retirement in good health. There's a good chance that many of us won't become sick or frail until we reach the far end of retirement. So the third box keeps getting stretched out to contain a greater proportion of the total life span. Only the last part may need to look like the original idea of retirement: a well-deserved rest for people who are worn-out.

Some retirees (who happened to notice that they are *not* worn-out) have realized that dividing life up and making each stage about just one thing doesn't make any sense. So they're doing something revolutionary: mixing everything up together. They're putting ingredients from all three boxes into their retirement. It looks like this:

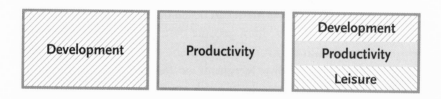

They combine self-development, productivity, and leisure in whatever combination works best for them. This gives them the greatest freedom to create a retirement that brings a greater sense of fulfillment if that's what they want. Unfortunately, in Western society it's still difficult to do this in the other two boxes—at least in a balanced way. For many people, retirement will be the only time when they can really do all three. Because of this opportunity, these ingenious people are making retirement into the highest point of life. Instead of being *over-the-hill*, they're *climbing the summit* of their lives. They recognize that life can be seen as a journey to freedom, that each box represents the opportunity for greater and greater freedom, and that retirement offers the most freedom of all—if we choose to see it as such and prepare for it. It looks like the figure on the next page.

More
Freedom

Should We Even Call It Retirement?

If you decided to put learning and work (instead of just leisure) into your retirement, an interesting thing might happen. You might need less retirement income. After all, full-time leisure may not be cheap! In our consumer culture, in which we're bombarded by seductive pitches that try to convince us happiness can be found only in buying things or paying to be entertained, full-time leisure can be quite expensive. It can take tons of money to fund a retirement that's based on *all leisure all the time.* You could be saving up *forever* to afford such a retirement.

In contrast, self-development can be a *bargain.* Public universities and community colleges often provide courses at nominal cost for retirees. Many faith communities sponsor programs for both self-exploration and socializing. Nonprofit entities like Elderhostel sponsor low-cost opportunities to explore and learn about the world. Senior-level athletic events are also becoming more common. On a more individual level, you're free to explore hobbies or activities that are based on self-development rather than entertainment.

Productivity is even better than a bargain. It can cost as little or as much as you're willing and able to spend, and the result is often *making* money rather than spending money. One form of productivity is paid employment—some of us will need to keep working to make ends meet. If you can afford to, you may choose to be productive as a volunteer, for no pay. And you may even find something in the middle—like a job that pays less than you'd normally accept—so you can do something more important to you than just a paycheck.

For each of us, the right kinds of self-development and productivity can be just as satisfying as leisure—or even more satisfying. Add all this up, and it's easy to see that a retirement based on three types of activities—leisure, self-development, and productivity—may not require as much annual retirement income as the old-fashioned leisure-only retirement did. Could this possibly mean you could start your retirement sooner? Not only would that change what's in the retirement box, but it would make that box *longer* in proportion to the other two, by shortening the work box (which would require more *years* of retirement income). Or you could also say you're overlapping the work and retirement boxes—dissolving the barrier between them. If you decide to take this approach, as some ingenious people have, you will be remaking retirement into something completely new and different. Something that those factory workers (and factory owners) could never have imagined. Good for you!

This revolutionary new approach to retirement has many variations. Because it's so different from the original idea of retirement, some people don't even want to call it retirement. They've come up with new labels to try to articulate what a huge shift it represents. Here are some of the terms that you might see:

- The New Retirement
- Re-Firement
- Re-Wirement
- Rest-of-Life
- The Second Half of Life
- The Third Age
- Unretirement

A change is under way that may be even more momentous than the original retirement spawned by the Industrial Revolution. As more and more people take the new approach—of greatest freedom, mixing it all up, development and productivity and leisure—it will begin to seem *normal*. It will eventually become the well-worn path. People will ask, "Wasn't retirement always about development *and* productivity *and* leisure?" The original idea of retirement as all leisure all the time will have faded away, and this revolutionary new approach won't even need an alternative name. It will come to be called simply *retirement*.

When Can You Start?

If you're thinking this new path to retirement might work for you, then the next question is, when can you start? If you're not going to be "over-the-hill" at any particular age but will still be climbing the summit, then you don't need to retire based on some arbitrary calculation of how many years you've been on earth. After all, *chronological age* is only one way to think about where you are in your life's journey. (Biological age is another way—but we'll get to that in chapter 9.) You may be able to retire "early" for your age, or you may need to retire "late" for your age. So instead of thinking about chronological age, try thinking in terms of your life stage—what's actually going on in your life.

If you're still carrying the heavy burdens of raising children (or paying their expenses), pushing to get ahead in your career, and paddling to keep your financial head above water, you're squarely in the second box. (Keep making plans and keep going—you'll get there!) On the other hand, if your children have flown the coop, if you have the choice at work of pushing hard or easing off, and if you've salted away enough money to make a paycheck optional, you may be able to start considering this new version of retirement. And instead of the all-or-nothing Industrial Age approach, perhaps you can make a more gradual transition—as humans once did, naturally, for millennia. You can mix and match work, learning, and leisure however you want!

Just to get your third-box imagination going, here are some questions to ask yourself about the three types of activities:

1. **Self-Development.** What do you really want to learn about, or how have you dreamed of developing yourself? Can you imagine exploring career options that would allow you to somehow *get paid to learn or develop in this way?*

2. **Productivity.** If you were determined to work at something that you absolutely love, what might that be? Could you afford to earn less money doing it, or even do it without pay—solely for fun and satisfaction? Can you imagine exploring career options that would allow you to *get paid to work at something you love?*

3. **Leisure.** What have you wanted to do, just for the sheer pleasure of it, but productivity and self-development seemed always to take precedence? As crazy as it may sound, can you imagine exploring career options that would allow you to somehow *get paid to play?*

If none of this mix-it-up approach sounds interesting to you, and you just want to think about taking it easy, don't feel guilty. All leisure all the time may be just what you're longing for. You may be just plain worn-out from all the work of the second box. You may really need to do absolutely nothing but enjoy yourself—without trying to be productive or self-developing—for a while after you retire. Farmers know that a field that's allowed to lie fallow for a year will yield a better crop the following year. That may be the case with your retirement; you may find you want to do something else later, after you're fully rested and recharged.

Supplies for the Journey

We can travel along on our journey to retirement without making many preparations and, by hook or by crook, probably figure out a way to *survive*. But most of us would like to do more than just survive. We'd like to *thrive*.

In traditional retirement planning, we may have short-changed ourselves by focusing primarily on money. In contrast, planning for Retirement Well-Being means focusing on three dimensions: our prosperity, our health, and our happiness. In our changing world, thinking that retirement is only about the money would be like thinking that a journey is only about the supplies! The right supplies make it easier to survive, and even to thrive, along the way. *But the journey is definitely not just about the supplies.* That would be missing the whole point.

Because you want more from your retirement than earlier generations did, you need to put more into it, too. Not necessarily more money, but more of *yourself*. A longer, healthier retirement that keeps you productively engaged in life, and developing in a meaningful way, takes more research and reflection. For all of us, in this changing world and with our expanded expectations, retirement planning is more than financial planning—it's *life planning*.

Life planning isn't about creating some rigid formula and laying out your future. Rather, it's about uncovering your *VIPs*: your *values, identity, and priorities*. Life planning is about recognizing the landscape of your journey and the terrain that you need to cross. The truth is, even when you do life planning, you still pretty much need to figure it out and make it up as you go along. But when you can see the big picture of your retirement (which is what this book is for), it's easier to make decisions that support your VIPs. *And you're free to live a more authentic life.*

No matter how carefully any of us plans, life—and retirement—never happens on the exact schedule or in the exact way that we expect. So rather than thinking that retirement will turn out just the way you plan, it's more realistic, and more practical, to remember that it's a journey. You can't know for sure where the path will lead you, or when you'll arrive. The most important thing is to heed the call to adventure, and to embark!

Resources on Life Stages

At the end of each chapter, look for a box like this with additional relevant resources. And at the end of this book, look for an invitation to the ultimate additional retirement resource: www.ParachuteRetirement.com.

If you're interested in a thorough yet lighthearted and engaging discussion of the three stages of life, the definitive guide is still Richard Bolles's book *The Three Boxes of Life and How to Get Out of Them: An Introduction to Life-Work Planning* (Ten Speed Press, 1978). This book created the field of life planning.

Originally published in 1976, the most widely read book about adult life stages and transitions is Gail Sheehy's *Passages: Predictable Crises of Adult Life* (Bantam, 2006). It approaches the subject by life decade—twenties, thirties, forties, fifties. It puts a very human face on the subject.

Probably the most influential scholarly approach to life stages is that of Erik Erikson. Although models of child development have been around for a long time, Erikson's eight-stage model was the first to address the full human life span, from birth to old age. Relevant to retirement planning, an accessible version of this very deep model can be found in *Vital Involvement in Old Age* (W.W. Norton, 1994).

Looking to the future, Peter Laslett identified how modern society may be replacing the three-stage model with a four-age model. His landmark book *A Fresh Map of Life: The Emergence of the Third Age* (Harvard University Press, 1991) would be considered heavy reading.

A lighter but still scholarly approach to the same subject— on a more personal level—is William Sadler's *The Third Age: Six Principles for Personal Growth and Renewal After Forty* (Perseus, 2001).

"I've been rich and I've been poor, and rich is better."
—Mae West

CHAPTER TWO

Your Retirement Stool Is Getting Wobbly

A h, money. It's been around for a long time—but it hasn't always made the world go 'round. For most of human history, in most places in the world, working people could live their whole lives with little need for coins or currency. They could grow their own food, build their own houses, make their own clothes, and create their own entertainment. What they didn't know how to do on their own, their family or friends did—and everyone helped each other out, in turn.

As societies began to adopt forms of legal tender, people began to need a *little bit* of money, to buy things they couldn't produce themselves. But for most of history, humans (being the adaptable, creative, resourceful creatures that they are) have been amazingly self-reliant—and they made do with what was close at hand or easy to trade for.

Most of us don't live like that today.

Modern life in the three boxes isn't about making the stuff we need for our daily lives. It's about making the money to buy the stuff that we need for our daily lives. Nowadays, in the industrialized nations most of us use money to pay for just about all of those things that people used to produce for themselves. We've shifted from a do-it-yourself (or do-it-with-others) orientation into a do-it-with-money orientation, so we live in a financial cycle of earning and spending.

Dick Wagner, a leading thinker in the realm of financial planning, observes that the skills humans need to survive have changed. Survival skills were once about safely navigating in a natural environment. If you didn't know how to find food and protect yourself from predators, you were in deep trouble. But in the twenty-first century, survival skills are about safely navigating in a *financial* environment. If you don't know how to find and manage money and protect yourself from financial risks, you're in deep trouble. There may have been something in our genes that helped us to learn about surviving in the natural environment. For example, deep down, we're drawn toward food and we're frightened of predators. But Wagner suggests that our genes don't seem to help us in acquiring financial survival skills. There's nothing *natural* about money!

The Three Boxes of Life Are Also the Three Boxes of Money

The Three Boxes of Life represent the stages of our life span in modern society. As we learned in chapter 1, each box is named for the one main activity that is expected of us in that stage. The three boxes can also describe our relationship with money at each of these life stages. In the first box of life, when you're oriented toward self-development, you don't fully support yourself. Your family supports you (more or less) while you're preparing to earn money in the future. In the second box of life, when you're oriented toward being productive, you're earning money to support yourself—and, often, others in your family. But in the second box you also need to save the money that will support you in the third box (or you need to build up future sources of retirement income). Then, in the third box, you get to enjoy the fruits of your labors, spending the money that you saved up while you were in the second box.

The Three Boxes of Money look like this:

Preparing to Earn Money	Earning and Saving Money	Spending Saved Money

What about the new approach to retirement we introduced in chapter 1—the one that lets you mix up life's activities in whatever way works best for you as an individual? How does putting self-development, and productivity, and leisure into the third box affect money? Well, it *may* change the money equation. If you plan to be productive in retirement by continuing to work for pay, then *theoretically* you don't need to save up as much money while you're in the second box. But in practice, because your ability and opportunity to work for pay in retirement is unknown, you shouldn't count on it. The safest approach is to save up all the money you'll need for life's essentials while you're still in the second box. Don't gamble that you'll be able to keep earning money for essentials in retirement!

The Three-Legged Stool

So how do you save up all that money while you're in the second box? The good news is that you haven't been completely on your own in that task. In the United States, the basic assumption is that you have primary responsibility for your personal financial security. But even in the United States, there's recognition that it's not always easy to save all the money that you may need. So in 1935, the Social Security Act created a system for providing old-age benefits for Americans. The goal wasn't to completely support people in their old age, but to provide a foundation. President Franklin Roosevelt, three years

THE THREE-LEGGED STOOL

after signing the Social Security Act into law, explained the rationale this way: "Because it has become increasingly difficult for individuals to build their own security single-handed, Government must now step in and help them lay the foundation stones."

Also beginning in the 1930s, it became more common for employers to provide pensions for retiring workers. The number of plans increased steadily over the decades of the twentieth century. In 1940, about four million workers were covered by pension plans. By 1960, that number had grown to over twenty-three million![1]

By the mid-twentieth century, the three separate approaches for providing retirement income—Social Security, employer pensions, and personal savings—had acquired a name. They were called the *three-legged stool* of retirement security. Although the origins of this metaphor aren't completely known, the concept of the three-legged stool has become very well-known—at least among retirement geeks.

Taken as a whole, this three-part financial retirement system is a marvel of engineering. (Some would say social engineering.) Before it was developed, retirement was relatively uncommon. Now, this system supports millions of retirees, and retirement is so common that it's all but taken for granted. Yet we may not give a lot of thought to how all those millions of retirees are able to get along without working until we draw closer to that age ourselves.

Every individual doesn't necessarily have all three sources, and even for those who do, the sources aren't likely to provide equal amounts of income. However, this system of retirement income provides support and stability for retirement in general.

But the Three-Legged Stool Is Getting Wobbly

In general, this system has worked well for our parents and grandparents. Now that you're planning for your own retirement, you may

---

1. For more on the creation and development of retirement over the twentieth century, read the source of these statistics, "Economic History of Retirement in the United States" by Joanna Short of Augustana College, accessible on the Economic History website, www.eh.net. Short reviews the research literature and shows how increasing prosperity allowed retirement to become commonplace.

want to know how the old three-legged stool is holding up. When it's your turn to use it, will it support you, as it has prior generations?

The unfortunate truth is that the stool is getting *wobbly*. Here's why.

THE FIRST LEG: SOCIAL SECURITY

In the United States, Social Security is getting wobbly for two reasons. The first reason is very high-profile; it has made headlines for years and will probably continue to do so. Social Security was designed primarily to be a pay-as-you-go-plan, meaning that the current contributions going in are used to pay the current benefits going out. And the ratio of workers paying into the system has fallen in comparison to the number of retirees collecting benefits. This is mostly due to a decreasing birth rate in the United States (holding down the number of workers paying in), combined with an increasing life span (pushing up the number of retirees receiving payments, and how long they receive them). Not surprisingly, this means that the total contributions are shrinking in proportion to the total benefits— which puts the system on a kind of internal collision course.

We'll need to either increase the contribution percentage or the income cap (or both), or reduce the benefits, or some combination of the two. The sooner that course corrections are made, the less drastic they'll need to be. If no changes are made, as of 2006 the Social Security Administration projects that benefits will need to be cut significantly in 2040 (the Social Security Commissioner offers a fresh prediction on the first page of each annual statement; see the box on page 28). As so often happens, whatever measures are taken to address this problem will probably be driven more by political science than actuarial science. Only time and the prevailing political winds will determine how much and how soon you should be concerned about receiving your projected Social Security benefits.

The second reason that the Social Security leg is getting a bit wobbly is much more low profile, but also much more concrete and personal. It has to do with something called the *replacement ratio*. Your replacement ratio is simply the amount of your working paycheck that will be replaced by your Social Security check. And over time, for many of us, the replacement ratio is becoming lower.

This has to do with the way that Social Security benefits are designed and the way they are taxed. Alicia Munnell, the brilliant director of the Retirement Research Center at Boston College, analyzed how much of a worker's wages Social Security will replace in the future. (By the way, Social Security benefits provide a greater replacement ratio for low earners than for high earners.) She found that for medium earners who retired in 2000, the replacement ratio was 41 percent, on average. But workers retiring in 2030 should expect only 37 percent of their pay to be replaced, on average. Take into account the increasing premiums for Medicare and the taxation of Social Security benefits, and the replacement ratio drops all the way to 31 percent. So the net monthly benefit that you receive will probably replace a smaller percentage of pay for you than it has for past generations.

Combine the challenges of the funding imbalance and the falling replacement ratio, and it looks like the first leg of the three-legged stool is indeed getting a bit shorter.

THE SECOND LEG: EMPLOYER PENSIONS

The term *employer pension* refers to a traditional plan that's funded, or paid for, by the employer, and provides a monthly retirement check—usually for life. In the future, *a smaller percentage of retirees will receive a pension benefit* than in the past. Fewer workers are being covered by this type of plan because of two trends in the U.S. workplace. One trend is from the *employee* side. Because employees tend to move around from company to company more than they used to, they are less likely to stick around long enough to earn this type of pension. It takes many years of service to build up a benefit. Since fewer and fewer employees consider themselves to be "lifers" at a given job, they don't reap the benefits of this type of long-term benefit structure.

The other trend is from the *employer* side. The number of employers still willing to foot the bill for a traditional employer-funded pension is steadily decreasing. Government employers have generally stayed with the traditional approach and are still likely to sponsor pension plans. At the opposite end of the spectrum, smaller companies typically never have. Large companies are somewhere in between, historically sponsoring pension plans, but with many now freezing or terminating them. The total number of traditional pension plans reached a peak of over 114,000 in 1985 but had dropped to just over 35,000 by 2001. In recent years, this trend has been highlighted in the news, as some large, well-known employers have reduced or eliminated these benefits.[2]

2. The consensus among experts is that the era of traditional defined-benefit pension plans is fading, because the total number of plans, and the number of new plans, is declining. However, the fade-out will take a long time, as the number of workers covered by these plans has been relatively stable for years at about 44 million. You can find these numbers and some background on the federal insurance program for these plans in the Annual Report of the Pension Benefit Guarantee Corporation, at www.pbgc.gov.

Why are employers doing away with pensions? First, the regulatory compliance for these plans became so complex that employers decided it wasn't worth the bother. Second, plans designed to reward long-term service were simply out of touch with the need to attract and retain new talent. Third, employees themselves seemed to have a better understanding of, and appreciation for, profit-sharing and 401(k)-type plans. Another reason—one that's less cited, but pretty obvious—is that many employers who have eliminated their traditional defined-benefit pensions were simply looking to reduce costs. (This is echoed in the emerging trend of employers eliminating or reducing medical insurance coverage for retirees.) In any case, the combined result of these two broad trends (employee and employer) is that *fewer people can look forward to getting a monthly pension* for as long as they live. For U.S. workers, the second leg has gotten shorter.

What about 401(k) plans? Is the 401(k) an employer pension (second leg) or personal savings (third leg)? When the subject of money for retirement comes up, the discussion almost always turns to these hybrid employee-employer retirement savings accounts. The 401(k) is a specific type of plan, but the term *401(k)* is becoming something of a catchall that's sometimes applied to any employer-sponsored, salary savings retirement plan. The actual technical names, and the technical details, vary according to where you work. In the private sector (at a for-profit company), the 401(k) is the most common type of savings plan; if you work for a small business, you may contribute to a "Savings Incentive Match Plan for Employees" (SIMPLE). In the public sector (government entities), the most common type of plan is the 457; for federal employees, it's the Thrift Savings Plan. Finally, if you work in the nonprofit or education world, the 403(b), which in some settings is called a *teacher's annuity*, is the most common.

Although the details vary, all of these 401(k)-type plans, in all these environments, are really about the same thing: your employer providing an easy way for you (*you, you, you!*) to save for your retirement. The cornerstone of these plans isn't an employer contribution, like in a traditional pension. No, the cornerstone is your own savings. Technically, these plans are *salary reduction* plans. (Guess whose *salary* gets the *reduction* to fund them? You get only one guess.)

If you're fortunate, your employer may match part of your contribution or make other types of contributions. However, in general, there are *no required employer contributions* in these salary savings plans. If your employer is generous, you could be on the receiving end of some hefty contributions—every bit as valuable as anything you might get from a traditional pension. But if your employer is stingy, you could be carrying the ball all by yourself—with no contributions at all from your employer. (Do you know which camp you're in?) A 401(k)-type plan simply provides a framework for you and your employer to make contributions into your retirement account, and each of you decides whether to put in a little or a lot. So if your employer only puts in a little, *you'd* better put in a lot!

Back to that sixty-four-thousand-dollar question: "Are these plans part of the second leg or part of the third leg?" The answer is yes. They don't fully measure up to the original concept of the second leg, employer pension, because in those the employer paid for all the benefits. But they *are* like an employer pension in that they're maintained by the employer, who does have significant responsibility to make sure everything is on the up-and-up—and who may make some contribution. And they're like personal savings in that you're the one who needs to save the significant money (through payroll deductions) to create a retirement benefit. So you could think of these plans as a hybrid of the second and third legs.

THE WOBBLY STOOL

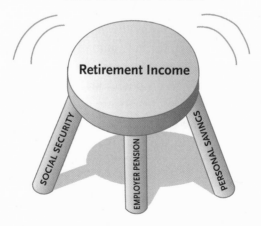

However, in most discussions of the three-legged stool, you'll see the 401(k) and its cousins counted as part of the second leg—perhaps because they are a popular employer choice to replace the traditional employer pension. And indeed, they are replacing pensions at a rapid rate. If they *are* the new second leg, we'd better be careful. Some workers will build a solid leg with them, but others will shoot themselves in the foot! If they are the new second leg, then a lot of us have a lot of work to do. ("A lot of us," in this case, means employers, and workers, and politicians, and retirement educators. Maybe I should make that "all of us.") We need to keep improving these plans so they'll do a better job of providing financial security for *all* workers. Without continual improvements, the plans won't deliver the retirement security that a true *employer plan* should provide. The recent trend of automatically enrolling eligible employees will result in more people building up benefits, and that's a step in the right direction. (More on this in chapter 5.) Still, as of right now, all these changes in the world of employer retirement plans have made the second leg of the stool more wobbly.

THE THIRD LEG: PERSONAL SAVINGS

In general, in the United States, the third leg of the stool has gotten shorter, too. Over the last twenty-five years, the aggregate percentage of our income that we've set aside as personal savings has steadily declined. When you look at the graph on the opposite page, you might even say it has plummeted—from a peak of about 14 percent in the early 1980s to almost nothing by the year 2000. In the year 2005, the unthinkable happened: the rate actually became negative. That was the first year since the Great Depression that we collectively spent more than we earned. To accomplish that feat, some Americans are spending out of their savings; others are borrowing money, whether it be with credit cards, interest-only mortgages, car loans, college loans, or home equity loans or lines of credit. The true opposite of saving isn't spending, it's *borrowing*. Borrowing sets people up for a double whammy. It's even more difficult to increase your rate of savings when you also need to pay off debts.

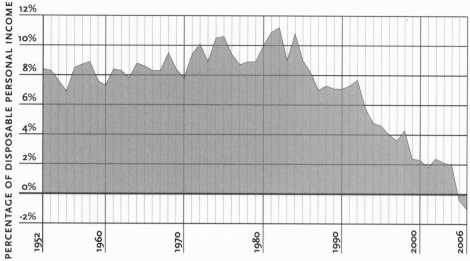

PERSONAL SAVINGS RATE IN THE UNITED STATES

Source: U.S. Department of Commerce, Bureau of Economic Analysis.

The dynamics of the third leg—personal savings—are the most personally varied of the three legs. You may have saved until it hurt and be sitting on a *mountain* of cash. Or maybe you've just started and you only have a *molehill*. Ideally, though, you haven't dug yourself into a hole with debt.

Why Is It So Hard for Us to Save, Anyway?

Why does saving for retirement seem to be such a challenge? After all, we all *know* about saving. We save all the time. Most of us don't spend our entire paycheck on the same day we get it. If we get paid on Fridays, we don't live like royalty on Friday night and like paupers by the following Thursday. No, we typically try to level things out so that we don't have such drastic peaks and valleys in our spending. Most of us get pretty good at leveling it out. From day to day, paycheck to paycheck, month to month, and over a whole year or longer, we more or less level out our spending. Through trial and error, we learn how much to spend right away and how much to save so that we can spend it later. We learn to base our spending not on how much money we have *at the moment*, but on how much money we *expect to have*, over time.

Franco Modigliani won a Nobel Prize in economics for coming up with a good explanation of how people typically save, which he called the *Life Cycle Hypothesis*. He suggested that most people spend based not on their current level of income but on the level they expect to average *over their lifetime*. When we expect to have a higher income in the future, we're more likely to dip into savings—or borrow money—to spend more than our current income. That is, in the early part of our lives, we tend to *spend more than we earn*. On the other hand, when we expect to have a lower income in the future, we're more likely to put money into savings and spend less than our current income (like when we save for retirement). Modigliani suggested that even if we overspend in the early part of our life cycle, we make up for it by underspending in the middle part. Similar to the approach of leveling things out from paycheck to paycheck, the Life Cycle Hypothesis suggests we try to level things out over our entire life cycle or lifetime.

But there's a big difference between a weekly (or monthly or annual) cycle and an entire lifetime. Because we get so much practice at leveling things out over the *short run*, most of us become experts at short-term spending and saving. In the short term, we get plenty of chances, over and over, to figure things out. But when it comes to the big enchilada—saving for retirement—*we only get one chance*. It's a very high-stakes test. There is no trial and error, so *we can't learn from our mistakes*. We just have to live with them.

Modigliani saw humans as rational decision makers, able to make spending and saving decisions across the life cycle. But according to the statistics, that's not what most people are doing. Most of us aren't saving enough. We're not acting . . . *rational*. What's the problem?

It could be that, for many of us, a human lifetime of eighty years or more is too long to really plan out in advance. (Historically, most humans have never needed to do that!) Or it could be that because our incomes have increased in the past, our *expectation* is that they'll keep increasing in the future, too. (So we figure it'll be easier to save tomorrow, and tomorrow never comes.) Or it could be that we plan to keep working in retirement, and so we think we won't need as much retirement savings. (Which could be true, or overly optimistic.)

On the other hand, the problem could be that there is a lot going on in modern society that the Life Cycle Hypothesis wasn't designed to address. For example, what if *marketing and advertising* have gotten so darned good that they blow the Life Cycle Hypothesis right out of the water? What if marketers manage to subvert our rational decision-making powers with their siren songs, and so instead we just keep *buying more stuff* than we can ever use? (John DeGraaf, the definitely walks-his-talk author and public television producer, calls this modern malady *affluenza*.)

Or what if *consumer credit* has become so darned plentiful that debt sinks the Life Cycle Hypothesis in the early years? When you turn eighteen, a steady stream of credit card offers begins arriving in the mailbox, and it never lets up. Never before has credit been marketed so heavily, so expertly, or so successfully. What if lenders entice us to *borrow too much* in the early part of the life cycle, and so we never get our heads above water again, to clearly see where we are? (Lee Eisenberg, an insightful observer of emerging cultural phenomena and a clever and urbane writer, calls this quantum phenomenon *debt warp*.)

Or what if instead of paying attention to our *own income*, as the Life Cycle Hypothesis suggests, instead we're paying attention to what we overimagine *other people's* incomes are? Have we gotten into a rat race of working hard and spending big, on a treadmill that never stops—because we believe the illusion that our peers live better than we do? (Juliet Schor, the groundbreaking researcher, linked these in her brilliant concepts of *The Overworked American* and *The Overspent American*.)

And there are other factors at play, beyond the scope of this book: things like the soaring costs of housing, health care, and fossil fuels, which keep some very hardworking lower- and middle-income folks from ever getting ahead.

Regardless of the factors operating at the societal level, in the end what really counts for each of us personally is how we come to terms with our own patterns of earning, spending, and saving for retirement. (More on this in chapter 5.)

So we've got a three-legged stool with all three legs getting shorter and shorter. Either way, if we're not paying attention, our retirement could be spent sitting on the cold, hard ground!

A RETIREMENT CRISIS?

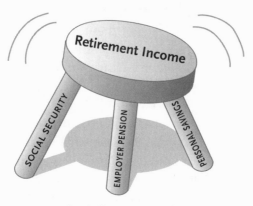

Are You Headed for a Retirement Crisis? Are We All?

This may be the first you've heard of the three-legged stool. After all, it's not a hot topic of conversation in most social circles. Many Americans may not know that earlier generations were able to retire because of it. More important, they may not realize that the legs are getting shorter and that the stool is getting wobbly. More and more of the burden is being put on *workers* to financially prepare for retirement, and yet *many workers haven't heard the news*. Is our society headed for a *retirement crisis?*

That's the phrase being used by entities that seek to provide retirement education, such as foundations and research organizations. They are stepping up their efforts to encourage workers to address their increasing personal responsibility. They're offering more financial education than ever before. Government agencies and public interest groups are mounting national savings initiatives. Financial service companies are cranking up new advertising campaigns. And employers are supporting more workplace education. Although everyone behind these efforts agrees that workers need to take more responsibility for their retirement savings, there is no agreement on what actually helps people do that.

Three Scenarios for Learning Our Way Out of the Retirement Crisis

Most retirement education uses one of three basic scenarios. You may have seen and heard them. Which of these financial responsibility scenarios makes sense to you?

1. THE "TEACH AND TRAIN" SCENARIO

The assumption behind this scenario is that if workers are taught the *financial facts* about preparing for retirement and then trained how to do it, they will naturally follow through and get the job done. However, the well-intentioned folks using this approach tend to be people who personally enjoy learning about finance. Because they find the subject—in and of itself—interesting and compelling, they assume that other people should, too. In their own lives, these folks wanted financial knowledge and wanted to learn financial skills, and then they wanted to use their financial knowledge and skills to better prepare for their own retirement. Naturally, it seems to them that it would be enough to simply provide other people with the financial "facts of life." Like telling them about the birds and the bees and then letting nature take its course. But for some reason, the *facts of life* seem to be more compelling for the average person than the *financial facts of life*.

One term that's often used for the Teach and Train approach is *financial literacy*. In the same way that reading literacy programs target adults who can't read, financial literacy programs target adults who can't *count*. Or at least *can't count on having enough money for retirement*. Although this terminology makes sense to the well-meaning educators who sponsor financial literacy programs, it's probably not very inviting to the audience they're trying to reach. The term itself creates a barrier: for you to participate in a financial literacy program, you're essentially admitting that you must be financially *illiterate*. That's a lot to ask of someone, just to sign up! So *financial literacy* is not a term that wins friends and influences people. Something accurate and positive, like *financial knowledge*, would be more inviting.

If you happen to be interested in the financial aspects of retirement but just haven't had a chance to get the knowledge and skills you need, this approach may be perfect for you. Just sign up for a financial literacy workshop. Your brain may soak up the financial knowledge like a sponge. But if you're not interested in financial topics per se, this approach may only succeed in putting you to sleep. Or making you sneak out of the classroom.

2. THE "SCARE AND SCOLD" SCENARIO

The assumption behind this scenario is that providing financial information by itself isn't sufficient, because *people are generally complacent*. Probably even lazy. At the very least, they're somewhat clueless. Anyway, the well-intentioned folks behind this approach tend to believe that people are motivated primarily by *doom and gloom*. That only a potential catastrophe will awaken them from their stupor. So the core theme of the Scare and Scold scenario warns people about the *retirement crisis* and urges them to take action to avoid disaster. The Scare and Scold approach to retirement education sounds something like this (and really means *this*):

- "Most people aren't saving enough for retirement." (Translation: You aren't saving enough for retirement.)
- "You need to plan ahead." (Translation: You haven't planned ahead, have you?)
- "Building retirement security takes time." (Translation: It may be too late for you, anyway.)
- "Saving is easier than you think." (Translation: Can't you at least try?)
- "Start today!" (Translation: Or you'll be living in a tar-paper shack and eating dog food.)

If this motivates you to increase your knowledge and skills, it's not because you suddenly *love* finance. No, it's probably because dire warnings tend to grab your attention and get you to imagine nasty outcomes that you don't want. If you're the type of person who, when confronted with a potential threat, actually takes steps to safeguard against it, then this could be exactly what you need. Although not an especially *enjoyable* way to get motivated, it can be just the ticket, sometimes. It may be good to scare the dickens out of ourselves, now and then.

3. THE "INQUIRE AND INSPIRE" SCENARIO

One underlying assumption behind this scenario is the same as for the Scare and Scold approach: that providing financial information by itself isn't sufficient. But the financial information isn't sufficient because it's usually offered in a completely *disconnected* way (like high school algebra). Financial information works best when it's offered in the *context of people's own lives*. The educators behind this approach (OK, I'll admit it, I'm one of them) tend to think that humans are pretty good at accomplishing things. But first, they need a *meaningful personal vision* of what they want. "Meaningful" and "personal" are the tricky parts, because each of us is unique. As the purposeful career coach and author Richard Leider says, "we're each an experiment of one." That's why it's not easy to help people develop a meaningful personal vision of retirement. It's not enough to simply dangle *generic* versions of a pleasant retirement in front of them. That's just advertising.

Instead, the Inquire and Inspire approach helps you create a clear, detailed picture of your Ideal Retirement, based on your desired *Ways to Live* and using your own personal VIPs: your values, identity, and priorities. The assumption behind this scenario—right or wrong—is that when you *clearly envision the retirement you really want*, you'll be resourceful enough to work toward it. You'll seek out the financial information (or anything else you need) that will bring you closer to your dream. This book, in fact, is based on that very premise!

All Three Financial Responsibility Scenarios Are True

It's a fact that the stool is getting wobbly. And it's a fact that most of us, for whatever reason, have a tough time saving money. So, which of these three scenarios will be most helpful in getting us to take action? Research shows that *we need all three.* But they must work together as a team. For most of us, the three approaches work best in the following order. (Try this on for yourself.)

Step One: You need to pay attention. Seeing a *negative* vision of what you *don't want* will usually do that. The Scare and Scold approach does that the best.

Step Two: You need to focus your energy and enthusiasm. Developing your very own *positive* vision of what you *do want* will usually accomplish that. The Inquire and Inspire approach does that the best.

Step Three: You need a way to *reach* your vision. Acquiring knowledge and skills will usually do that. The Teach and Train approach does that the best.

The Three Big Surprises for Your Retirement Savings

When you create a picture of your Ideal Retirement and start working toward it, keep in mind that there are three emerging trends that may catch you off guard. Even when you become aware of them, they're the kinds of things that people tend to not fully appreciate until it happens to them personally.

The first big surprise is that maintaining your standard of living will require *a higher annual income* in retirement than you imagine. Why? When you think back on all the financial projects you've ever been involved with, didn't most of them end up costing more than you anticipated? Well, retiring is definitely a major financial project, so the same will probably hold true. If only your life would stick to the budget! It's the unexpected events that throw the budget out the window. And you could be looking at ten or twenty or thirty years of unexpected events. For example, when you plan what your cost of living will be, the conventional wisdom is that it will be less than in your working years. That's because it actually costs money to work and earn. For years and years, there's even been a rule of thumb about it: people need about *70 percent* of their preretirement income to *maintain the same standard of living* in retirement. However, rules of thumb often point in the wrong direction. The latest research on people who are actually retired suggests that it may be costing them more like *85 percent* of their preretirement income.[3]

So if maintaining your preretirement standard of living is important to you, it will probably cost more than you think. If you're forced to cut your cost of living *after* you retire, that will feel like *involuntary poverty*; you won't like it, and it may be too late to do anything about it. So try to leave yourself a bigger financial cushion than you think you'll need. (Or, instead of *involuntary poverty*, you could try something called *voluntary simplicity* to achieve a lower cost of living. But if you want to base your retirement on *voluntary simplicity*, you'd better try it out in advance, right away! You'll find more about this in chapter 4.)

The second big surprise is that you will probably need *more years of retirement income* than you think. That is, you'll be retired for longer than you anticipate. There are actually two reasons for this; one at the beginning of retirement, and one at the end.

The beginning reason is that you may *retire sooner than you plan to*. The latest statistics suggest that four out of ten people retired earlier than they intended—mostly for unhappy reasons.[4] Some lost their health, but instead of being *disabled*, they're retired. Some lost their jobs (got fired, laid off, or downsized, or their employer shut down or relocated), but instead of being *unemployed*, they're retired. They never found another job. Most of these four out of ten who retired early didn't have a choice. They would have liked more time to prepare, surely. Fortunately, some workers who retired earlier than planned did so for happier reasons. They won the lottery, or received an inheritance, or had some other financial windfall, and were able to call it

---

3. This approximation is from the 2004 version of the ongoing Retirement Ratio Study conducted by AON Consulting and Georgia State University. The average percentage is greater at lower incomes and less at higher incomes. For a thorough discussion of replacement ratios, the percentages at different levels of income, and how they've changed over the years, you may want to check out the study, available from AON Consulting at www.aon.com.

4. This disturbing statistic isn't from a survey aimed at individuals or policymakers. It's from *Cracking the Consumer Retirement Code*, a 2006 report by the prestigious consulting firm of McKinsey & Co. (www.mckinsey.com). The report is intended for financial services companies—which may make it even more interesting for you.

quits. But whether it was due to unhappy or happy circumstances, almost half of retirees began earlier than they thought they would. All things being equal, that makes retirement longer and requires more years of retirement income.

The *end* reason retirement may last longer is that *you may live longer than you imagine.* We all know that average life expectancy (how long the average person lives) has been getting longer. In contrast, the maximum life span (how long the very oldest people live) hasn't increased by all that much—it's about 120 years. A hundred years ago, most people didn't live even one-half of the maximum life span. The average lifetime was only about fifty years. But the average lifetime has been inching further and further out toward the maximum life span. It's not that the very oldest people are making it to a greater age; it's that the *average* person is now living to a ripe old age.

Also, statistically, the longer someone lives, the greater their life expectancy becomes. According to data compiled by the Center for Disease Control, a baby born in the United States today has a life expectancy of age seventy-six. Once you make it to sixty-five, though, your life expectancy increases to eighty-three. Then when you make it to seventy, it increases to eighty-five. And if you make it to the age of eighty, your life expectancy is eighty-nine. The older you get, the older you're likely to get! Or, to think of it another way, if the life expectancy at birth is seventy-six, half of those born will die before they reach that age. But the other half will still be alive and kicking (well, maybe not kicking) *past* the age of seventy-six.

What does all this actuarial mumbo jumbo mean? It means that, for most of human history, really old people were rare. Now they're common. You'll probably be one of them!

If you add these beginning and end factors together, you can sum it up this way: you just may have a longer retirement than you would have ever believed. At the beginning, it can start with a bang. And at the far, far end, it can end with a whimper. In between, you could need twenty, or thirty, or more years of income. Who would believe it?

The third big surprise is that *access to medical care will cost more* than you imagine. Now, the book you are holding is based on the idea that retirement can be the high point of life—the zenith, the apex, the climax, the great earthly reward. Even so, it's also true that retirement is a stage of life that happens while you're *aging*. You get older through the course of your retirement. Aging brings an increased incidence of disease, and that has major financial implications. Getting sick leads to doctors and prescriptions and hospitals, and those are expensive—even when you have medical insurance. If you need long-term care outside of a hospital, those costs aren't covered by insurance unless you have specific long-term care insurance. When one partner in a marriage or other committed relationship dies before the other (almost always the case), the survivor often faces additional financial challenges.

We all hope to stay completely healthy throughout our retirement and then pass away peacefully in our sleep. (That really is the goal: to make our *health span* last as long as our *life span*). Just the same, to prepare for the unexpected, and to make financial arrangements, is part of retirement planning. The statistics show that for most of us, medical expenses in retirement could be *enormous*. One credible study estimated typical out-of-pocket costs for a couple at $200,000![5] Although attempting to project your own likely costs for medical care in retirement could be an exercise in frustration and uncertainty, you can sum it up as "more than you think!"

These three big surprises, taken all together, mean that even with good financial planning you can underestimate how much money you will need for retirement. Retirement planning requires a balance between the vision of your Ideal Retirement and the risks that threaten it. You're probably *inspired* by the sunny side of the retirement street—the fun, engaging, meaningful things you want. But you may also find *motivation* for planning and preparing in the dark alleyways—the likely risks that you don't like to think about. Ignoring the risks doesn't make them go away. Worrying about them doesn't

5. Each year since 2002, Fidelity Investments has estimated the cost of basic health care for a couple that retires at age sixty-five. The estimate has increased each year, beginning at $160,000 in 2002 and topping $200,000 in 2006. Assuming you're not already age sixty-five, just extrapolate how high this amount could possibly be for you. Access to basic health care will be the biggest expense category for many retirees.

reduce them. Frankly, making sure that you have *enough money* is the surest way to address them.

What's Your Number?

Perhaps you're just getting started on your retirement journey. Or maybe you're well along the path. Or you may be nearing the end, and you're about to retire, or already have. Regardless of how far along you are, there is something you should do for yourself if you haven't already. You should calculate your Number. That's the price tag on the retirement that you want. It's the amount of money you need in savings to live the life of Retirement Well-Being that you want to live. Lee Eisenberg described what a bugaboo this is for most of us in his book *The Number*.

We often go to great lengths to avoid figuring out what our Number is. We usually save only what we think we can afford to put away. That's a good way to get started, because any amount of retirement saving is good saving. But saving without a specific goal means that, when it's time to retire, we may or may not have saved enough. That's why you should have at least some rough idea of what your Number is. Is this mandatory, or is it possible to save up enough without calculating your Number? You bet it's possible! Some folks will do just fine without making any calculations. But they tend to be the kind of penny-pinchers who save money with both hands and spend it with only one. They're the ones who somehow always manage to save, at every life stage. Apparently, they're wired that way. If you're one of those people, you may not need to calculate your Number. But it's still a good idea. That's why you'll find three approaches for doing so in chapter 5.

I suggest you calculate your Number (using whichever of the three approaches you prefer), because knowing your Number will have a positive effect in more ways than one. Once you know your Number, you have a definite goal to work toward. You can see how close to it or far away from it you are. You can break it down into how much you need to save each year, each month, or each payday to get there.

So, you've got a wobbly stool, the task of calculating your Number, and the challenge to save enough money to reach it. Is it starting to seem like Retirement Well-Being *is* all about enough money? Not so. As the next chapter will explain, simply having "enough money" to stop working is no longer enough. Money is just one of three important dimensions that make up the new Retirement Well-Being Model.

And that brings up the final important reason for calculating your Number: it will also help you *visualize the life you want to live in retirement*. Being the adaptable, creative, resourceful human being that you are, your vision of your Ideal Retirement is a powerful thing. *It draws you to it, and it to you.* The stronger your vision, the more likely you are to have the money you need. After all, you do need supplies for your journey. And money makes the world go 'round.

Resources on Saving (or Not)

For a well-researched theory about why it may be so difficult to save for retirement in modern society, read Juliet Schor's *The Overspent American* (HarperCollins, 1999). This is a companion to her earlier book, *The Overworked American* (Basic Books, 1991).

It's a challenge for many people to get ahead financially, but it's almost impossible for folks on the bottom rung of the economic ladder. For a personal account about those who will someday be relying completely on Social Security in their retirement, read Barbara Ehrenreich's *Nickel and Dimed: On (Not) Getting By in America* (Owl Books, 2002).

Even at the opposite end of the income spectrum, saving for retirement—and, particularly, knowing when you've saved enough—isn't easy. Lee Eisenberg's *The Number: What Do You Need for the Rest of Your Life, and What Will It Cost?* is the first truly entertaining story about the process of preparing—or not preparing—for retirement (Free Press, 2006).

---

*"The only thing money gives you is the freedom
of not worrying about money."*
—Johnny Carson

CHAPTER THREE

Why "Enough Money" Isn't Enough

I
f life is a journey and retirement is a journey, what does that mean for you?

How will you prepare?

What do you want to take along?

How will you end up?

Is having enough money going to be enough?

People have thought of life as a journey for a long time, so when you think about what you might want for your own journey, you have quite a bit of history to draw on. You can tap into those thousands of years of human experience and find out what all such journeys have in common—and what other travelers have wanted and needed to see them through the journey.

First, a true journey always has an element of the *unknown*. If everything is planned out and known in advance, it's not a journey—it's a guided tour. Who would want a life like that? It's like the difference between an actual safari and the safari ride at a theme park. The unknown—the adventure—is part of what makes the experience real rather than synthetic. Even a well-planned, well-prepared-for journey embraces an element of the unknown.

Second, when embarking on an adventure into the unknown, humans have always sought to maintain their *well-being* along the way. It seems to be a basic truth of human existence: *we all want well-being*. So what is *well-being*? The definition has evolved as human culture developed. Over time, it's become clear that well-being has three distinct dimensions: *prosperity* (material abundance), *health* (a sound body), and *happiness* (a positive subjective experience).

The question is, do we need all three to have well-being, or is any one of the three good enough? Can we achieve well-being if we have enough prosperity, by itself? Or enough health, by itself? Or enough happiness, by itself? Or do we need all three, together, to truly have well-being? We as a culture haven't come to a final conclusion about this. Indeed, if you look around at the people you know and those you see in the media, you can probably name some who are focused on just two, or even just one of those three dimensions. But you need to answer this question for yourself. Are you personally OK with planning for *just one dimension* of well-being, or does your Ideal Retirement include *all three*?

To answer this question, you need to know more about how each one works, separately and together, in the new model for Retirement Well-Being. In this chapter you'll learn about the specialized research fields that are focused on exploring the three dimensions, and you'll get a first look at the Retirement Well-Being Model. This is the model you will use to map out your Ideal Retirement journey as you complete the exercises in the chapters that follow.

Enough Money Used to Be Enough

It's actually quite a luxury to be able to worry about your retirement lifestyle. Not so long ago in the history of the world, life was an elemental struggle for survival. People worked hard every day just to satisfy their basic needs—food, water, shelter. Until quite recently, the vast majority of people (those who weren't of the "leisure class") needed to focus their daily lives on acquiring those basics. In much of the developing world today, this is still true. And even in the developed world, some people have it very, very tough. If you're reading this book, you're part of a privileged minority, fortunate enough not to have to worry about survival at a basic level. For you, it's not so much a question of *whether* you'll get by, but of *how well* you'll get by. For you, the fundamental question has evolved from "How will I be able to live?" to "How will I be able to live the lifestyle that I want?"

When we're at the subsistence level and just getting by, money is everything. Every little bit is important, and any additional money leads directly to better health and more happiness. When an entire country is operating at a subsistence level, more money in the economy as a whole will generally translate directly into better health and more happiness for the overall population. Governments need to know whether there's "enough money" both at the national level and in the hands of individual citizens, because that's an indicator of whether people have (1) enough to survive and (2) beyond survival, enough to prosper. (Prosperity allows the original "enough money" kind of retirement—or even, ideally, the new model of Retirement Well-Being.) So governments have developed economic measures to do just that. The most familiar one is the gross domestic product (GDP). Though GDP is a very high-level, macroeconomic measure, increases in economic production have historically meant increases in the quality of life for individual citizens, too. (To measure *that*, there's the GDP per capita—but it's too simplistic to be a measure of individuals' true standard of living, let alone their overall well-being.)

But Now, Enough Money Isn't Enough

As humans have moved up from the subsistence level to a complex and highly industrialized culture, and as our material standard of living has soared, having more money doesn't automatically equate to more health or more happiness. After we reach a certain level of security and prosperity, each increase becomes less significant. Each additional influx of money makes an incrementally smaller difference to our overall well-being. For example, at the low end, upgrading from an outhouse to an indoor bathroom will dramatically increase a family's health and happiness. Upgrading from one indoor bathroom to two can certainly make a big difference, but it's far less significant. And upgrading from two bathrooms to three—more prosperity—may not really increase health or happiness at all. (There may actually be a negative effect on happiness: more bathrooms require more cleaning!)

The more bathrooms (or just about anything) we accumulate, the less positive effect each incremental addition will have on our lives. It won't necessarily directly translate into more health or happiness. That's true for each of us individually, and it's true for us collectively as a nation. The gross domestic product is still an important measure, to be sure. But it's too narrow a measure to tell us about our overall well-being (in terms of prosperity, *and* health, *and* happiness). That's why Daniel Kahneman, the only psychologist to ever win a Nobel Prize in economics, is working on another national measure. It will probably be called the *Well-Being Indicator,* and it will measure how we're doing overall rather than just economically.[1] We're learning that, even in economics, money isn't everything.

A Recipe for Retirement

Here's an analogy for how the dimensions of well-being combine. Many dessert baking recipes call for four basic ingredients: flour, sugar, eggs, and butter. It's amazing how many varied and delightful desserts you can create by using just these four ingredients in different amounts and proportions (plus different flavorings and spices). But no one of these ingredients can take the place of any of the others in the recipe. Not only does each contribute a different sensory pleasure to the eating experience, but each also plays an essential, irreplaceable chemical role in the transformation from dough or batter to baked dessert. If you don't have any eggs, you can't just add more butter and expect the recipe to work. If you're a bit short on sugar, you can't increase the amount of flour to compensate. When you choose your recipe, you must make sure you have enough of each of these ingredients on hand— no substitutions!

---

1. See a press release about this from the National Institutes of Health, "How Are We Doing? Researchers Aim to Measure National Well Being," at www.nih.gov/news/pr/dec2004/nia-02.htm.

When you're planning for well-being in retirement, think of the three key dimensions of well-being—prosperity, health, and happiness—as essential baking ingredients. You can't just keep adding money and expect it to turn into health or happiness. Don't wait for our culture to figure out whether well-being means any one of the ingredients or all three. In your life and in your retirement planning, don't waffle on this issue—demand your just desserts.

Besides Money, What Do You Want?

When you really think about it, what does the idea of retirement mean to *you*? Does it mean just having enough money to stop working? In 2004, AARP conducted a survey of baby boomers who had not yet retired and asked them that very question. Here's what they said retirement meant to them:

An opportunity to spend more time with family	72%
More time to pursue interests and hobbies	71%
More time for leisure	63%
A chance to travel	57%
A chance to socialize with friends	54%

All of these responses ranked higher than the idea of retirement as pure economic enjoyment: only 48 percent said that retirement meant a "time to indulge yourself." For most of us, retirement is not chiefly an opportunity to have a deeper, more fulfilling relationship with our money, or with the indulgences that money can buy. Perhaps we've come such a long way from the subsistence level that some of us are starting to get the lure of material indulgence out of our systems. We've tried it, over and over, chasing after the happiness promised us by all those commercial images of beaming, ecstatic consumers. And when buying those things doesn't make *us* just as happy as the people in the advertisements, we end up asking ourselves, "Is that all there is?"

The survey respondents did recognize the second dimension of Retirement Well-Being: health. Over half of them predicted that retirement would be a time of increased concern about health and increased attention allocated to it. They recognized that retirement is a time of getting older. And diseases do become more common as we age. For most of us, thinking about retirement will also mean thinking more and more about our health.

Then there's the third dimension, happiness. When we look at the top responses for what retirement means to us, we see that it *is* mostly about doing things that we hope will bring us happiness. We think of spending more time with family and friends. We think of spending more time with ourselves, too—pursuing interests or leisure. And we think about exploring the world. At the same time, we know that we won't get there unless we have enough money. And we won't get there unless we have enough health, too.

How can we combine all of this in a way that's easy to grasp? After all, it's much easier to work toward something when we have a singular, striking image of it—and we're much more likely to get it, too. So if we bundle all three together, what do we get? A retirement model that encompasses all three dimensions of well-being. This is what you'll be mapping a route to.

The Retirement Well-Being Model

Let's recap a bit. Retirement came into existence because there was enough prosperity to allow people to stop working later in life. So at that stage in the evolution of retirement, retirement planning was entirely about money. Then, as work for many became less physically rigorous and our life span kept growing longer, a whole generation gained the wherewithal to think of retirement as more than just "not working." Now we're entering the next stage in the evolution of retirement. A stage in which, instead of just planning for enough retirement money, we can plan for Retirement Well-Being.

The possibility of well-being in retirement always existed, but very few planned how to attain it. Naturally, a few people have always found it, because they were either unusually lucky or unusually wise.

Now you're the lucky one, because you have the recipe—the secret formula—for Retirement Well-Being. Graphically, it looks like this:

THE RETIREMENT WELL-BEING MODEL

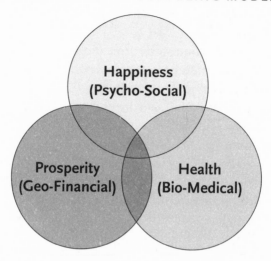

Notice that the three dimensions of well-being overlap. Although the dimensions are each essential and distinct, they connect to, affect, and interact with each other. Your prosperity affects your happiness and health, your happiness affects your health and prosperity, and your health affects your prosperity and happiness. In your life, you couldn't separate them if you wanted to. Now, most retirement planning tools have been strictly financial—things like portfolio management models and retirement savings calculators. But economics and finance aren't the only fields that are relevant to retirement planning. It's about time we had some tools for the *health* and *happiness* dimensions, too.

We're fortunate, at least, that we're getting closer to comprehensive retirement planning. Researchers have been studying a variety of topics that, one way or another, relate to retirement. We can turn some of these scientific findings into tools and guidance that will help us plan for our Retirement Well-Being. That's what I call progress!

Now, although in the real world the three dimensions are interconnected, research scientists don't see the world in quite the same way that you and I do (unless you, dear reader, are a research scientist).

For the most part, science breaks things into parts—and into further subparts—to be better able to study them. After all, you can't fit an elephant under a microscope, can you? Science usually needs to break things down into smaller chunks to get a better look at them. (Remember the old riddle "How do you eat an elephant?" Answer: "One bite at a time.")

So scientists focus on one of the three dimensions of well-being—or one aspect of that dimension. Economics, for example. Or biology. Researchers in each field pose theories, conduct research, and create useful knowledge—but usually only within the boundaries of their own field. The knowledge piles up, but it doesn't connect with the knowledge piling up in other fields.

So what can science tell us about each of the three dimensions of Retirement Well-Being? For one thing, there are actually *two fields* of research for each of the three dimensions, as shown in the next figure. So when you plan your retirement journey, you need to look at all six fields. Each plays a vital role in your Retirement Well-Being.

THE RETIREMENT WELL-BEING MODEL

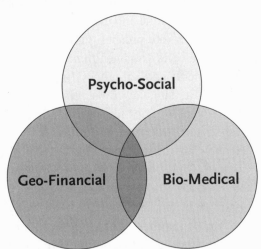

You can think of health as the Bio-Medical dimension; happiness, as the Psycho-Social dimension. And for prosperity, we'll use a new term: the Geo-Financial dimension. These labels identify the specialized fields of research into the three dimensions of Retirement Well-

Being and offer the tools that can help us realize each of them. These six fields are full of good ideas for retirement planning.

GEO-FINANCIAL

The Geo-Financial dimension (prosperity) is based on geography and finance. The original scope of retirement planning was finance, all finance, and nothing but finance, and of course that remains a key component. Now why, you may ask, is geography included? First, because your financial circumstances are greatly affected by where you happen to be on the face of the earth. (If you live in Manhattan, you probably couldn't afford to retire on a million dollars. But if you live in Manhattan, Kansas, you could live like royalty!) And second, because your home is often one of your largest retirement assets. Figuring out how to use your home equity and still have a place to live is both an opportunity and a challenge for the prosperity dimension of retirement. To have the money you want for retirement, you need to be able to think both financially (see chapter 5) and geographically (see chapter 8).

BIO-MEDICAL

The Bio-Medical dimension (health) is made up of biology and medicine. Medicine, of course, studies diseases and how to treat them. Where would you be in retirement without access to medicine? However, quite apart from the necessity of treating disease, it's helpful to understand the basic biological processes of your body. Health means not just the absence of disease, but *vitality*. You'll also see it called *optimum health*. To support that for yourself, you need to understand how your body works, how that changes as you age, and how you can support your body through those changes. Whether you're healthy or sick, knowledge from biology and medicine can help you achieve optimum health—which translates to greater well-being. The sooner you start acting on your Bio-Medical knowledge, the more health (strength, stamina, flexibility, good habits, you name it) you'll establish for your retirement. And the more health you build up, the longer it's likely to last. (You'll find more on this in chapter 9.)

PSYCHO-SOCIAL

The Psycho-Social dimension (happiness) is made up of psychology and sociology. Psychology has often studied unhappiness, rather than happiness—similar to the way that medicine has studied disease rather than health. But psychologists are finally conducting solid research into how happiness actually works and how we can build it into our lives. How's that for useful? On the social side, psychology has studied interpersonal relationships, and sociologists have studied retirement within society and among groups of people. We can use findings from these fields to come up with specific plans for our personal happiness and our happiness with other people. That's the kind of planning that can pay off now as well as later. (More on this in chapters 6 and 7.)

THE SIX FIELDS OF KNOWLEDGE FOR WELL-BEING

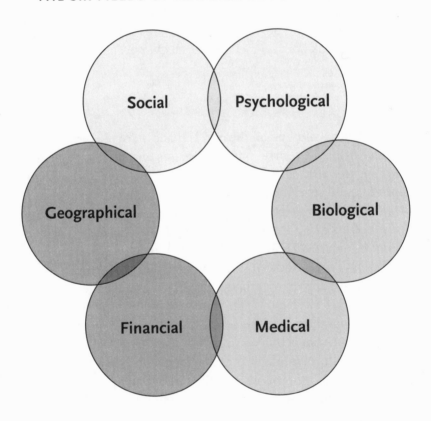

Just because these six fields study topics that are important to your personal well-being doesn't necessarily mean that their findings, in and of themselves, will do *you* any good. On occasion, a field can be like a pipeline, pumping vital information out into the popular media, telling us just what we need to know. But more often, only the insiders in each field know about the latest developments in that field. The lines of communication between the insiders in the field and the outside world usually aren't very good. Because so much of this research goes on at universities, you could even say the information is locked inside the ivory tower. So loads of good information that we all could have used in our retirement planning has not been readily available. We've been trying to plan in the dark.

Well-Being Is Like an Elephant

It's not just retirement planning that's been in the dark. These six fields have more or less been in the dark about each other, too. They're so specialized that they don't often talk with one another. And when they do, sometimes they don't even speak the same language. For example, *well-being* is a term commonly used in these fields. But medicine has one understanding of what it means, psychology has another, economics has yet another, and so on.

This means that there are medical researchers who spend their time studying "health and well-being." They've learned a lot about how to keep our bodies healthy as we approach retirement and progress through it. And there are research psychologists who spend their time studying "subjective well-being." They've learned a lot about how to conduct our lives in order to be happier as we travel along our journey. And, yes, there are economists who spend their time studying "economic well-being." They've learned a lot about how we can more easily accumulate money for retirement and how we can make it last as long as we need it to.

Unfortunately, little knowledge from one particular field's version of well-being gets connected up with the other fields' version of well-being. For example, how does health affect prosperity? How does happiness affect health? Those questions have been asked only recently, and only by a few pioneering researchers. For the most part, knowledge about the dimensions of Retirement Well-Being isn't connected into a comprehensive, intelligible whole.

It's a bit like the old story of three blind men who encounter an elephant. It's a completely new experience for each of them. Not being able to see the elephant in its totality, they each must settle for learning about just one part:

- The first man encounters the side of the elephant. He runs his hands back and forth across the elephant's hide and stretches his arms out as far as he can reach but doesn't find anything else. He concludes that an elephant is similar to a wall.

- The second man encounters the elephant's leg and runs his hands around it. It won't budge; it seems to be planted in the ground. He concludes that an elephant is similar to a tree.

- The third man encounters the elephant's trunk. It coils around his arm, and he feels how long and flexible it is. He concludes that an elephant is similar to a snake.

Our society has studied well-being in much the same way. Economics sees it one way, medicine sees it another way, and psychology sees it a third way. (This flows through to practitioners in the field, too. How often do financial planners, medical doctors, and counselors get together to help their clients plan for retirement? In a word, *never!*) These researchers and practitioners are doing the best they can, and they are now beginning to reach out to each other, to describe to each other the characteristics of the elephant from their own perspectives. But if you want to plan for all three dimensions of well-being for your retirement, *it's up to you to put it all together*. Even though researchers study well-being in a *disconnected* way, you can create a *connected* well-being in your own life, for your own retirement. You, and you alone, can connect the dots for your ideal version of retirement.

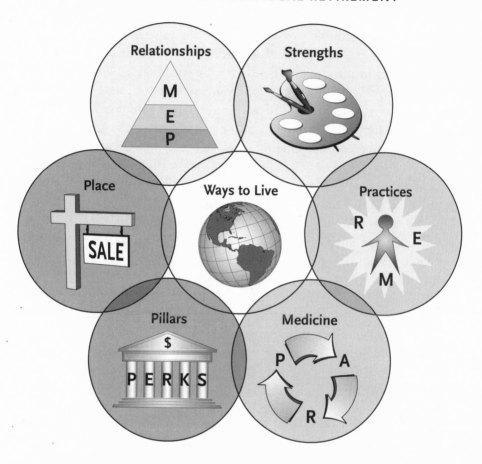

A Map for Your Retirement Journey

This brings us back to the Retirement Well-Being Model. It's not some esoteric theory or hypothesis. It's a practical, down-to-earth tool for planning your retirement in all three dimensions. You might think of it as a literature organizer, collecting information from different fields all in one place. Or as a puzzle, showing you where and how the different parts of your retirement can fit together. Or as a checklist, helping you make sure you've taken care of everything you were supposed to. Or even as a Swiss Army knife—you may not know which tool you'll need to use, or when, but you'll be glad it's in your pocket.

Personally, I like to think of it as a map to take with you on your journey. When you heed the call to adventure, the Retirement Well-Being Model reminds you of the provisions you need and where to look for them. Your journey to retirement will take you into unknown territory, no matter how carefully you research and plan. To ensure your well-being on the way, you'll need a good map. (It might even be a treasure map.) And as promised in chapter 1, you'll create that map for your retirement journey as you work through the remaining chapters. The chapters and exercises provide you with the *processes* for retirement planning; the *content* of your retirement is something that only you can create. Taken all together, these parts make up your Retirement Circles exercise—a picture of your Ideal Retirement. When you complete your own circles, you'll fill in your own content. A picture of the Retirement Circles exercise, with symbols that stand for the key concepts of each circle, is on the previous page.

Looking ahead, chapter 5 addresses the financial part of the prosperity dimension, showing you how to replace the wobbly three-legged stool with five sturdy pillars. Chapters 6 and 7 offer guidance on the two aspects of happiness: the psychological (the happiness that arises from engagement and from using your strengths) and the social (the happiness that comes from a supportive network of rewarding relationships). Chapter 8 complements the financial preparation of chapter 5 by exploring retirement geography at the level of your region, community, and residence. Chapter 9 explores both domains of health: your access to medicine for when you're not feeling up to par and your practices for maintaining biological vitality as you age. Finally, chapter 10 gives you the opportunity to pull all the elements together. You'll create a picture of your Ideal Retirement on One Piece of Paper. After all, the clearer your vision of what you truly want, the more likely you are to manifest it in your life.

But before you start filling in your map with your plans for Retirement Well-Being, in chapter 4 we'll look at something even more fundamental. At the center of the Retirement Circles, and connected to all of them, you'll find your preferred *Ways to Live*. This circle describes a certain way of being in the world and includes your VIPs—

your values, identity, and priorities. These are at the center of the circles because they're at the center of your life. When you're in the second box of life, you may not always have the ability to act in alignment with your values. But the third box offers you the freedom to finally choose your preferred Ways to Live. Even with all this planning and preparation, following your own path to Retirement Well-Being is more like a voyage of discovery than a luxury cruise. It is, in the truest sense, an adventure.

Resources on More Than "Enough Money"

For a well-written take on how people in modern society haven't gotten any happier even though they've gotten more prosperous, consider Gregg Easterbrook's *The Progress Paradox: How Life Gets Better While People Feel Worse* (Random House, 2003).

One of the first—and still one of the best—examples of collaboration between fields of research relevant to retirement is *Successful Aging* (Dell, 1999). John Rowe, a medical doctor, and psychologist Robert Kahn analyzed the long-term results of the MacArthur Foundation study. This isn't as stuffy as it sounds, and it really connects the Psycho-Social and Bio-Medical dimensions.

In 2004, I met an amazing fellow named Steve Vernon when we discovered that we had independently arrived at similar conclusions about comprehensive retirement planning. His book is *Live Long and Prosper! Invest in Your Happiness, Health, and Wealth for Retirement and Beyond* (Wiley, 2004). Steve, an actuary, deeply explores the relationship between life expectancy and managing retirement investments.

"Pay no attention to that man behind the curtain!"
—The Great and Powerful Oz

CHAPTER FOUR

What the Retirement Industry Doesn't Want You to Know

D id you know that you're a target? A target market, that is. In fact, if you're a member of the baby boom generation, you're part of the most targeted market that has ever existed.

Marketers came up with the term *target market* to describe a group of people that they have determined have enough in common to need or want the same things. Businesses use those similarities to design new products and services, then sell them to that target market.

On the one hand, target marketing by businesses is good. It means they're thinking of you when they decide what to offer. And it's nice to be thought of. On the other hand, no one really enjoys being thought of as a target. It sounds too much like warfare. Perhaps it really *is* a type of warfare. Marketers talk about penetrating a market and, they hope, dominating it. They think in terms of dividing and conquering—splitting markets up into smaller chunks to more effectively target them.

The businesses, the marketers, the advertisers, the salespeople who see you this way are attempting to bypass your brain. They've known for decades that advertising and sales are most effective when they use triggers that get you to react emotionally instead of rationally. They are not your friends, no matter how friendly their communications may seem.

Not that the products and services they are marketing to you aren't valuable; many of them are. Some of the stuff that they're selling, you truly want. Some of it, you even truly need. It's just that you'd like to decide rationally, based on what's best for you, rather than emotionally, based on what's best for them. What's best for them is always, always more and more and more sales. These businesses are, in a word, insatiable.

Marketers Know All About the Three Boxes of Life

You and I think of the three boxes as stages of life; marketers see them as target markets. When the baby boomers were kids, marketers realized how many of them there were and that it was a huge business opportunity. It's as though they asked themselves, "What can we sell to kids and young people who are in the first box?" The answer, of course, was kid cereals, and toys, and dolls, and tennis shoes, and fast food. They carefully researched how to package products and where to place them in retail stores to be more attractive to children.

Television arrived with the boomer generation, and marketers studied how to make TV commercials that would be most persuasive to children—first during Saturday morning cartoons, much later on the cable channels oriented toward children and families. They figured out how to use the youngest members of the family to shake the money tree and generate sales. They mapped the psychology of persuasion and emotion in children and the dynamics of power between children and their parents. They knew that children—being emotional rather than rational, and the least skeptical members of any family—were the exposed flank in marketing warfare. They learned the importance of establishing the little consumers' *brand loyalty* at an impressionable age. In short, the marketers became experts at penetrating the child market.

As the boomers became teenagers, marketers became experts at penetrating the teen market. Even though those in the first box of life usually don't have a lot of their own money, they have discretionary spending money because they don't yet have financial obligations. And of course, young people in the first box of life have influence, beyond their own small piggy banks, on the much larger family piggy bank.

Marketers have really targeted people in the second box of life, too, because those are peak earning and spending years. They know what we're doing in that box—starting careers, getting married, and buying cars, then buying homes, furnishing them, and taking vacations to get away from them. They know we need clothes, groceries, dinners out, and lots and lots of coffee.

Some very clever people have made a science and a billion-dollar industry out of studying how to get you to buy more stuff. And the latest trend in marketing is about how to get you to buy *experiences*, rather than just products and services.

Consuming to Infinity

Where will these marketing geniuses turn their attention next? Just as they followed the baby boomers from the first box of life to the second, they have been making war plans and strategies for the transition from the second box of life to the third. Millions of people and trillions of dollars will be in transition. It's when your life is changing and you're moving through life transitions that you particularly need new products and services.

It's also true that, in general, you may be at a financial high point when you're in the later part of the second box and the early part of the third box. You may still be pulling down a full-time salary and be at the peak of your earning power, but (ideally) you're finished with the financial obligations of raising your children. You're cashing out of employer retirement plans and moving to a new house. Transitioning from the second to the third box of life, you may have more access to more liquid cash than you've ever had in your life. Access to all this liquid cash can even make you a bit giddy and impulsive. Marketers, of course, have been studying all this. And making plans for you.

Their plans don't have anything to do with actually optimizing your well-being. Or making your retirement engaging or meaningful. Or making sure you're socially connected or live in a vital community. Or keeping you healthy or physically active. Not that they don't want you to have these things—they just don't particularly care one way or the other. What they do care about is that you keep buying their products and services and experiences. And when you approach the end of your retirement, marketers won't know and won't care whether your retirement was ultimately fulfilling or not. They just want to make sure that you keep consuming—to infinity and beyond (if possible).

Their Secret Weapon Is Lifestyle Marketing

Marketing has changed over the years. One thing you may have noticed is less use of the so-called hard sell—a pushy, obvious, obnoxious approach. Particularly in the branding of companies and products, you may have noticed more use of the so-called soft sell—a more gentle, subtle, sometimes even witty approach. This didn't happen because the billion-dollar advertising industry decided to be nice and give consumers a break. It didn't happen because companies decided it was OK to sell less of their products and make a smaller profit. Just the opposite: marketers figured out how to sell us just as much, or even more, with a breakthrough concept: *psychographics*.

We're all familiar with marketing *demographics*—the practice of profiling us by age, gender, income level, and other external characteristics. The idea is that those of us who are similar in those respects will be similar in the products and services that we need and buy. More to the point, the idea is that we'll also be susceptible to the same marketing approach. Marketing based on demographics works, of course, and is still widely used. However, researchers have discovered that beyond our external characteristics, our internal characteristics—based on psychological research—are the most effective way to profile us. We're actually more likely to fall for a given pitch based on our psychographics than our demographics. After all, we make decisions—including buying decisions—from the inside, not the outside.

This comes down to what most of us would call *lifestyle marketing*. We've all seen it, over and over. A company positions itself and its products (cars, coffee, clothes, condos, you name it) as a gateway to a certain lifestyle. The marketing message to consumers is that when we purchase that company's products, we automatically get the lifestyle that's implied. Research tells the companies about the lives we want to live (party animal, cultured connoisseur, loving caretaker); then they project that lifestyle onto their products. Instead of using a hard sell to push the features and benefits of specific products, they can use the soft sell to get us to buy into a lifestyle. It works because the lifestyles they invite us into are based on our own human longings. Psychographics and lifestyle marketing may seem subtle, but don't be lulled by that subtlety—this is powerful stuff.

For Your Retirement, Do You Want a "Lifestyle" or a Way to Live?

The battle plans for retirement lifestyle marketing are now being laid out. Until recently, marketers have mostly used a simple attack to sell retirement products and services—a carefree, leisure-based lifestyle. However, just as they knew about the Three Boxes of Life, they know about the New Retirement and all of its variations. They're coming up with a variety of retirement lifestyles (lifelong learner, youthful athlete, wise elder, and so on) to dangle in front of you, attached to their products, services, and experiences. The almost subliminal message is this: If you want that particular retirement lifestyle, you can have it. Just get out your credit card.

Is there anything wrong with making purchases to improve your life in retirement? Absolutely not! However, you need to make a fundamental decision about planning your retirement: Do you want to be *sold* a lifestyle dreamed up by an advertising agency to sell products? Or do you want to *choose* a Way to Live based on your own core values, then make conscious purchases that support your choice?

The *Ways to Live* exercise that follows is based on work that was begun by Charles Morris at the University of Chicago in the 1940s (and since then has been more or less forgotten). Morris was among the first to systematically study human values. Recently, values have been addressed primarily by psychologists, and in the small-chunk fashion that makes research easier. For example, which do you value more: freedom or power? That type of values research, and the tools that result, can be interesting and insightful and can help us to know ourselves better. However, they can also be at such a granular level that they're not up to the task of guiding us in our major life decisions. That's why this exercise isn't like that.

Philosophers and others have struggled to make philosophy more relevant to life in modern society. Most of us don't have the opportunity to engage in Socratic dialogue with a learned mentor who challenges us to develop our own philosophy of life. If we could do so, that philosophy of life might guide us in our retirement planning and in designing the life we want to live. Sometimes, though, a philosophy of life can be too far removed from day-to-day life to offer much practical help. For example, do you lean toward existentialism or pragmatism? Even when you know the answer, it may not help you plan your retirement. So this exercise isn't about a philosophy of life, either.

Morris was a philosopher, but he took an unusual approach in designing the original Ways to Live assessment. He didn't use simplistic, single-word "values," and he didn't use esoteric, ontological positions. Rather, he asked a very practical question, one almost tailor-made for retirement planning: What is your idea of "the good life"? Answering that as an essay question—from scratch—could take a lifetime (and often has). So Morris turned it into a multiple-choice questionnaire (which takes considerably less than a lifetime to answer). He identified major *paths of life* or *ways to live in the world* that have been used by people in various times and places across human history.[1]

These Ways to Live grew organically out of human cultures over thousands of years. They've been associated with a variety of different religious, ethical, and philosophical traditions—but the Ways are not those exact traditions or belief systems. Some of the Ways have been practiced in a number of different religious and philosophical traditions but are not tied to any particular one. The Ways are more historical and anthropological than psychological; closer to philosophy,

---

1. See *Varieties of Human Value* (University of Chicago Press, 1956). Morris offered long descriptions of the twelve historical ways, plus a thirteenth he had synthesized. That's what you'll do—synthesize your own!

art, and literature than to science. Each represents not a single value, but a *values system*. They are simply ways of being in the world, paths to follow in conducting one's life.

The following exercise is adapted from Morris' original Ways to Live assessment. It is much simpler and shorter than the original, and it serves as an excellent introduction to thinking in terms of a path of life or way to live. This exercise is up to the task that we'll give it within the scope of this book. Just remember that these descriptions of the Ways are simply a taste, and that each is also a doorway to an entire way of living in the world. Each is an answer—or a part of an answer—to the question "What is the good life?" After you complete the Ways to Live exercise, you'll also identify your VIPs—your values, identity, and priorities. (Note: You can make a copy of each exercise, enlarging it if you'd like more space for writing, and use the copy to fill in your responses.)

CHOOSING MY WAYS TO LIVE

Listed on the next page are twelve Ways to Live that have been followed by groups of people at various times and places. Each Way is a different path to what has been called "the good life."

First, assign each Way a letter grade from "A" through "D," according to how much you prefer that way to live. It's not a question of whether you live that way *now*, or how you think people *should* live. Simply grade them according to how closely each one fits the kind of life *you personally would like to live*. As there are twelve ways, you may assign each letter grade more than once.

Second, assign each Way a number rank from "1" through "12," from your most preferred to your least preferred. Start by ranking all of your "A" grades, then your "B" grades, and so on. Use each number rank only once.

Letter Grade	Way to Live	Short Description	Number Rank
	Refinement	Understanding, appreciating, and preserving the best in society	
	Improvement	Working continuously for realistic solutions to specific problems	
	Altruism	Sharing sympathetic concern and affection for others	
	Service	Devoting yourself to the great cosmic purposes and to others	
	Community	Actively merging yourself into a social group with common goals	
	Action	Using physical energy to accomplish things in the world	
	Enjoyment	Immersing yourself in sensuous pleasures and festivities	
	Simplicity	Enjoying easy, wholesome comforts and friendship	
	Receptivity	Patiently opening to joy and peace through nature	
	Contemplation	Turning inward to cultivate a rich and rewarding inner world	
	Self-Sufficiency	Gaining self-knowledge through independence from persons and things	
	Self-Control	Holding yourself firm through reason and high ideals	

Each of the Ways can be a path in life unto itself. However, for planning your retirement in modern society, you don't need to choose just one path. You can consider how to create your own path by integrating your three most preferred Ways to Live. So after you rank all the Ways to Live, enter your top choices—the Ways you ranked 1, 2, and 3—into the Retirement Circle to use for your One Piece of Paper in chapter 10.

**My Ideal Retirement
includes choosing these
Ways to Live:**

_____ ,

_____ ,

and _____ .

MY VALUES, IDENTITY, AND PRIORITIES

Congratulations! You've identified your three most preferred Ways to Live, using the quick and easy, multiple-choice method. Now it's time to move on to the short-answer questions. (Good news: no essay question!) Look at your Ways to Live Retirement Circle, and think back to the times in your life when you were most able to actually live in those Ways. Sometimes, circumstances may have prevented you. But focus on those times, however brief or seldom, when you were able to follow those paths in life. Create a label or short phrase to name one, two, or three of those examples, to clearly identify them in your memory.

Time #1 when I was following my Ways to Live path:

_____

Time #2 when I was following my Ways to Live path:

_____

Time #3 when I was following my Ways to Live path:

_____

Now, from the perspective of those times, answer the following questions about your VIPs:

1. **Values.** When I was following my Ways to Live path, what did I value? What did I hold most dear?

   _____

   _____

2. **Identity.** When I was following my Ways to Live path, who was I being on the inside? What was my role on the outside?

   _____

   _____

3. **Priorities.** When I was following my Ways to Live path, how did I allocate my time? My money? My other resources?

_____

_____

Your life now, and your life in retirement, may be quite different from the times when you were able to follow these Ways to Live. Still, look for the tiny seeds of those experiences that you can carry with you on your journey to retirement. Who knows where you may be able to plant them in the future?

Six Retirement Industries That Are Targeting You

The Ways to Live exercise and your VIPs help you do retirement planning from the inside out. They start with you, to help you to bring your inner values out into the world and incorporate them into the decisions that you make about your retirement. However, sometimes you need to start on the outside, with a specific marketing pitch, and see how well the product or service fits your needs. In these next sections we'll turn things around and look at a tool for doing that.

For as long as retirement has existed, there have been businesses seeking to serve the needs of those approaching and entering retirement. As the number of people in retirement has grown, a growing variety of businesses have sought to penetrate the retirement market. Collectively, let's call this otherwise very diverse group of businesses the _retirement industry_—a hodgepodge of other industries, each with an interest in providing products and services related to retirement. Some retirement industry companies market to people who are still in the second box of life (for example, financial companies selling investments for retirement). Others market to people who are transitioning to or already in the third box (for example, retirement communities). The list of industries and companies could probably go on forever, but there are six main ones that expect to make a bundle from the baby boomers' retirement:

1. Investments   4. Travel

2. Insurance   5. Retail

3. Real Estate   6. Antiaging

Many other industries will naturally benefit from serving the needs of a growing number of retirees—health care, for example. However, the six listed are worth noting because they are—and will be—aggressively marketing products and services to you. Some of these may be wonderful, and some may be not so wonderful. Each of us is unique, so only you can decide which products and services will genuinely increase your well-being—and which are essentially a waste of money. Or, even worse than a waste of money, a waste of your attention, your focus, or possibly even your hopes and dreams.

The Retirement Industry Wants You to Have the Right Stuff

The benevolent aspect of marketing is to make you aware of things that you may want or need. If it weren't for marketing, you might never find these things or even know that they exist. (If this book weren't marketed, you probably wouldn't be reading it right now.)

The less benevolent (dare we say malevolent?) aspect of marketing is to influence you to buy things that you really *don't need*. Or to influence you to buy things that, in that moment, you think you want—but that, if you had a chance to reflect on it, you'd realize you don't really want at all. The marketing is just so darned good that, almost before you know it, you've bought something—or made a big life decision—without considering the alternatives.

The retirement industry wants to define your retirement for you. Instead of choosing a Way to Live, they want you to buy a lifestyle. Instead of reflecting on your values, they want you to value consuming the right investments, the right insurance, the right real estate, the right travel, the right retail goods, and the right antiaging products. Instead of discovering your identity, they want you to simply identify yourself as a consumer. They want images of products and services dancing in your head so that you make acquiring them the goal and the purpose of your retirement. They want consuming to be your highest priority. They want you to believe that if you buy all the right stuff, you'll live the right lifestyle, have "the good life," and have *their* idea of a good retirement. And if you *don't* buy all the right stuff, you'll have a bad retirement—an impoverished retirement, an unsafe retirement, a nowhere retirement, a boring retirement, a nobody retirement, an old person's retirement! That's no one's idea of "the good life." In short, they want you to believe that you'll be in pain if you don't buy into their definition of what retirement should be. In fact, more ingeniously, they want you to believe you're in pain already if you haven't yet acquired all the stuff they want you to buy.

The retirement industry isn't bad or evil, any more than a predator like a wolf or a shark is bad or evil. Marketing and selling are just in their DNA. But that doesn't mean that you want to get gobbled up by them, either.

How to Spot Retirement Hogwash

You absolutely, positively will want to buy some of what the retirement industry is selling. But you probably want to design your own Retirement Well-Being first. Then you can make decisions about which products, services, and experiences will support *your* idea of well-being in retirement. You can base those decisions on careful reflection rather than on the insidious marketing approaches that try to slip one by you by appealing solely to your emotions.

The primary way that the retirement industry tries to influence you is through advertising and direct sales. And most of these ads and sales pitches are good old-fashioned hogwash.

"What exactly is hogwash?" you may ask. Hogwash is communication that at first seems plausible, or even persuasive, but doesn't hold up under closer scrutiny. Hogwash is sometimes a bald-faced lie. But more likely it contains just enough truth to have some credibility. It's only when you pick the communication apart and examine it that you discover the hogwash.

Hogwash isn't reserved for just marketing communications, by the way. Some hogwash becomes deeply engrained in the media, the culture, and people's belief systems. It can bubble up from all around and then can even seem like common sense or received wisdom. That can make the hogwash even more difficult to detect.

There's a story about Ernest Hemingway. Supposedly, a group of journalists asked him the single attribute that is most important to becoming a great writer. Hemingway's response was, reportedly, "The most essential gift for a good writer is a built-in, shockproof bullshit detector."

A similar tool is essential to becoming a great consumer of products from the retirement industry. But most readers of this book are far more polite than either novelists or journalists, so let's instead call it a *hogwash detector*. After all, it doesn't matter which form of residue or which particular farm animal you're talking about. Once you know how to use the detector, you'll be able to smell it from a mile away.

So here is your very own Retirement Hogwash Detector—a worksheet that you can use to break apart, or deconstruct, communications from the retirement industry. When you break these messages apart, it's easier to see how marketers are trying to influence or manipulate you. It's easier to see what the product or service really is and what it can or cannot do. And once you've designed your own concept of Retirement Well-Being (using the rest of this book), you can determine whether the product or service supports that.

Each time you consider making a major purchase or a major decision, you can use the Retirement Hogwash Detector to help you decide. You'll reach one of four possible conclusions:

1. You don't need what's being marketed. Sorry, Charlie!

2. You do need what's being marketed. Get out the checkbook.

3. You need something similar to what's being marketed, but want to consider alternative purchases.

4. You have a *higher need* that cannot be fulfilled by what's being marketed—or by any other purchase. You need to fill the need in another way.

Here's the Retirement Hogwash Detector. To help you get a feel for using it, we have included some completed examples at the end of this chapter.

The Retirement Hogwash Detector

Don't be manipulated! You're being bombarded nonstop with advertising and sales pitches. Some decisions you make for retirement are once-in-a-lifetime events, so you can't learn through trial and error. You need to get them right the first time. Many pitches seem reasonable on the surface but appeal only to your emotions. They're designed to make you feel inadequate, dissatisfied with your life, or fearful that you'll be in pain if you don't buy the product. That's *hogwash!*

To evaluate some pitches, you may need to get expert technical knowledge. But you can make a good start by reading between the lines and uncovering the hidden messages attempting to influence your emotions. Answer each of these questions about any ad, presentation, or live sales pitch that you find tempting (see examples at the end of this chapter):

Underwriter. Who's behind the pitch? What's the marketer's motive? Does the marketer want an ongoing relationship, or just a one-time transaction? Does the marketer really have any interest in your well-being?

Pitch. What are the facts and actual features? What are the greater *implied* benefits, as suggested by the pictures, music, style, or tone? What emotions are these designed to trigger?

Assumptions. What are the underlying messages about you or the world? What are the hidden values or beliefs? In your experience, are these really true for you in your own life?

Ideal Outcome. What's the most you can realistically, rationally expect? Could you actually get the implied benefits? What *can* this do for you and what *can't* it do?

Needs. Why might you really need it? Why might you *not* need it? What are the alternatives? Finally, what *higher need* can you identify that the pitch hints at, but could never fulfill? How might you *really* fill this need?

Two Final Words: Retirement Simplicity

Why has this chapter treated marketers so harshly, you may ask? The answer, dear reader, is that marketing is so pervasive in our mass-media-dominated culture that we've become desensitized to it. Because we've become desensitized, it's not easy to see the situation clearly, through fresh eyes. But it's essential that you do your retirement planning with fresh eyes, for two reasons.

One is related to Retirement Hogwash and to the wobbly retirement stool. If it turns out that many people truly aren't saving enough for retirement, they could be headed for a very difficult time. Although the answer seems to be simple—save more!—there aren't any signs yet that this is happening. If those same people arrive at retirement age to discover that they must live on significantly less income than they've been accustomed to, it will be a painful adjustment. They will long for the higher standard of living they enjoyed during their working years, and they will lament their diminished circumstances. Who wouldn't?

Of all the changes that these people could possibly make in their lives, there is one change that would have a profoundly positive effect on both phases of their retirement finances: *voluntarily reducing their expenditures*. Reducing expenditures—that is, consuming less—in the second box of life would help them to set aside more money for retirement. At the same time, voluntarily consuming less would help them prepare to live in the third box under the reduced circumstances they would still be likely to experience.

Voluntarily consuming less has two benefits. The first is purely economic: they will be able to save more. The second is more related to a sense of control over their lives. By consciously consuming less, rather than having it imposed on them, they will retain conscious decision-making power. That is one difference between voluntary simplicity and involuntary poverty: a decision to be satisfied with a lower rate of consumption. For those who suspect that they may be headed toward a retirement with insufficient income, a conscious choice to live with less is the strategy that allows them to retain the most control over their lives. The first step in making that choice is to confront the messages in our culture about how much they need to buy (buy! buy!) to experience "the good life." Of course, planning consciously for Retirement Simplicity puts them directly at odds with the world of marketing and the consumer culture.[2]

The second reason this chapter has dealt with marketers so harshly is related to the Ways to Live. Now we are talking about the many people who will arrive at retirement with plenty of retirement income. In fact, they will be loaded. They'll have the luxury of continuing to consume at the same rate in the third box as they did in the second box. Perhaps at an even higher rate. They won't face the economic challenge that the first group did. However, the second issue—control and choice—will still be a challenge. To the extent that they uncritically accept the marketers' messages about "the good life" and how to live in retirement, they will be giving up their control and choice in a subtle way. Only through the process of finding their own preferred Ways to Live and identifying their own VIPs will they gain a perspective for deciding how, and how much, they choose to consume in retirement. There are important life tasks associated with the retirement journey—and consumption is mostly a distraction from them. So, for a different reason than the necessity confronting the first group, Retirement Simplicity may be worth the consideration of these affluent folks, as well.

Besides, who would want to be a retirement *consumer* when they could be a retirement *adventurer*?

2. Although *retirement simplicity* is a new term, *voluntary simplicity* has become fairly common. The concept was introduced by Duane Elgin in his now classic 1981 book, *Voluntary Simplicity: Toward a Way of Life That Is Outwardly Simple, Inwardly Rich* (Harper, revised edition, 1998).

Retirement Hogwash Detector Examples

We've run the Retirement Hogwash Detector on a few common retirement industry pitches to give you a feel for how you can deconstruct the message, get to the underlying motive, and make the right choice for *your* Retirement Well-Being.

Example #1: The Romantic Getaway Cruise

Underwriter
Who's behind the pitch? *Travel agency.*
What's the marketer's motive? *Wants my booking.*
Does the marketer want an ongoing relationship, or just a one-time transaction? *Sure, they'd like me to cruise again.*
Does the marketer really have any interest in your well-being? *Doesn't care about me.*

Pitch
What are the facts and actual features? *Four-day cruise.*
What are the greater implied benefits, as suggested by the pictures, music, style, or tone? *Fun with beautiful people.*
What emotions are these designed to trigger? *Makes me want to escape.*

Assumptions
What are the underlying messages about you or the world? *They can create more fun for me than I can for myself.*
What are the hidden values or beliefs? *Vacations should be about indulgence, period.*
In your experience, are these really true for you in your own life? *But I've always had more fun when I've created it.*

Ideal Outcome
What's the most you can realistically, rationally expect? *See beautiful islands, eat a lot of food, relax, swim, and sun (if the weather's good).*
Could you actually get the implied benefits? *The other guests will be ordinary folks, not professional models.*
What can this do for you? *Can give me an adventure; I can meet new people, briefly.*
What can't it do? *Can't give lasting satisfaction.*

Need
Why might you really need it? *I may need a change of scene, a change of pace.*
Why might you not need it? *I don't need the letdown I may feel when I return.*
What are the alternatives? *I could create my own trip to explore an area I'm curious about but have never visited.*

Higher Need
What higher need can you identify that the pitch hints at, but could never fulfill? *I'm bored, in a rut.*
How might you really fill this need? *I need an ongoing interest instead of just a short vacation.*

Example #2: The Luxury Ride

Underwriter

Who's behind the pitch? *Luxury automaker.*

What's the marketer's motive? *Wants to sell or lease me a car.*

Does the marketer want an ongoing relationship, or just a one-time transaction? *Probably hoping I'll want the new model every few years.*

Does the marketer really have any interest in your well-being? *Doesn't care about me.*

Pitch

What are the facts and actual features? *Expensive, comfort, luxurious appointments, high-tech systems.*

What are the greater implied benefits, as suggested by the pictures, music, style, or tone? *I'll be admired and envied.*

What emotions are these designed to trigger? *Makes me want more social status.*

Assumptions

What are the underlying messages about you or the world? *People will look up to me.*

What are the hidden values or beliefs? *You are what you drive; this car will proclaim my superiority.*

In your experience, are these really true for you in your own life? *My friends don't care what I drive, and I don't need to impress strangers.*

Ideal Outcome

What's the most you can realistically, rationally expect? *Good for long trips.*

Could you actually get the implied benefits? *Not unless I change everything else about myself.*

What can this do for you? *Can give me comfort.*

What can't it do? *Can't give me social status.*

Need

Why might you really need it? *I do need a new car.*

Why might you not need it? *Probably don't need a luxury car.*

What are the alternatives? *Look at other models.*

Higher Need

What higher need can you identify that the pitch hints at, but could never fulfill? *I do want to be respected by others.*

How might you really fill this need? *Identify what in my life makes me proud, and how I can expand that.*

Example #3: A More Youthful You

Underwriter

Who's behind the pitch? *Cosmetic surgeon.*

What's the marketer's motive? *Wants me to undergo (and pay for) cosmetic surgery.*

Does the marketer want an ongoing relationship, or just a one-time transaction? *May hope for follow-up treatment and additional procedures. (I've read that people often get "hooked," never satisfied with the results.)*

Does the marketer really have any interest in your well-being? *Cares that I'm pleased with the improvement, to preserve the surgeon's reputation and generate referrals.*

Pitch

What are the facts and actual features? *Facelift gets rid of wrinkles.*

What are the greater implied benefits, as suggested by the pictures, music, style, or tone? *I'll look younger and feel better about myself.*

What emotions are these designed to trigger? *Makes me feel sad that I've aged, fearful about how others will see and treat me.*

Assumptions

What are the underlying messages about you or the world? *Old is ugly; young is beautiful.*

What are the hidden values or beliefs? *Old is less desirable and valuable; young is more desirable and valuable.*

In your experience, are these really true for you in your own life? *With maturity, I've become more comfortable with my appearance. "Inner beauty" is a reality.*

Ideal Outcome

What's the most you can realistically, rationally expect? *Would make me look younger.*

Could you actually get the implied benefits? *You can't turn back the clock; you are who you are.*

What can this do for you? *I may look younger and more rested (or I may have that stretched-tight, wide-eyed look).*

What can't it do? *Don't think it would change how I feel about myself, though.*

Need

Why might you really need it? *I may need a younger look to compete in the workplace. I may need to feel that my spouse is still attracted to me, and my spouse may like it.*

Why might you not need it? *It probably won't really change my life the way I hope it would.*

What are the alternatives? *Maybe I really need to renew my marriage in other ways.*

Higher Need

What higher need can you identify that the pitch hints at, but could never fulfill? *I need to accept myself on the inside, and feel confident and entitled to be a full participant in life at every age.*

How might you really fill this need? *Appreciate myself as I am and value all I have gained through life experience. Keep my body and mind active.*

Example #4: The "55 and Better" Planned Community

Underwriter

Who's behind the pitch? *Real estate developer for an "active adult community."*

What's the marketer's motive? *To sell properties.*

Does the marketer want an ongoing relationship, or just a one-time transaction? *Manages the association, so probably wants to keep me satisfied.*

Does the marketer really have any interest in your well-being? *Only to the extent I will refer other potential buyers to the marketer.*

Pitch

What are the facts and actual features? *Beautiful property—far away, though.*

What are the greater implied benefits, as suggested by the pictures, music, style, or tone? *Living there will be like a constant vacation, with attractive people.*

What emotions are these designed to trigger? *Makes me want to live that way—the good life, all ease and fun.*

Assumptions

What are the underlying messages about you or the world? *Retirees just want to be around other retirees.*

What are the hidden values or beliefs? *Retirement is about leisure.*

In your experience, are these really true for you in your own life? *I enjoy being around people of all ages. And what if I want to work part-time?*

Ideal Outcome

What's the most you can realistically, rationally expect? *A livable home in a benign climate.*

Could you actually get the implied benefits? *Depends on the actual quality of the home. Real people, not professional models, will be my neighbors.*

What can this do for you? *Can give me the experience of living in beautiful surroundings with maintenance taken care of.*

What can't it do? *Can't really sustain the vacation feeling over the long term. I've got to create my own life in retirement, and a development alone can't do that for me.*

Need

Why might you really need it? *I do need to relocate to a better climate when I retire.*

Why might you not need it? *I don't need that distance from my family and friends.*

What are the alternatives? *I could look for a smaller town or city neighborhood in this area.*

Higher Need

What higher need can you identify that the pitch hints at, but could never fulfill? *I want to have a "sense of place" and a connection with the other people who live there—to realize the true meaning of the word community.*

How might you really fill this need? *Look into other options at my own pace, comparing them based on my criteria. Spend time in the potential locations.*

Example #5: The Unbeatable Investment Opportunity

Underwriter

Who's behind the pitch? *Investment company, selling a mutual fund.*

What's the marketer's motive? *To get my retirement funds invested in the marketer's company.*

Does the marketer want an ongoing relationship, or just a one-time transaction? *Wants to keep me as shareholder.*

Does the marketer really have any interest in your well-being? *No.*

Pitch

What are the facts and actual features? *Fund was a top performer for the last few years.*

What are the greater implied benefits, as suggested by the pictures, music, style, or tone? *It will keep performing that way (but read the fine print, which specifically warns me not to invest based on past performance).*

What emotions are these designed to trigger? *Makes me want to get in on those high returns and not miss out on a good thing.*

Assumptions

What are the underlying messages about you or the world? *Finding high returns is the most important thing.*

What are the hidden values or beliefs? *You'll be sorry if you let this pass and it really pays off.*

In your experience, are these really true for you in your own life? *I've gotten burned before, so I think it's better to stay diversified.*

Ideal Outcome

What's the most you can realistically, rationally expect? *Fund could do as well in the future as the past.*

Could you actually get the implied benefits? *Few investments perform well all the time; they're subject to market cycles.*

What can this do for you? *Would make some difference to my finances.*

What can't it do? *It's not an investing cure-all.*

Need

Why might you really need it? *I need to choose a mutual fund.*

Why might you not need it? *But I don't need something that volatile—I'd be lying awake at night worrying.*

What are the alternatives? *Maybe make it just one part of my investments.*

Higher Need

What higher need can you identify that the pitch hints at, but could never fulfill? *I want to have some peace of mind that I'm doing the right thing.*

How might you really fill this need? *I need to either learn more about investments or get advice that I can trust.*

Example #6: Insurance for Nursing Home Costs

Underwriter

Who's behind the pitch? *Insurance company.*

What's the marketer's motive? *Selling long-term care insurance.*

Does the marketer want an ongoing relationship, or just a one-time transaction? *They would want me to keep the policy in force—but if I ever actually need the care, will the company be as eager to pay the claims as they were to get my business?*

Does the marketer really have any interest in your well-being? *No.*

Pitch

What are the facts and actual features? *Premiums are high, but could pay off.*

What are the greater implied benefits, as suggested by the pictures, music, style, or tone? *I won't need to worry about the cost of getting old.*

What emotions are these designed to trigger? *Makes me afraid that if I don't buy it, I'll end up liquidating my home to pay for long-term care expenses.*

Assumptions

What are the underlying messages about you or the world? *There's a good probability I'll need long-term care.*

What are the hidden values or beliefs? *I'd go into an institution rather than work it out with family. (I need to find out what the policy would pay in either case.)*

In your experience, are these really true for you in your own life? *My parents stayed at home until their deaths. But my mother-in-law was in a nursing home.*

Ideal Outcome

What's the most you can realistically, rationally expect? *If I need long-term care in an institution, at least it's paid for, and I won't lose my house.*

Could you actually get the implied benefits? *It's not the whole answer. We need to address other issues: end of life, heirs, and so on.*

What can this do for you? *Could save us from spending down all of our assets and going on Medicaid.*

What can't it do? *The policy won't keep me from becoming old or disabled.*

Need

Why might you really need it? *The policy may make financial sense based on my situation and my health issues (current and potential, based on my family history).*

Why might you not need it? *I may not need it if I have enough savings to cover long-term care expenses or if I qualify for Medicaid.*

What are the alternatives? *Look at other long-term care insurance plans. Try to stay healthy. Choose or adapt the right home and town for aging in place.*

Higher Need

What higher need can you identify that the pitch hints at, but could never fulfill? *I want to be self-sufficient as long as possible.*

How might you really fill this need? *Make the changes that I can now to improve my chances of being healthier for longer.*

Resources on "Lifestyles" and Ways to Live

Probably the most entertaining look at consumption in modern society is *Affluenza: The All-Consuming Epidemic,* by John de Graaf, David Wann, and Thomas H. Naylor (Berrett-Koehler, 2005). This clever concept—affluenza—is also articulated by two companion PBS documentaries, which may be available at your public library.

If you'd like to learn about demographics and psychographics from the marketers' perspective, check out David Wolfe and Robert Snyder's *Ageless Marketing* (Kaplan Business, 2003). The culmination of many years of research, this book will help you see yourself from the other end of the microscope—as a target market.

If you're interested in the opposite perspective—retirement as an opportunity to consider life's biggest questions—explore Ronald Manheimer's *A Map to the End of Time: Wayfarings with Friends and Philosophers* (Norton, 1999). This book introduces classical philosophy through group discussions with retirees from all walks of life.

Finally, for an integrated perspective on how you might develop a philosophical approach to living in the modern world, read *Money and the Meaning of Life,* by Jacob Needleman (Currency Doubleday, 1994). This book delves deeply into timeless wisdom about money and materialism while also telling an interesting story.

"I would rather spend my time enjoying my income than bothering about investments."

—Clive Granger, winner of the 2003
Nobel Prize in economics[1]

1. Granger was quoted by Peter Gosselin in the *Los Angeles Times* on May 11, 2005.

CHAPTER FIVE

Retirement Money: When to Use Autopilot and When to Take the Controls

D oes the subject of money interest you?

Of course, we're not talking about all the wonderful things you can do *with* money—having a nice place to live, going shopping, doing fun things with your friends and family. No, we're talking about money as a subject in itself. Are you interested in money's inner secrets? Where it comes from, how to get more of it, what makes it grow, and so on?

If the answer is yes, then you're a *money enthusiast*. You may have a job working with money—which would be a good thing, for both you and others. If you're a money enthusiast but it isn't your work, then it's probably your hobby. You buy financial books and magazines, gleefully open your account statements, and swap money stories at social gatherings.

On the other hand, if this doesn't sound like you at all, then you're probably *not* a money enthusiast. Money, in and of itself, doesn't interest you one bit. The subject may bore you, frustrate you, or even scare you a little. If you're not an enthusiast, you're not likely to have a job focused on working with money, and it probably isn't your hobby, either. You don't open your account statements right away, and when you do, you see only the bottom line and ignore the rest. When money comes up at a social gathering, you either change the subject or make your way to another conversation.

If we took a poll, we'd probably discover that some folks are at these two extremes of money enthusiasm, but most of us are somewhere in between: some money topics interest us, some of the time, but it's definitely not our hobby.

Wherever you are along the money enthusiasm spectrum, you may find that this chapter is not what you expect. It doesn't list all the types of retirement plans, offer advice on choosing a mutual fund, or tell you how to minimize your income taxes. This chapter isn't about those kinds of financial nuts and bolts of retirement. Heaven knows, there are hundreds of those books already in existence, and new ones are published all the time. (I'll even suggest some good ones for you!)

This chapter is more of a companion to all of those highly detailed, financial nuts-and-bolts books. Mainly, this chapter is about getting crystal clear on the essential sources of retirement income that you plan to use. Whether you're a money enthusiast or not, you need to know what your own particular sources of retirement income are. If you're like most people, you may have a variety of financial holdings—but just a few main ones. These are your pillars. You need to know your pillars so well that you could instantly rattle off their names, write down their approximate values, and even remember the web address or telephone number to check up on them. Even if you don't like the financial element of retirement, if you want Retirement Well-Being, you need to get a handle on these sources of income.

Trade Your Wobbly Old Stool for Secure Financial Pillars

Remember society's original three-legged stool for retirement income, which supported generations of workers and helped them acquire financial security for retirement? Although not every worker was able to make use of all three legs, they did a good job for society and provided opportunities for individual workers. But in chapter 2 we saw how all three legs of the stool are getting wobbly, and why retirement income will probably need to be different for you and other retirees in the future:

- For Social Security, the challenge is the shrinking replacement ratio and the funding crisis of fewer and fewer workers paying in for more and more retirees.

- For employer plans, the big change is a migration from traditional employer-funded pensions to 401(k)-type plans that shift much of the funding (that is, responsibility for saving) and decision making to employees.

- For personal savings, the looming concern is the statistical fact that Americans, on average, are saving less out of their personal income than they have historically.

Now it's time to turn from the past and look toward the future. Rather than pinning your hopes on this wobbly, seventy-year-old stool, let's look at how you can build your retirement financial security on some solid, secure pillars. Pillars that allow you to have as much direct control and security as possible. Five of these pillars, or sources of retirement income, are most common in our society today. You need to look at all of them to determine how large a role each is likely to play in your retirement finances.

Your Retirement PERKS

In your working life, have you ever enjoyed any perks? A perk is a benefit, a right, or a privilege that you receive over and above your regular compensation. Perks are usually doled out to bigwigs in corporations; they can be anything from a key to the executive washroom to a million dollars in stock options. The word *perk* is short for *perquisite*, which originally meant property that you didn't inherit. So according to the original idea, if you didn't inherit your perks, apparently you had to earn them, somehow. Then you were entitled to them.

That's exactly what you need to do to create your financial pillars for retirement. So we'll even call them PERKS—an acronym for the five most basic ways you can create security for your retirement income. Three of them are the twenty-first-century versions of the three legs of the stool; two of them were never recognized as parts of the stool, even though they've been around for a long time.

Here are the PERKS.

P IS FOR PERSONAL SAVINGS

This pillar is just like the leg of the same name from the olden days. *Personal savings* is the pillar that you have the most direct control over. Which also means, of course, that it's the one that demands the most from you. This pillar won't even exist unless you resolve to save your money and invest it—and then do just that.

E IS FOR EMPLOYER PLANS

For some, this pillar will still be like the employer plans leg from the olden days, but for most of us it won't be. Increasingly, *employer plans* are 401(k)-type employee saving plans, with some employers kicking in a little, others a lot. Even though these are sponsored by employers, you can think of them as joined at the hip with personal savings. As with your personal savings, this pillar may not even exist unless you take the initiative to save through payroll deductions, and you're usually in charge of making the investment decisions, too.

R IS FOR REAL ESTATE

This pillar was never recognized as a leg in the olden days, even though it existed. For most people, building retirement security through *real estate* means owning their personal residence. (Although some enterprising real-estate tycoons build retirement security through other types of real estate, too.) Throughout the era of the three-legged stool, workers were buying homes and building home equity. But in the olden days people thought of their home solely as a place to live in retirement. Their goal was to pay off the mortgage before they retired. As home values have climbed and home equity has become a larger share of people's total assets, many have begun to realize that home equity can be used for retirement income.

This pillar is a bit like personal savings, in that it won't exist unless you take the initiative to purchase a home and build up equity. But unlike personal savings, retirement security isn't the primary motivation for owning your home. It's an incidental, but possibly essential, part of your retirement finances. Also unlike personal savings, it doesn't usually require making ongoing investment decisions. (But it may require you to do odd jobs on the weekend. Which is worse?)

K IS FOR KEEP WORKING

In the really, really olden days, before the Industrial Revolution, this was the only pillar (except for the kindness of family and friends). More recently, in the olden days of the twentieth century, *keeping working* as a source of retirement security almost disappeared. It definitely wasn't part of the three-legged stool. In fact, the stool metaphor underscores the assumption that retirement meant sitting on your duff and not working! But these days, keeping working is a viable option for many retirees, and we can expect it to grow ever more common in the future. Continuing to work is a little bit like personal savings, in that it's up to you to make it happen. The other four pillars would be broadly classified as financial capital, whereas this pillar could be classified as human capital. If you plan to keep working, you need to be healthy, and you need to offer value to employers. There's a big difference between assuming that you'll keep working and actually being prepared to do it when you retire. The best way to be prepared to keep working is to follow the career and job-hunting recommendations in the companion to this book—the original *What Color Is Your Parachute?*

S IS FOR SOCIAL SECURITY

In the olden days, *Social Security* was originally intended to be a safety net for the relatively small proportion of people who lived long enough to become too old to work. Then it morphed into a very broad-based retirement program that ended up being the foundation of retirement income for many. In the future it may not be as much of a pillar as it has been for retirees in the past, but it may be essential. Of all the pillars, this is the only one that's almost completely automatic. Just by earning income that's subject to FICA (or self-employment taxes), you're accruing future retirement benefits automatically. Isn't that nice? No gumption needed.

So there you have them: your Five Pillars of Retirement Financial Security. Whether or not you've ever been fortunate enough to get any perks from your employers, you'll definitely want to make sure you get these PERKS.

Put Your PERKS on Autopilot, If You Can

Social Security became such a foundation largely because it was automatic. Workers didn't need to remind themselves to contribute, and then get around to doing it, and then follow through to keep Social Security going. It just happened. That's also why traditional pension plans have provided so much security to generations of workers. If the employer provided a pension, the employee was accruing benefits automatically, sometimes without realizing it until later on. It was automatic, and the pension was doing the right thing to ensure retirement income without the employee needing to know what the right thing was. Two legs of the old three-legged stool were pretty much on autopilot, and that's one reason they worked so well.

The Five Pillars aren't like those legs. In the future, retirement security will depend much, much more on *you* and the actions that you take. You're the one who's in charge. But you can learn from the past, and you can resolve to look for ways to use automatic and autopilot approaches to building your pillars, whenever and wherever possible.

Now we'll take a deeper look at the strategies you can use to build your pillars. Personal savings and the emerging version of employer plans are quite similar: both require you to take the initiative on saving and investing. Because those activities are so fundamental—yet they're a major bugaboo for the majority of workers—most of this chapter is devoted to saving and investing. But we'll also touch on real estate, keeping working, and Social Security.

Finally, there's an exercise at the end of this chapter that will help you get crystal clear on which of the Five Pillars you'll focus on to create your Ideal Retirement. After all, you'll want to be able to rattle off their names, write down their approximate values, and remember their web addresses.

Is There a Personal Savings Gene?

We generally do one of two things with each and every dollar that we receive: save it or spend it. Yes, the concept of saving—setting aside a portion of whatever comes in—is straightforward, but for most of us the *practice* is difficult. Even some money enthusiasts (with financial knowledge coming out of their ears) have trouble getting themselves to save in the first place. On the other hand, there are people who aren't really money enthusiasts and aren't interested in or knowledgeable about the intricacies of money, but nevertheless are very good savers. These people don't make money into a hobby—they just tuck it away.

Whether there's a "good saver" trait that will be discovered in the human genome or it's a habit that's created through life experience (like living through the Great Depression), saving certainly seems natural for some people—and very unnatural for others. Natural savers are somehow able to save whether they're young or old, low earners or high earners, happy or unhappy, married or single, and so on. For them, it's as though saving isn't a decision that they make, but something that just happens—*automatically*. We should all be so fortunate.

Now, we all recognize that there are economic circumstances beyond our individual control, and the list is a long one: erosion of middle-class earning power, stagnant wages in terms of inflation, recessions, unemployment, outsourcing, the steeply rising cost of essentials like housing and health care and near-essentials like a college education.

The interplay of social forces and personal finance can stack the deck, too. The boomer generation has been called the "sandwich generation," as its members have gotten squeezed by the double demands of caring for aging parents and raising the next generation (many of whom have lingered in the nest, or returned to it, long after they once would have been self-sufficient). All this would fill another book, so we won't try to tackle it here. No, what we are going to address is the part of spending and saving, over which you *do* have control. So let's get back to personal saving.

Budgets Don't Work

Have you ever created a budget? A budget is a spending plan that sets a target for how much to spend on different categories of expenditures. For example, businesses set up budgets so they can plan how much they'll need for payroll, how much for office expenses, and so on. You may have created a household budget, and if you're a money enthusiast you may have even enjoyed it, even if it was a lot of work. Popular software allows you to get very detailed in breaking down your household budget, line by line. Budgets are powerful tools.

There's just one glitch. When it comes to saving for retirement, those kinds of budgets don't work very well.

Budgets can help you do many things, especially in analyzing the past and planning for the future. But the best household budget doesn't actually put any money into savings. At the end of the day (or week or month or year), you may have followed your budget or not. Maybe you got around to putting money away for retirement or maybe you didn't. Walter Updegrave, the retirement answer man, suggests a much simpler approach: the *two-line budget*. It's OK to create a household budget with many lines for different kinds of spending, but there are only two lines that matter for retirement: the first is your income, and the second is how much of it you save.

There's another common term for this: *pay yourself first*. Normally, when you get your paycheck, you use it to pay the ongoing financial obligations that you've taken on—the phone bill, the electric bill, the car payment, the mortgage payment, and so on. Then you use it to pay for the stuff of everyday life—gas, groceries, clothing, and the "extras," whatever those may be for you. After you pay everyone else, you intend to pay yourself, too, by putting money into savings. But then you discover that everyone else got their share, but you didn't. At the end, there just wasn't enough money left over.

What's the solution? *Pay yourself first* by saving, then pay everyone else. In the short run, this tactic could force you to reduce your "extras." In the long run, it could force you to take on fewer ongoing financial obligations. But paying yourself first is the only way you can be absolutely certain that you'll get your fair share. Up front, and off the top. Ask those natural savers how they do it, and they'll most likely confirm this approach. The most painless way is to have a certain amount or percentage automatically shifted into savings. The employer plans version would be your payroll contribution to a 401(k)-type plan. The personal savings version would be an automatic transfer from your bank account into retirement savings every month or every payday. And the real estate version would be the home mortgage obligation that you pay right off the top, remember? You can take that one step further by setting up an automatic debit from your bank account. All of these pillars build up the best when you never have that money in hand to spend. It's out of sight and out of mind.

Put Your Employer Plan on Autopilot

In the world of 401(k)-type employer plans, doing the *wrong* thing (like not saving) has usually been the automatic thing. And doing the *right* thing (like saving) has usually required a manual override.

For example, let's say you start a new job. The default contribution for your retirement savings is zero, which is the wrong thing. To do the right thing, you need to do a manual override. You need to overcome your own internal inertia (the tendency to keep things as they are) and also the external inertia of your new employer's payroll and benefits department. You must complete the enrollment forms, choose a contribution amount, and allocate percentages to different investment choices. Under this traditional approach, the easiest thing for you, and for your employer, is to do nothing. And if you do nothing, the wrong thing happens, which is something bad—you aren't saving for retirement. Under this traditional approach, it takes willpower and deliberate action to manually override the system and initiate the right thing so that something good can happen: you save for retirement.

Behavioral economics is a new way of thinking that turns all of this on its head; it suggests we set up systems to do the opposite of the traditional approach. What if we made the right thing into the default? Then doing nothing would allow the good thing to happen, automatically— and doing the wrong thing would require deliberate action.

How does behavioral economics address the new job scenario we just analyzed? With something called *automatic enrollment*. In contrast to the traditional approach, when you start a new job, a certain percentage of your pay is automatically withheld from your paycheck and contributed to your retirement savings. There's no remembering to sign up. No filling out of election forms. Of course, your employer must fully inform you that this will happen, and you must consent. And you can always manually override the system to fine-tune the amount of your contribution, or how it's invested. In fact, you can even override the system to not save at all. But at least automatic enrollment puts inertia and the status quo to work *for* you instead of against you. To shoot yourself in the foot, you'll have to do it on purpose.

Ideas from behavioral economics have been bubbling up for decades, but they are only now breaking through into applications that can do us some good. Thanks to the buzz that behavioral economics is generating, more and more aspects of retirement preparation will be changed so that doing the right thing becomes automatic. Laws are even being changed to allow for arrangements like automatic enrollment, which is very encouraging.

But what if you're not starting at a new employer and you're already contributing to your retirement account—how could behavioral economics help you? Well, there's a related approach called *automatic increases*. Even though you're saving for retirement, you know you should probably save more. What if you increased your contribution percentage every time you got a raise? That would be the perfect opportunity, because you wouldn't even feel the pinch of the higher contribution. That's what automatic increases do. They make doing the right thing automatic, instead of requiring you to make a manual override.

Are you beginning to wonder exactly how much of this financial stuff you could automate? The number and type of automatic saving options that your employer or investment provider can offer is evolving rapidly. Talk with them to explore what new options may be available. And for your real estate pillar, you can look into setting up mortgage payments based on your paycheck cycle, instead of monthly. You'll actually build equity faster.

The best thing about putting your saving on autopilot is that instead of having to concentrate on remembering to save, you can sit back, relax, and enjoy the view!

But How Much Should You Save?

If you've been expending energy and effort on remembering that you should save more and then getting yourself to actually follow through, you've been taxing your brain cells. Once you automate your savings, what should you do with that freed-up brain capacity? Turn to another, equally important part of saving: figuring out *how much* to save. Unlike the mechanical process of saving, deciding how much money you're going to need in retirement is something unique to you. It's a task you should *not* put on autopilot.

In the early part of your savings life cycle, the most important thing is to get started. If you have an employer plan that offers a matching contribution on a certain percentage of your pay, then it's a no-brainer to save at least that much to make sure you get the full employer match. For example, your employer might provide a 25 percent match on the first 4 percent of your pay you contribute into the saving plan. That is, when you contribute 4 percent of your pay, your employer then contributes 1 percent. The total contribution is 5 percent. The match is essentially free money—and you should always take free money.

An even better way to get started is to make a commitment to having a grand total of 10 percent contributed for you, between your personal savings and employer plan. For example, if your employer contributes 1 percent of your pay, you need to contribute or save 9 percent. If your employer contributes 5 percent, you need to come up with only 5 percent. But if your employer isn't contributing anything, then you're on the hook for saving the whole 10 percent. (Makes you want to work for an employer that makes a contribution, doesn't it?) If you're not accustomed to saving this much, 10 percent may sound like a lot. But if you're in the later part of your career, there's a good chance you need to be saving at least this much to be on track for the retirement you want. (Using automatic increases over several years—if you have access to them—can make getting all the way up to 10 percent a bit less painful.)

On the other hand, if you're in the early part of your career and you can't imagine locking away money until retirement, take heart in knowing that it could end up being useful for something else, too, like a first home purchase or extraordinary medical expenses. Using your retirement money for nonretirement expenses is almost never a good idea; it should be a last resort. But if retirement is so far away for you that you can't get yourself to save for it yet, keep this in mind.

A major danger point is when you switch jobs and have a chance to withdraw the money from your employer plan. Unless you're in dire circumstances, don't even *think* of using that money. See that it's transferred safely—"rolled over"—into your new employer's plan or your personal IRA.

Saving: When to Switch Off Autopilot and Take the Controls

Matt Greenwald, the mastermind behind the Retirement Confidence Survey, observes that for people in the early years of their career, a rule of thumb like 10 percent may be just dandy. But by the time they reach midcareer (and certainly late career), they should go beyond the rule of thumb and actually base their savings on how much money they'll need to retire. Lee Eisenberg calls this amount of money *The Number*.

Some of the tools for figuring out your Number are available for free, and you could use them to do the calculation yourself. This may sound like it's not all that difficult. But just because scissors are available at the discount store and you could use them to cut your own hair doesn't mean you should. Depending on how far away you are from retirement, how complex your situation is, and how savvy you are at using financial tools, you may or may not be able to do a good job on your own. You only need to live with a bad haircut for a few weeks. How long will you need to live with a bad retirement calculation? So although you may want to do this on your own, at least consider getting some help.

Once you're serious enough about all this to calculate your Number, note that there are *three basic methods* for getting the job done, ranked from least intelligent to most intelligent.

THE LEAST INTELLIGENT METHOD: A PIECE OF PAPER

Even though this approach is on the bottom rung, it's better than just guessing. Most paper worksheets for calculating your Number are based on that old rule of thumb about having 70 percent of your pre-retirement income. Your Number may be expressed as a monthly income you're saving up for, or the lump sum needed to generate that monthly income. You might use the back of an envelope to calculate this, but I wouldn't recommend it. Instead, use an *intelligent piece of paper* in the form of a prefabricated worksheet from a reputable organization. You may have access to one through your retirement plan at work. (Many of these are limited in that they consider only three of your pillars—Social Security, employer plans, and personal savings.) As paper worksheets go, the best one is from EBRI, the Employee Benefits Research Institute, (202) 659-0670. Or go to their website, www.choosetosave.org, and click on "Ballpark E$timate," where you can download a printable PDF file.

A MORE INTELLIGENT METHOD:
A COMPUTER PROGRAM

This approach is better than using a piece of paper, and it's easier, too. These days, computerized retirement calculators have pretty much replaced paper worksheets. They're likely to take into account more data about your finances, such as your real estate pillar and your keep working pillar. They allow you to select from various assumptions about the future, and they make it easier to run multiple scenarios. That allows you to get a range of possible answers about your Number. Doing all of this on a computer, or online, will definitely be more accurate than a paper worksheet. It's no crystal ball, though. Any of these calculators are just mathematical models. Remember, "garbage in, garbage out." However, the more intelligent the program is, the less garbage it will let you load in. For example, it will suggest reasonable assumptions, rather than force you to make uneducated guesses about them.

You may have access to one of these through your retirement plan at work or through an investment company where you have an account. The EBRI Ballpark E$timate mentioned earlier, which originated as an intelligent piece of paper, is now also available as an even more intelligent computer program. This interactive online version is available at www.choosetosave.org; click on "Ballpark E$timate." The AARP (the organization known pre-2000 as the American Association of Retired Persons) offers its own free retirement calculator at www.aarp.org. The AARP calculator can accommodate a spousal calculation. The trail to it is "Money and Work" → "Financial Planning and Retirement" → "Retirement Planning Calculator" (under the heading "Retirement Planning").

THE MOST INTELLIGENT METHOD:
A FINANCIAL ADVISOR

This approach is better than using a computer program, because even the most intelligent computer program is no match for a human expert. Using a financial advisor to calculate your Number really amounts to getting someone with more knowledge and experience than you have to do the computerized calculation for you. One reason it's the best method is that only a human being can ask you the questions in a thoughtfully probing way. The computer mostly accepts whatever information you enter; a good financial advisor challenges you and gets you to think more deeply. The first answer we come up with to retirement planning questions is often shallow. It's the second or third answer to the question that turns out to be really useful. Also, the calculation isn't really in the realm of pure mathematics; rather, it's where financial planning intersects with our VIPs (values, identity, and priorities). It's at the confluence of outside factors, like the cost of living, and inside factors, like our preferred Ways to Live. It takes a conversation with another human being to arrive at retirement planning *wisdom* instead of mere *accuracy*.

Should You Use a Method That's Free, or Pay a Fee?

If you're at the stage of doing this on your own, whether with the paper or computer method, using a free resource is probably fine. But if you're serious enough to use the financial advisor method, free is probably not good enough. A calculation from a financial advisor is often worth exactly what you pay for it. If the advisor is willing to do it for free, it's probably because the advisor earns a living by selling investments on commission. These advisors are more likely to be sales experts than financial planning experts. On the other hand, if the advisor charges you a fee to do the calculations, it's probably because the advisor earns a living by doing calculations for a fee. These advisors are more likely to be expert planners than expert salespersons.

If You Need Help Calculating Your Number

When it comes to choosing the right financial advisor to do these high-stakes calculations for you, expertise is more important than convenience. There are only three places you should look. The first is www.fpanet.org, the website of the FPA (Financial Planning Association), where you can find a member who holds the CFP (Certified Financial Planner) designation. Some of these advisors earn commissions, but the best ones—for this purpose—work on a fee-only basis. Whether they work on commission or fee-only, as long as they hold the CFP designation, they've had the proper training. The second place to look is www.napfa.org, the website of NAPFA (the National Association of Personal Financial Advisors). This is a much smaller association, for financial planners who have sworn off commissions completely and pledged to work on a purely fee-for-service basis. The third place is the website of the AICPA (the American Institute of Certified Public Accountants). Although most CPAs work in business accounting and taxation, a tiny percentage have taken additional training to become Personal Financial Specialists (PFSs). Visit www.aicpa.org and choose the "Personal Financial Planning Center," under "Professional Resources," then click on "Find a CPA/Personal Financial Specialist."

Are there *reputable* financial advisors who don't belong to any of these three associations? Yes. Are there *knowledgeable* financial advisors who don't hold the CFP or PFS designations? Definitely. Are there even *trustworthy* financial advisors who work on a commission-only basis? Absolutely. But your chances of finding a *reputable, knowledgeable,* and *trustworthy* financial advisor are much, much greater if you use one of these three websites.

However, it's almost never quite this black and white; many financial advisors fall somewhere in the middle. You may have access to a financial advisor through your retirement plan provider at work. Or you may have an existing personal relationship with an advisor. The most convenient is not necessarily the best, though (see the box on page 104 for ways to find the right expert for your needs).

The Next Step: Retirement Investing

Calculating your Number gives you a figure (or more likely, a range) to save toward. But of course, you don't just put that money in a sock or under the mattress. You invest it.

Saving and investing are related, but when it comes down to it, they're two different things. Saving is setting aside money so that you can spend it *later*. And investing is what you do with that set-aside money between now and the time you'll be spending it. That time could be lunchtime tomorrow or fifty years from now. In employer plans, it turns out that even when workers do a good job of saving money for retirement, they often don't do a good job of investing it.

Who's on Your Investment Team?

Why is it so important to focus on investing? The main reason is to be fair to yourself. You work hard for your money. It's only right that it work hard for you in return. When you invest your money, you need to make sure it's doing its fair share so you don't end up doing all of the work by yourself. Here's a secret about getting to your Number: the more your savings grow on their own through investment gains, the less saving you need to do—but the less they grow through investment gains, the more saving you'll need to do.

One of the biggest challenges in managing your investments is that the terminology gets in the way. There are so many technical terms that they often obscure the basic underlying principles. There's one such principle that you've certainly heard, even if you know absolutely nothing about investments: "Don't put all your eggs in one basket." But agriculturally speaking, investing for retirement is much more like vegetable gardening than like gathering eggs.

Your Retirement Victory Garden

Here's an analogy. In the vegetable garden of financial preparation, the first task, *saving*, is like planting seeds. There are three ways to go about planting—or retirement saving:

1. Planting in an unstructured way, placing the seeds randomly, whenever it's sunny and you find the time.

2. Planting in a structured way, with seeds carefully counted and spaced at intervals in rows. This is more efficient, with a more predictable outcome.

3. Not getting around to planting the seeds at all.

Either #1 or #2 gets the seeds into the ground and on their way to becoming vegetables. Way #1 translates into saving when you get around to it or get some extra money. Way #2 is the equivalent of an automatic saving plan like a 401(k) or automatic transfers from your bank account. With #3 you'd go hungry if we're talking about your garden, or you'd be working forever if we're talking about your savings.

Growing vegetables from seeds and saving dollars are very similar tasks in that both crops need time to grow. Certainly, there are many other factors that affect *how* both will grow (that's *investing*). But getting those seeds into the ground as soon as the season starts for each vegetable gives you a longer growing season and makes sure your seeds have the maximum time to grow and produce a good harvest. Sooner is better than later, but later is better than never. There are fall and winter crops too. So whether you're in the spring, summer, or autumn of life, it's not too late to plant.

If saving is like planting seeds, then investing is like choosing what to plant and tending to your growing crops. In choosing what to plant, you could decide on a single vegetable. You might choose your personal favorite. Or you might analyze which single crop is likely to give you the highest yield: You test the soil, consider your climate, find out what diseases and pests are most likely to threaten your garden, and select the one crop that should do the best. Then you bet the farm on that one vegetable. If your bet is correct, you'll do great. But if, despite your careful analysis, something goes wrong—the weather, diseases, insects—you could lose your whole crop. In that case, you'd face a long, hungry winter. (The same thing can happen if you place all of your retirement money in a single investment, like your employer's stock. Don't do it!)

There's another, less risky approach to gardening. Instead of betting on just one crop, you can grow a variety of vegetables. You plant some tomatoes, because although they aren't reliable, if they grow well they'll have a very high yield—a bumper crop. Tomatoes out the wazoo. And you also plant some carrots, because they seem to grow OK no matter what, although the yield on carrots is lower. You've learned that the best years for tomatoes are hotter and wetter, and the best years for carrots are cooler and drier. Also, the diseases and insects that plague tomatoes don't seem to affect carrots much, and vice versa. So regardless of what the season brings, between the two different plantings your garden is likely to produce a decent crop.

That's diversification. You've given up the chance to strike it rich with all tomatoes. But you aren't playing it overly safe with all carrots, either. Your garden is balanced between the two. If you find a third vegetable that doesn't share the characteristics of either of the first two, you can create an even better balance. (With investing, too, choosing *asset classes* that historically do well or poorly at different times creates a balance.) Diversification is essential. After all, you don't want to bet the farm.

Achieving true diversification can be tricky, though. You might think you're getting a balance across different crops when you're really not. Take broccoli and cauliflower. They have different names, different colors, and different shapes, so planting both broccoli and cauliflower might seem like diversification—but it's not. Master gardeners know that these two cruciferous vegetables are more alike than they are different. Good growing conditions for broccoli are good for cauliflower, and bad conditions for broccoli are bad for cauliflower. Planting these two vegetables together creates a kind of naive diversification, instead of the true diversification that you're trying to achieve.

With investing, some people feel they've diversified by parceling out among different funds or different brokers, but they've really got everything in one asset class—large-cap growth stocks, for example. If you're a master gardener (or a money enthusiast), you can probably figure out how to get true diversification. But if you're not an expert, you need expert advice about diversification—either from a live expert or from investor tools, books, and newsletters.

It can also be tricky to achieve the right balance. How much of your garden should you allocate to those boom-or-bust vegetables like tomatoes, and how much to those steady-Eddie vegetables like carrots? Fifty-fifty? Sixty-forty? Seventy-thirty? It depends how much risk you can afford to take. (For investments, your appropriate level of risk comes from how long until you expect you'll need the money, and also the chances that you might need to pull it out early.) Some of us can afford to take a lot of risk, and some of us can't. You've got to determine the right level of risk for *you*, over time, to know the right balance between boom-or-bust and steady-Eddie.

Tending your garden is important, too. You can't just plant it once and then ignore it. What if the tomatoes are taking over your garden? You need to keep checking to make sure that your crops actually stay in the balance that you selected. (With investments, this is called *rebalancing*.) And if your life changes in some way—for example, you develop a chronic medical condition—then your desired level of risk will change too. You need to change the balance in your garden—or in your investment account.

Then there's the need to weed. Weeds suck up the water and nutrients that your vegetables need to grow, and they'll crowd them out too. A well-weeded garden will produce more vegetables than a weedy garden will. (In your retirement account, the weeds are investment expenses.) Fewer weeds equals more produce, pure and simple—especially over time. Planting the right crops in the right balance to start with is definitely the most important part, but tending and weeding will make a difference, too.

Saving is like planting seeds, investing is like tending your crops, and spending, once you've retired, is like harvesting—and eating!— your crops. *Bon appétit.*

Five Rules of Investing (That Could Be Learned from Gardening)

The most basic principle for managing your personal savings and employer plan pillars is something called *modern portfolio theory* (MPT). Don't imagine, just because it has *theory* in the name, that it's some far-out possibility, like string theory in physics. No, over the last fifty years MPT has become the basis for managing retirement investments, and you need to know at least a little bit about it. Harry Markowitz won a Nobel Prize in economics for setting forth the basic structure of MPT, which showed that managing a portfolio is a lot like gardening. Instead of different crops, though, MPT uses different asset classes: *stocks, bonds, and cash.* Or, to say it another way, *equity, debt, and money markets.* Whether you think about investing in terms of economics or gardening, there are five rules you should know about that could be drawn from either field.

1. By diversifying, you can avoid the boom-or-bust scenario. You're better off with multiple types of investments than with a single type. (And don't ever, ever consider a single, solitary investment, like employer stock.)

2. By choosing types of investments that react differently to different conditions, you can make sure that you'll weather the ups and downs of good and bad times. *Some* part of your portfolio will be holding its value or even increasing in every financial climate.

3. By determining the right level of risk for your situation (how long you expect to let it grow, and how likely it is that you might need it early), you can figure out the appropriate balance of investment types. Perhaps your neighbor is comfortable at a seventy-thirty split between stocks and bonds (tomatoes and carrots), but you should be at fifty-fifty. Rather

than guess, use whatever assessment your investment provider makes available. It might be a questionnaire or software program that suggests a specific split or points you toward one of a set of pie-chart allocations.

4. By periodically *rebalancing* your portfolio, you can maintain the suggested allocation, instead of letting one type of investment take over your garden. Annually (or at another periodic interval), as your different classes of investments grow or decline at different rates, rebalancing shifts amounts to restore your original allocation. (If the string beans are overshadowing the cucumbers, you'll need to cut them back and let the light in.) In the long term, as you get closer to actually spending your money, you'll probably want to become more conservative—because you'll have less time left to make up for any losses from market downturns. That means adjusting your split, or allocation, to a new mix that you choose.

5. By reducing expenses, you enable your portfolio to grow more quickly. Although the most important factor is having the types of investments that are right for you, it's also important to keep expenses low. Expenses are like weeds competing for garden space, sunlight, nutrients, and water; they inhibit growth by sucking the life out of your market gains and dividends. Lower expense ratios allow greater investment growth; over time the difference can be enormous.

Learning how to do all these things, and making sure you actually do them over the long haul, may interest you if you're a money enthusiast. If you're not a money enthusiast, you may want to switch your investments over to automatic—and spend your time out in your garden instead of inside managing your investments.

Investing: Switching to Autopilot

Remember automatic enrollment? Fortunately, the same kind of automatic breakthroughs are happening in managing investment portfolios too. At last, it's possible to choose an investment account that does everything you are supposed to be doing, but it does it all by itself, automatically. (It's like a robotic master gardener!) Your employer plan may already offer an account that automatically splits up your money to the right allocation of asset classes based on how much risk is appropriate for you. Then it automatically rebalances them back to that split as the investments go up or down in value. It even automatically changes the split to become more conservative as you get closer to retirement.

Until the advent of automatic investing, it wasn't easy—or cheap—to accomplish all this. It took a lot of investing knowledge and skill to set up an account with the right allocation. And then it took a lot of boring operational follow-through to keep up with it, rebalance it, and then shift it over time to become more conservative.

Before, the choices were either paying significantly higher fees to have this done for your account or taking it on yourself. Understandably, many people opted to have it all done for them by a service or an investment representative, but they paid a huge price—often 1 percent of their account balance every year. Over the span of a career, that significantly reduces the value of a portfolio. And workers who didn't pay to have it done but opted to do it themselves usually wound up not doing it. They had good intentions, but it was just too complicated. Then they still devoted a lot of time and energy to *worrying* about what was happening to their investments because they weren't managing them!

But with the breakthrough in automatic investment management, the cost is falling. Instead of an expensive service that might cost 1 percent annually, the kind of management just described is now available as an automated account or fund, without the extra charges. The terminology for these accounts isn't as standardized as it could be, and not all investment providers offer all the types. However, these are the five most common variations that you'll see:

1. **Balanced Fund.** The most old-fashioned type of automatic investing, this usually just keeps the account at the same split between stocks and bonds; say, sixty-forty. This is more automatic than having to manually split your money between two funds, but it's a one-size-fits-all approach.

2. **Auto Rebalancing.** This automated service periodically shifts your investment allocation back to whatever split you had originally selected. However, if you did a poor job of allocating your investment split in the first place, this service just keeps replicating that error.

3. **Lifestyle Funds.** This is like having a range of balanced funds to choose from, instead of just one. There could be several that are more aggressive, like seventy-thirty or eighty-twenty (if you have more time until retirement), and several that are more conservative, like fifty-fifty or forty-sixty (if you have less time until retirement). Unlike the one-size-fits-all balanced fund, you're more likely to find something off this rack that fits you well. However, even though there is a range of splits or allocations to choose from, each one stays the same over time. You might choose the eighty-twenty because it fits you at the time, but later on, if it's time to move to a more conservative sixty-forty, it's up to you to know that and remember to make the change.

4. **Lifecycle Funds.** This is like a lifestyle fund, except it automatically shifts from aggressive to conservative as you progress through your life cycle toward retirement. This is the most fully automated type of account. Some are called *target funds*, because you choose them based on your target date for retirement. As your target retirement date approaches, the fund automatically shifts into a more conservative split. However, if you don't plan to draw on your investments beginning at your target date, you may not need to make that shift. It would be better to choose a fund based on when you plan to start accessing your retirement account than on your official retirement date.

5. **Managed Accounts.** This uses technology to create a more personalized service than a lifestyle or lifecycle fund. Instead of investing your money into a particular fund whose assets are all managed in the same way, this approach can be more closely matched to your situation. However, just as when you

buy a custom tailored suit rather than one off the rack, you're likely to pay much more. If you're very hard to fit, it might be worth it. But most people are better off choosing something from the lifestyle/lifecycle rack and saving their money.

When you choose one of these automatic approaches, you free yourself from some of the ongoing work of managing your investment account. You shift the burden. You don't have to become an expert at using your investment provider's website or phone system. You also eliminate the trepidation and second-guessing that can plague you each time you make your own decisions about your investment accounts.

How Your Real Estate Pillar Grows

If you're a real estate tycoon, you probably have all the real estate investing books already. There's nothing that would fit in one section of a chapter that would be new to you.

If you're *not* a tycoon, though, and your real estate investing is restricted to just your residence, then there is one idea that's really important to understand about your home as a retirement investment: your home equity can result from two distinctly different processes, and most of the time comes from both. The first process is *amortization*; the second is *appreciation*.

Amortization works this way: For an extremely simple example, let's assume you purchase a home for $100,000 with a 10 percent down payment, and you borrow the remaining $90,000. Over the term of the mortgage, let's say fifteen years, you make monthly mortgage payments. As you make those payments, the mortgage balance decreases to $89,000, to $88,000, and so on. As that happens, your home equity is building up, slowly and steadily. *Amortization operates a lot like saving.* At the end of fifteen years, when the mortgage is paid off, let's assume the house is worth the exact same $100,000 that you paid for it. The good news is that you now have

$100,000 of home equity, essentially because you saved it up over time. That's amortization.

But appreciation has been getting a lot more attention lately. We'll use the same example but ignore the slow, steady amortization process for a moment. Let's say that in the first year, the value of your home increases from $100,000 to $110,000. That 10 percent appreciation in home value caused your equity to increase from $10,000 to $20,000—it doubled. Appreciation is a much more exciting way to create home equity than amortization, wouldn't you say? It's actually appreciation combined with leverage, and it's important to remember that the lever can move both ways. If the value of your home had instead decreased (and that *can* happen), from $100,000 to $90,000, your equity would go from $10,000 down to $0. Still exciting, but in a different way. This is more like investing than saving.

Historically, even outside the currently hot real estate markets, most homes have increased in value over the term of a fifteen-year mortgage. So the combination of these two factors—the steady saving effect of amortization and the more volatile investing effect of appreciation—work together to create home equity.

Investing: When to Take the Controls

Remember how automating the mechanical process of saving frees you to think of higher-level concerns, like your Number? Well, automating your investing frees you to think at a higher level, too. An automatic account works because many, many people have a similar need for that type of investment management. Chances are your need in the area of investment management is fairly generic. So now that you're free to think about other things, the question is this: In what area is your need *not* generic? What's unique and special about your situation? Which decisions do you personally need to take control of? What should not be on autopilot?

There are two investment-related issues that are unique to you and are *key decisions*. They're about *when* and *how* to retire. When do you plan to leave your full-time or long-term employment? How do you plan to make that transition: all at once or little by little? What age or date makes sense for you, based on the topics you're exploring in this book? Customizing the timing of your retirement—earlier or later—could change your target date for choosing a lifecycle fund, couldn't it?

Also, since Social Security may be an important pillar for your retirement, you don't want to make those decisions on autopilot. For example, the timing of when you apply affects the amount of your monthly benefit for the rest of your life. Is it better to begin sooner and thus receive more monthly checks, or to begin later and receive a larger monthly check? That question is part of managing your investment in Social Security. The answer is particular to you: your health, your hereditary life expectancy, how strong your other pillars are (which will affect when you absolutely must have that Social Security check for your survival), and so on.

Next, think about your retirement transition. If you retire all at once, as an event, you'll need to start drawing from your retirement accounts right away. But if you retire little by little, you may be able to wait longer before drawing from your accounts. This could allow a later target date and more aggressive investment allocation. On the other hand, if your plans involve a big withdrawal when you first retire (perhaps for buying another home or an RV), you may actually need to be more conservative and liquid in your investment allocation. You can see that these are definitely not autopilot decisions. The closer you get to retirement, the more you may need to shut off the autopilot and take over the controls.

By thinking clearly about the life that you want to live in retirement, you'll be more realistic about your Number, more accurate about your saving, and more appropriate with your investing.

MANAGING MY FINANCIAL PILLARS

Your PERKS—the Five Pillars of Retirement Financial Security—are the sources of retirement income that you manage over the course of your working life and also over the course of your retirement. Managing your pillars includes consciously planning for them in advance, consistently taking action to build them up over time (automatically, if possible), and carefully drawing on them to provide a retirement income for as long as you live.

This exercise isn't about creating a detailed list of your financial resources. That's something you should do with another piece of paper, a computer program, or a financial advisor. The purpose of this exercise is to crystallize in your mind the financial pillars that you need to manage. If your situation follows the Pareto principle, about 20 percent of your retirement income sources will provide about 80 percent of your income. Knowing what your largest resources are, and managing them, is your highest priority.

If you're still at an earlier stage in your career, this exercise will help identify which pillars you think you'll be able to build in the future. By focusing your attention on those pillars that offer you the greatest potential, you increase your chances of managing them to create sufficient financial resources.

If it's later in your career, this exercise will help identify which pillars you've already built or are in the process of building. By focusing your attention on those pillars that will provide the largest share of your retirement income, you increase your chances of managing them effectively.

(Note: Make a copy of the exercise to fill in, enlarging it if you'd like more space.)

Personal Savings. What are the types and names of the specific personal accounts that offer the greatest potential for me?

_____

_____

_____

How great a share of my retirement income are they likely to provide?   ❏ Small   ❏ Medium   ❏ Large

Employer Plans. What are the types and names of the employer-sponsored retirement plans that offer the greatest potential for me?

_____

_____

_____

How great a share of my retirement income are they likely to provide?   ❏ Small   ❏ Medium   ❏ Large

Real Estate. What are the types and names of the residences or investment properties that offer the greatest potential to produce retirement income for me?

_____

_____

_____

How great a share of my retirement income are they likely to provide?   ❏ Small   ❏ Medium   ❏ Large

Keep Working. What type of work and specific jobs offer the greatest potential to produce retirement income for me? How long could I keep working?

_____

_____

_____

If I'm able to get a job, how great a share of my retirement income is it likely to provide?

❏ Small   ❏ Medium   ❏ Large

Social Security. What types of Social Security benefits will I be eligible to receive?

_____

_____

_____

How great a share of my retirement income are they likely to provide?   ❏ Small   ❏ Medium   ❏ Large

Other. In addition to these sources of retirement income that I create for myself, will I have other financial resources to draw on, like an inheritance or passive business income?

_____

_____

_____

How great a share of my retirement income are they likely to provide?   ❏ Small   ❏ Medium   ❏ Large

Now review the information about your pillars and consider which *three* are most likely to provide the largest share of your retirement income. Enter these in the Retirement Circle to use for your One Piece of Paper in chapter 10.

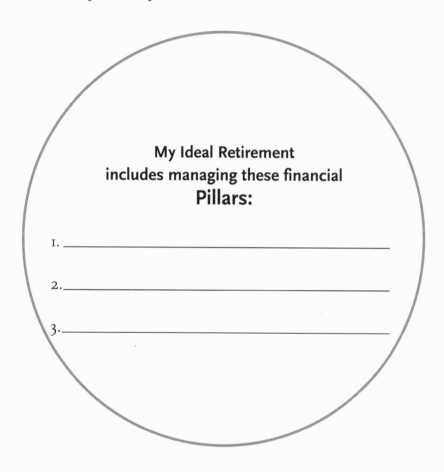

**My Ideal Retirement
includes managing these financial
Pillars:**

1. _____

2. _____

3. _____

Your PERKS on the "Other Side"

What about your PERKS on the "other side"—*after* retirement? In the olden days—the era of the three-legged stool—we thought of the retirement event as the end point. All the work went into financial preparation, and once you retired, things were pretty well set. Money after the retirement event was relatively simple (as long as you had enough of it, that is). One reason it was simple is because it wasn't supposed to last all that long. The other reason is that the sources of retirement income didn't require much decision making during retirement. Let's look at the Five Pillars to see how things will be different for you in retirement from the way they were for people in the past.

PERSONAL SAVINGS

This pillar hasn't changed that much. In the olden days, even after they retired people did need to make decisions about how to invest and how much of their savings to spend so their money would last. However, the investment options keep expanding, so you'll need to keep learning about investing even after you retire. Also, the retirement income phase introduces the need to minimize income tax on your withdrawals, which requires you to get a handle on an entirely new subject.

EMPLOYER PLANS

Traditional pensions not only accumulate the funds for workers' retirement income automatically, they typically pay it out to them automatically, too. Pensions provide a monthly "retirement paycheck" for life. Unless you're one of the few who will still enjoy a traditional pension, in retirement you'll probably need to make all the same ongoing decisions for your employer plans that you do for your personal savings. No automatic retirement paycheck for you. (Unless you structure things that way—what an idea!)

REAL ESTATE

This pillar has become much more complex. As a potential source of income as well as an abode, your residence must do double duty.

How can you access your equity and still have a place to live? You'll need to get savvy about reverse mortgages and other new financial instruments.

KEEP WORKING

In the olden days, retiring workers were worn out—and needed to rest their old behinds on the three-legged stool. But for you, continuing to work is a distinct possibility. So even in retirement, you'll want to keep managing your career—whether it's for pay or for fulfillment.

SOCIAL SECURITY

For the retirement phase of life, this pillar hasn't changed much. Prior to retirement, you need to manage your Social Security benefits in advance—by securing your eligibility and carefully choosing when to begin. But once those monthly payments start rolling in, this pillar will be about the same for you as it always has been—unless the funding problem doesn't get resolved and your benefits get cut by 25 percent once you're already retired.

Conclusion: Provisions for the Journey

Remember that your financial pillars are just the supplies, or provisions, for your journey. They are not the journey itself.

If you're a money enthusiast, you run the danger of becoming so interested in the provisions that you don't notice all the other parts of the journey. You could shortchange yourself and your retirement. Even though the financial element is a powerful force for getting the retirement that you really want, it also provides the least opportunity for true fulfillment in life. Ultimately, money by itself isn't meaningful.

If you're at the opposite end of the money enthusiasm spectrum and you don't like dealing with money issues, you run the danger of neglecting them. You may be aware of all the other potentially fulfilling parts of your retirement journey but get bogged down because you don't have enough money. It's difficult to enjoy the journey when you're making do without adequate provisions.

Making absolutely sure that you've gotten the financial element taken care of and your pillars well established will free you to explore the other elements of your Retirement Well-Being. In the chapters that follow, you'll continue to fill in your One Piece of Paper (see chapter 10) as you discover what those elements mean for you:

- Chapter 6, the psychological, and chapter 7, the social, which make up the happiness dimension
- Chapter 8, the geographical, which, combined with this chapter's financial element, makes up the prosperity dimension
- Chapter 9, the medical and biological elements, which make up the health dimension

In chapter 10, you'll pull all these elements together to create the complete picture of your Ideal Retirement.

Resources on Spending, Saving, and Investing

Most discussions of behavioral economics still are found in textbooks and academic treatises. But Gary Belsky and Thomas Gilovich offer a more accessible introduction in *Why Smart People Make Big Money Mistakes and How to Correct Them: Lessons from the Science of Behavioral Economics* (Simon & Schuster, 2000).

These days, the most common opportunities for automatic saving and investing are found in employer-sponsored retirement plans. However, a popular book for individuals that advocates an automatic approach is David Bach's *The Automatic Millionaire: A Powerful One-Step Plan to Live and Finish Rich* (Broadway, 2005).

Many books offer a how-to formula for becoming financially successful, but very few offer a "how-did," based on empirical research of those who've already made it. Thomas Stanley's account, *The Millionaire Mind* (Andrews McMeel, 2001) is the real deal. Like his earlier work with William Danko, *The Millionaire Next Door* (Pocket Books, 1998), this isn't really a guidebook; it's about setting the facts straight.

On the other hand, most people don't do what it takes to become wealthy. And even those who do often find they still have a strange relationship with money—whether about saving it, investing it, spending it, or ultimately giving it away. George Kinder has explored this inner landscape more deeply than anyone I know of, and *The Seven Stages of Money Maturity: Understanding the Spirit and Value of Money in Your Life* (Dell, 2000) is his map for the journey.

For a refreshingly contrarian view, check out the classic *Your Money or Your Life: Transforming Your Relationship with Money and Achieving Financial Independence* (Penguin, 1999), by Joe Dominguez and Vickie Robin. Although most readers won't follow the authors' Spartan philosophy of spending, saving, and investing, most will come away with new beliefs and attitudes about those activities. And that's a good thing!

*"Your vision will become clear only when you can
look into your own heart. Who looks outside, dreams;
who looks inside, awakens."*

—Carl Jung

CHAPTER SIX

Discover Your Retirement Strengths

C an you really *plan* how to be happy in retirement? Hasn't happiness been likened to a butterfly that you can chase but never capture—that will land on your shoulder when you aren't looking?

Yes, you really *can* plan how to be happy. And yes, happiness has been likened to a butterfly that lands on your shoulder only when you aren't looking. But that analogy is only half true. It's a poetic truth, and poetry is one important form of truth—but another important form of truth is investigation. If happiness really were a butterfly, you could learn more about it, couldn't you? You could study it scientifically: where it lives, what it eats, when it's mostly likely to be flying around, the types of things it's drawn to—even who it's most likely to land on. If you do this research and put it to use, there's no guarantee that the butterfly of happiness will alight on your shoulder, but you will be able to actually plan how to go about increasing the probability. (And if science doesn't work, there's always poetry!)

Of course, a cynic would say that neither science nor poetry is necessary for happiness. In terms of the Retirement Well-Being Model, cynical thinking would conclude that if you have prosperity and you have health, you'll automatically have happiness. To which there is only one answer: hogwash!

When people dream about creating a happy retirement, and when marketers engineer their images of what that happy retirement looks like, they tend to focus on carefree fun and enjoyment. But scientific inquiry into lasting happiness has identified a critical factor that the fun-and-enjoyment approach overlooks: engagement.

Engagement is the missing ingredient in lasting retirement happiness. And the key to engagement is identifying your *strengths*—those talents and abilities that you excel in and get great satisfaction from using.

You can certainly find out what your strengths are by happenstance—by letting them alight on your shoulder. But when you're actively planning for your well-being, particularly for a new stage of life that offers your greatest potential for freedom and fulfillment, the scientific method is your best bet.

So let's forget the cynical approach, honor the poetic approach, and roll up our sleeves to get to work using the scientific approach.

Happiness in the Laboratory

As it turns out, happiness is being studied at least as rigorously as butterflies—but only in recent years. Instead of studying happiness, most psychological research over the previous five decades studied its opposite: depression, addiction, neurosis, and so on. Some very smart and well-intentioned people have spent billions of dollars to create a mountain of detailed knowledge about the thousand and one ways that people can be unhappy. This is important information, to be sure. But it doesn't help you learn about how to create happiness or plan for it in retirement. Trying to prevent or avoid unhappiness isn't the same as creating happiness.

To balance out all this knowledge about unhappiness, a new discipline called *Positive Psychology* emerged around the turn of the new millennium. This is not just a variation on "positive thinking." The inquiry into Positive Psychology was championed by the renowned research psychologist Martin Seligman and others. They take a clear-thinking, hard-nosed, let's-measure-it-and-see-if-it-stands-up approach to the study of human strengths, positive emotions, and other aspects of optimal human experience. Positive Psychology has really caught on, and these days there are many more researchers who are studying how humans thrive.

Thanks to systematic research in other fields, we know about approaches for increasing our economic well-being and our health and well-being. Now, thanks to Positive Psychology, we know there are specific approaches for increasing our psychological well-being, too.

Seligman suggests that there are, essentially, *three approaches to happiness*; that is, three *basic ways* to be happy. Although there are, thank goodness, an unlimited number of specific ways in which you can be happy, each comes under one of these three basic approaches.

The Three Approaches to Happiness

What, you ask, are these three approaches to happiness?

- Pleasure
- Engagement
- Meaning

Let's explore them one by one.

PLEASURE

This one sounds obvious, doesn't it? When you first think of happiness, it's usually pleasure and enjoyment that come to mind, right off the bat. An afternoon at the ball game. Eating a delicious meal. Watching an entertaining movie. Buying something that you want. These involve being comfortable and having fun in an easy or relaxed way. Pleasure like this brings a burst of positive emotions that usually come and go quickly, usually not lasting much longer than the event itself. When you use this approach (and I sincerely hope that you do), you need to keep going back and doing enjoyable activities, over and over again, to get more of that happiness.

ENGAGEMENT

This one isn't very obvious. Another word for engagement is *involvement*. Positive Psychology researcher Mihaly Csikszentmihalyi uses still another word for this experience that you can almost feel: he calls it *flow*. (His name, by the way, is actually easier to say than it looks; it sounds like "Me high. Chicks sent me high.") Flow happens when your abilities are well matched to some challenging task. You get so deep into an activity, whatever it is, that you lose all track of time. You may feel like it's been only a few minutes, but it's been much longer. Or a few seconds may feel like an eternity. Either way, when you're engaged, you lose yourself in what you're doing. You may not even be aware that it makes you happy while you're doing it, but afterward you say, "That was great!"

Engagement involves challenge, and it demands something from you, so it's not as simple as pleasure. It can't be purchased or consumed in the way that pleasure can be. When you use this approach (and you may be using it more than you realize), it can stick with you longer than pleasure does. Over time, it can build up into a lasting satisfaction with life.

MEANING

This approach to happiness is somewhat more obvious than engagement, but it's not so easy to pin down. Of course having meaning in your life would make you happy! But how do you get it? The way you get it, my friend, is to use your abilities in the service of something larger than yourself. This approach requires something from you, too. Note that meaning doesn't come from just *believing* in something larger than yourself; it comes from being *in service* to that something.

What's larger than yourself? Take your pick, depending on your belief system: God, your family, the environment, your political party, your ethnic culture, the free enterprise system, your community. Or it may be service not so much to something larger than yourself as to something *beyond* yourself: a neighbor who needs help with chores, a child who needs help with school, a litter-free walking path, a safer neighborhood, the sick, the needy. You can't buy or consume meaning, just as you can't buy or consume engagement. And giving your money to something you believe in doesn't provide the same sense of meaning or happiness that *working* for it provides (although giving money is still a good thing). You can be aware of this happiness before, during, and after a meaningful experience. When you use this approach (and I highly recommend it), the sense of satisfaction can last a lifetime.

Important Note

Look carefully at the three approaches to happiness. You'll notice that "fixing your weaknesses" appears nowhere on the list. Rooting out and eliminating your imperfections is not an approach to happiness. With the best of intentions, your loving parents, your well-meaning teachers, and every straight-shooting boss you've had since high school have attempted to correct your deficiencies. It's finally OK to place a bit less emphasis on that. In retirement, you won't need to focus on fixing your weaknesses. So take a lesson from Positive Psychology—develop and expand what's *right* with you. Focus on what you like about yourself, rather than what you don't like. Concentrate on what you *do* want, instead of what you *don't* want. Those are the scientific recommendations, anyway.

For Retirement, Think of Them as Three Levels of Happiness

If you'd like to increase your happiness in retirement (or even right now!), you can use the three approaches to make plans. All three are equally valid—one of them is not better or more important than the others. But there is a connection between them and what society tries to tell you retirement happiness *should* be about. Society is stuck with a lot of old-fashioned ideas about retirement. Remember, it was invented primarily for people who didn't have all that many years to live and weren't in the best of health. Those folks were like worn-out cogs of the Industrial Revolution, or beasts of burden ready to be put out to pasture. For them, just retiring *from work* was a blessing; the notion of retiring *to another stage of life* probably never occurred to most of them.

So society has created expectations about what kind of happiness is appropriate for worn-out old people in retirement: the easy, relaxing, leisure-oriented kind of happiness. The message from society has been that happiness in retirement should be based on pleasure.

That message may have made sense years ago (and still may for those who earn their living with hard physical labor), but for the legions of modern workers whose sedentary lives require the intervention of gym workouts, a good long rest is not what they need from their retirement.

So even though there is no hierarchy among the three approaches to happiness, society has created a hierarchy for *retirement* happiness. Society's expectations are that enjoyment and pleasure should be enough. If your expectations are higher than that and you want engagement and meaning in retirement, you have some work to do.

If a *pleasant* retirement is all that you want, that's perfectly OK. But if you decide that you'd like to set your sights higher and plan for a retirement that's *engaging*, or possibly even *meaningful*, that's OK, too. You should realize that if you haven't worn yourself out on the job, those two approaches give you a better chance at achieving a more lasting kind of happiness—the true Retirement Well-Being that this book is all about.

The three approaches create the Three Levels of Retirement Happiness shown in the figure.

THE THREE LEVELS OF RETIREMENT HAPPINESS

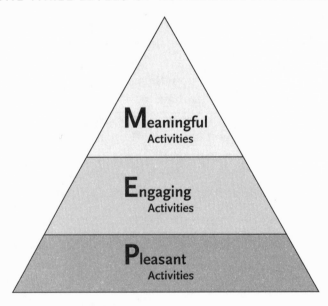

Pleasure:
The First Level of Retirement Happiness

When you initially imagine the retirement you want, it's probably a *pleasant* retirement. You want to be secure and comfortable, and to simply enjoy yourself. You want to spend time with friends and family. You want to *play*. A pleasant retirement is based on leisure, and relaxation, and finally getting a chance for some fun in life. Like a vacation.

This is the original idea of retirement, as people have imagined it, for generations. You probably already know a lot about what it would take to create this level of retirement happiness. It's usually based on your *interests* in the world outside of work. It's the same kind of stuff that you pursue whenever you have enough free time: hobbies, entertainment, spectator events, travel, socializing. These things are enjoyable partly just because they're *not* work. And they're enjoyable partly because there's something about the subject or pastime that you find interesting.

Some of these interests may keep you tuned in for years or for a whole lifetime. Others you may casually pick up, explore, and let go again, moving on to new explorations and new interests, as those interests aren't necessarily a very fundamental, or lasting, aspect of yourself. (Think how much your interests have already changed over the years.)

During your working life, these low-involvement activities bring a welcome *counterbalance* to your work. In retirement, though, these activities are no longer counterbalancing work (unless you are still doing some work to pay the bills), and they may not have enough weight to stand on their own. They may not be rich enough to bring the amount of happiness that you expect from them. They were up to the task of filling your all-too-short weekends and a week or two of vacation. And it helps if you can choose from a wide range of pleasurable activities that you've already lined up and experienced. But they may not be up to the task of filling weeks and months and years and decades of retirement.

FIRST REMEMBER, THEN IMAGINE

How do you go about actually *planning* for the first level of happiness—pleasure and enjoyment? You'd think it would be as easy as falling off a log! After all, you're naturally drawn toward what's fun and enjoyable, and no doubt you've found ways to fit it in during your free time. You've done it in your preretirement life, so you should be expert at planning for it in your retirement life. (If you're one of those who have taken little or no time out for fun and enjoyment during your career—and sadly, there are more than a few—it *will* take some effort to reconnect with your natural inclinations and rekindle your interests.) So for your retirement, can't you simply imagine how to do more of it—a *lot* more of it?

The answer is yes, you can and should use your imagination. And that's the tricky part. It's easy to imagine all sorts of new activities for the first level that seem like they would be fun, but you've never tried them before. They're unrelated to your actual experience. It's great to try new things in retirement and discover new ways to have fun. However, the bad news from the research front is that we humans are spectacularly inaccurate at predicting what will make us truly happy.

Low-stakes experiments into new ways to have fun are no big risk. (For example, trying a new sport or a membership organization.) On the other hand, high-stakes experiments that aren't based on experience can be disastrous. (Like buying a boat, an RV, or a vacation home. We've all heard horror stories, haven't we?)

So when you're planning for the first level of retirement happiness, don't rely solely on your imagination; use this three-step process:

1. Remember previous fun experiences. After all, when you plan how to create a pleasurable retirement, you have lots and lots of information to go on. You've been accumulating data on yourself whenever you pursued your favorite leisure activities outside of work. So the first step is to search your memory bank. Cruise back in time for some of the most fun experiences you can remember having.

2. Identify, specifically, what it was about these experiences that brought you the most enjoyment. Use the basic questions you

Consuming Happiness versus Creating It Yourself

Because pleasure can easily be packaged and sold to you as a product or service, the first level of retirement happiness is a very big business (as we explored in chapter 4). Magazine advertisements and television commercials are filled with entertainment, travel, and luxury goods that were developed and marketed based on the narrow view that retirement happiness is based only on pleasure. It's a big business because the marketing works—we consume pleasure, and it generates a healthy profit.

Marketers know that we want other forms of happiness, too, like engagement or meaning, but those are difficult to package and sell because they require more involvement from us than just buying something. However, let the buyer beware: the marketing messages for products that can really provide only pleasure often imply that you'll get engagement or meaning if you buy the product. That's just hogwash.

It's not easy to buy engagement or meaning—they're more self-created. You need to build these kinds of happiness yourself, even if you do use a product—tools, books, sporting goods, learning opportunities—in conjunction with the activity. Even the simplest approach to retirement happiness—pleasure—has been a do-it-yourself project for most of human history. Not until the twentieth century did packaging and selling it become such a gigantic business.

When you plan for your retirement happiness, you can make a choice about how much to consume and how much to create yourself. It's a little bit like making food choices. The second box of life is so hectic that many of us end up eating a lot of fast food along the way. But the third box opens up new possibilities, so with planning (and a bit of luck) we'll all have the time for more of those good home-cooked meals.

learned in high school: Who? What? Where? When? How? These are hints, or clues, based on your real experiences, for how to create more enjoyment like this.

3. *Now* imagine new ways to have fun in retirement. You're not trying to recreate the old experiences, of course. But by using the hints and clues from your real life, you're pointing yourself in the right direction. Find opportunities to test out, in a low-stakes way, your ideas for new types of retirement fun.

Engagement:
The Second Level of Retirement Happiness

In addition to the first level of happiness that comes from pleasure, people are beginning to imagine something more: a second level that comes from engagement. This level introduces a new element: challenge. But why would you want challenge in your retirement?

Here's what Csikszentmihalyi's research discovered. When the challenges in your life are too far *above* your level of skill, they create anxiety. You've probably had a job like that at one time or another. But when the challenges in your life are too far *below* your level of skill, they create boredom. You probably wouldn't want a retirement like that. Perhaps you'd like more of a middle ground. That's what an engaged retirement is about. The secret is regularly finding interesting challenges that are a good match for your favorite skills and strengths. When you find these interesting challenges and become actively involved in them, you get a sense of accomplishment from doing them well.

What's that, you say? This sounds a bit like *work?* Yes, it does, except it's closer to "working" in the garden, or "working" on your golf game, than working for a paycheck. It's the aspect of working that we all hope to find when we look for engaging work. It's investing yourself in life and getting back more than you put in. It's investing yourself in your ongoing development and becoming more of who you really are. Even though an engaged retirement isn't just a long vacation like one based purely on pleasure, it can be more rewarding.

If there's a chance that you might need to keep working as one of your financial pillars of retirement income, finding *engaging work* could be your version of an engaged retirement. That would certainly be better than working at a job you don't like just to get a paycheck. If your retirement might include working for pay, you should also read the original *What Color Is Your Parachute?* It's for job-hunters and career changers (and is the inspiration for this book).

"GO WITH THE FLOW"
DOESN'T MEAN WHAT YOU THINK, DUDE

But what about planning for the second level of retirement happiness—engagement? Remember, flow is about enjoyable effort; it isn't even remotely like the laid-back, *whatever* attitude of "go with the flow." No, the second level is more like "*make* the flow."

Here's how you can begin to make plans for going beyond the first level to the second level. Pure enjoyment is most closely linked with your *interests*. And your level of involvement with an interest can be passive or active. Let's say you're interested in baseball. You could choose to be a spectator at a baseball game, or you could choose to play on a team. The low level of skill needed to be a spectator would produce a *pleasant* experience. But the higher level of skill needed to be a player would produce an *engaging* experience (not to mention the boost to your health from being physically active).

So when you're planning for the first level, you need to know what your interests are. But when you're planning for the second level, you need to know what your skills and strengths are. Because when you get an opportunity to use *those* parts of yourself, you tend to experience engagement—you go into the flow state. The surest way to successfully plan for the second level of happiness is to plan for ways to use your strengths. It does take more research and planning. You need to discover your strengths so that you can begin to investigate opportunities to use them in your retirement. The Retirement Circles exercise in this chapter will help you identify your top five strengths so you can be on the lookout for where to use them in the world.

STRENGTHS ARE LIKE SKILLS
WITHOUT A PAYCHECK

What's the difference between skills and strengths? Since you have more experience with skills, let's start there. Skills are the abilities or talents that you use to accomplish tasks with people, data, or things. In the world of work—the second box of life—skills are king. A key aspect of the job-hunter's *What Color Is Your Parachute?* is helping you identify your skills (especially the ones that you love to use). Knowing your skills and being able to effectively communicate them is the basis for showing a potential employer what you can do. How valuable you are as an employee depends, to a large degree, on your skills. *Skills have a paycheck attached to them.*

As you may already know, it's possible to have skills that you absolutely *hate* to use. Perhaps you became an expert at something, somehow, but you don't like to do it. Or you may have loved that task at one time and developed the skills to do it, but now you don't like it anymore. Or you may *never* have liked it. Competent, conscientious person that you are, though, you retained the skills.

However, for the most part, you probably like using your skills. In the second box of life, if you found a job made up entirely of tasks that used your skills, and those tasks had just the right level of challenge (this is obviously a fantasy), you'd be in job heaven. You wouldn't be spending (wasting?) your time on tasks that didn't make use of your skills. Because the challenge wouldn't be too high for your skill level, you wouldn't feel anxious. And because it wouldn't be too low, you wouldn't feel bored. In fact, you'd be feeling engaged all the time. You'd probably be in a perpetual flow state (if that's humanly possible). You'd be a model employee. Employee of the Month, over and over and over.

Of course, most jobs are a mere shadow of this. Yet people are more likely to experience flow *at work* than *outside of work*! How can this be? Because they typically get to use their skills more at work than they do anywhere else. If you experience much flow in your work, you'll undoubtedly miss it when you retire. The first level fun of a leisure-based retirement just ain't the same thing.

Now let's make some distinctions between skills and strengths. Your *skills* are mostly useful within some context—usually work. Your *strengths* are useful across all contexts—your whole life. Skills are narrow and specific enough that they often can have a paycheck attached to them. Strengths are broad and general enough that they usually don't. (Yet your strengths are the parts of yourself that you're happy to use, whether they have a paycheck attached to them or not.) Skills are related to being a worker, and they're most important in the second box; strengths are related to being a human, and they're important in all Three Boxes of Life. Strengths are more fundamental.

THE DIFFERENCE BETWEEN STRENGTHS AND PERSONALITY TRAITS

Strengths may sound a bit like something else that humans have: *personality traits*. These are intrinsic and enduring motivations or behaviors, like introversion and extroversion. Theoretically, personality traits are as unchangeable as physical traits, such as the color of your eyes. You don't have a choice with your personality traits—that's just the way you are. Strengths are a little like that, because you also have tendencies toward certain strengths, developed through both nature and nurture. But here's a big difference between traits and strengths: Expressing your personality traits is automatic, and you can't help it. But using your strengths is a choice, and you can choose to use them or not. (Skills are that way, too.)

Here's another distinguishing characteristic of strengths: They are always positive. In contrast, personality traits and skills can be either positive or negative. For example, one of the most widely used personality tests measures the level of neuroticism as a trait that's present in each person. Neuroticism may be useful in the world of personality traits, but it would never be classified as a strength. In the same way, there are workplace skills that would be valued only by unethical employers. For example, cooking the books and roughing up adversaries are certainly skills, but not positive ones. In contrast, strengths are abilities that are valued by the individual and by society at large.

Deep down inside, you know what your greatest strengths are. You are, without a doubt, the world's leading expert on yourself.

But you are also so accustomed to some of your strengths, so familiar with them, so at ease in using them, that you may have kind of forgotten about them. Perhaps you noticed when you were young that you could do something in life easily and effortlessly while others struggled trying to do the same thing. Then, because doing that thing or acting in that way was effortless, you didn't need to focus on it. It receded into the background of your awareness as you focused on the things that *didn't* come easily and effortlessly. You needed to really apply effort and attention to the areas that were not your strengths (we won't call them weaknesses), and so those other things may have stayed in the foreground of your awareness.

You probably have other strengths that you've never been aware of, even when you were young. They're so much a part of you, so automatic, that they've been in the background all along, quietly helping you to effortlessly excel in that particular area. What's more, they haven't stayed the same over time. As you've used them—whether you were aware of them or not—you've continued to develop them. You've probably gotten better at using them over time. In fact, retirement may offer the greatest opportunity for you to develop them to their fullest potential.

You can think of your strengths as being like the paint colors on an artist's palette (or in a kindergartner's watercolors box). If you were to look back at the scenes of your life, you'd notice that over the course of time you've been painting with mostly the same colors. You may have used red or blue over and over again. That's the way you use your strengths—they're your favorite colors in the pictures of your life. In the scenes of your life, sometimes your favorite colors, or strengths, were in the foreground. In other scenes they were in the background; less obvious, but there just the same. You may find it helpful to line up a bunch of your scenes alongside each other to notice which colors are the most recurring. Once you do, they just jump out at you: those same colors, those same strengths, are in so many of your life's pictures and in your best work—your greatest achievements.

THE SIX STRENGTHS THEMES

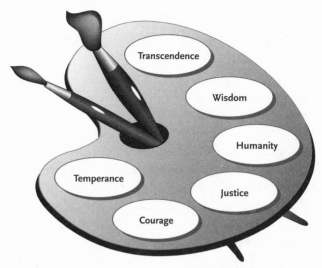

The three different methods in this chapter's exercise are designed to help jog your awareness of your own strengths so you can plan how to incorporate them into your retirement. The picture of your Ideal Retirement needs to include those best parts of yourself, so it's well worth a bit of reflection to identify them. Although, again, deep down you know what they are, these exercises are about naming them and more clearly articulating them, so they'll be easier for you to plan with.

The naming system we'll use is the VIA (Values in Action) Classification of Strengths. It's the most thoughtfully conceived, broadly researched, thoroughly developed, and painstakingly validated system for naming human strengths that's ever been created. You are very fortunate to have it as a tool for identifying your retirement strengths.

This system consists of twenty-four individual Signature Strengths, which are organized into six groups. The system's developers, Chris Peterson and Martin Seligman, call these six groups *virtues*; for our purpose here, you can think of them as Strengths Themes. Each of these six broader Strengths Themes contains three to five of the more specific twenty-four Signature Strengths. You could spend years learning about the relationship of all these (and some people have), but you'll get the general picture just by looking over the Strengths list on the following pages. Which sounds most like you?

The Strengths Themes and Signature Strengths[1]

TRANSCENDENCE
Strengths that forge connections to the larger universe and provide meaning

Appreciation of beauty and excellence *(awe, wonder, elevation)*
Noticing and appreciating beauty, excellence, and/or skilled performance in all domains of life, from nature to art to mathematics to science to everyday experience

Gratitude
Being aware of and thankful for the good things that happen; taking time to express thanks

Hope *(optimism, future-mindedness, future orientation)*
Expecting the best in the future and working to achieve it; believing that a good future is something that can be brought about

Humor *(playfulness)*
Liking to laugh and tease; bringing smiles to other people; seeing the light side; making (not necessarily telling) jokes

Spirituality *(religiousness, faith, purpose)*
Having coherent beliefs about the higher purpose and meaning of the universe; knowing where one fits within the larger scheme; having beliefs about the meaning of life that shape conduct and provide comfort

WISDOM AND KNOWLEDGE
Cognitive strengths that entail the acquisition and use of knowledge

Creativity *(originality, ingenuity)*
Thinking of novel and productive ways to do things; includes artistic achievement but is not limited to it

Curiosity *(interest, novelty seeking, openness to experience)*
Taking an interest in all of ongoing experience for its own sake; finding subjects and topics fascinating; exploring and discovering

Open-mindedness *(judgment, critical thinking)*
Thinking things through and examining them from all sides; not jumping to conclusions; being able to change one's mind in light of evidence; weighing all evidence fairly

1. The VIA Classification of Strengths is adapted with permission of the Values in Action Institute.

The Strengths Themes and Signature Strengths

Love of learning
Mastering new skills, topics, and bodies of knowledge, whether on one's own or formally; obviously related to the strength of curiosity but goes beyond it to describe the tendency to add systematically to what one knows

Perspective *(wisdom)*
Being able to provide wise counsel to others; having ways of looking at the world that make sense to oneself and to other people

HUMANITY
Interpersonal strengths that involve tending and befriending others

Love
Valuing close relations with others, in particular those in which sharing and caring are reciprocated; being close to people

Kindness *(generosity, nurturance, care, compassion, altruistic love, niceness)*
Doing favors and good deeds for others; helping them; taking care of them

Social intelligence *(emotional intelligence, personal intelligence)*
Being aware of the motives and feelings of other people and oneself; knowing what to do to fit in to different social situations; knowing what makes other people tick

JUSTICE
Civic strengths that underlie healthy community life

Citizenship *(social responsibility, loyalty, teamwork)*
Working well as a member of a group or team; being loyal to the group; doing one's share

Fairness
Treating all people the same according to notions of fairness and justice; not letting personal feelings bias decisions about others; giving everyone a fair chance

Leadership
Encouraging a group of which one is a member to get things done and at the same time maintain good relations within the group; organizing group activities and seeing that they happen

The Strengths Themes and Signature Strengths

COURAGE
Emotional strengths that involve the exercise of will to accomplish goals in the face of opposition, external or internal

Bravery *(valor)*
Not shrinking from threat, challenge, difficulty, or pain; speaking up for what is right even if there is opposition; acting on convictions even if unpopular; includes physical bravery but is not limited to it

Persistence *(perseverance, industriousness)*
Finishing what one starts; persisting in a course of action in spite of obstacles; "getting it out the door"; taking pleasure in completing tasks

Integrity *(authenticity, honesty)*
Speaking the truth and, more broadly, presenting oneself in a genuine way; being without pretense; taking responsibility for one's feelings and actions

Vitality *(zest, enthusiasm, vigor, energy)*
Approaching life with excitement and energy; not doing things halfway or halfheartedly; living life as an adventure; feeling alive and activated

TEMPERANCE
Strengths that protect against excess

Forgiveness and mercy
Forgiving those who have done wrong; giving people a second chance; not being vengeful

Humility and Modesty
Letting one's accomplishments speak for themselves; not seeking the spotlight; not regarding one's self as more special than one is

Prudence
Being careful about one's choices; not taking undue risks; not saying or doing things that might later be regretted

Self-regulation *(self-control)*
Regulating what one feels and does; being disciplined; controlling one's appetites and emotions

DEVELOPING MY PSYCHOLOGICAL STRENGTHS

Your choice of method for discovering your retirement strengths depends on how much time and effort you can spare for it. Naturally, the more of yourself you invest, the greater your likely return, and the more personalized, relevant, and meaningful the outcome will be. The good news is that the following three methods are not mutually exclusive. You could end up using all three methods over time. Speaking of time, they're listed in order from the smallest to largest investment of time and effort.

The Quickest Method for
Discovering Your Strengths

Choose them from a list. (Requires about ten minutes.)

You can use this method right now, with just this book. You'll jot down your answers, notes, observations, and so on, in the margins and spaces around the strengths listed on pages 140 through 142. Or if you prefer, make photocopies and write on the copies.

First browse the six Strengths Themes to get the big picture. Which of the themes are most likely to contain some of your strengths? The themes are a bit more abstract than the strengths, so you're starting at the broader level, then narrowing things down. Even the strengths may seem a little abstract to you, because they're more general than the kinds of narrow skills that relate to the context of work.

Next, browse through the twenty-four strengths, studying the synonyms and descriptions. As you consider each of the strengths, ask yourself, "Is this strength *not* like me? Is it *somewhat* like me? Is it *very much* like me?" Remember, you're looking for the parts of you that have shown up, over and over, across many different life situations. Make note of the strengths that seem *very much* like you. There should be no more than ten of these.

Now your goal is to identify the five strengths that are *most* like you. Go back through your list of "very much like me" strengths to narrow it down to five. One way is to ask yourself two questions:

1. Which strengths, when I'm *using* them, make me feel the most *engaged*?

2. Which strengths, when I'm *not able* to use them, make me feel the most *frustrated*?

The five that you ultimately select are your Signature Strengths, which you will fill in the Retirement Circle on page 150.

The Second-Quickest Method for Discovering Your Strengths

Take the VIA online survey at www.viastrengths.org. (Requires Internet access, completion of a free registration form, and about thirty minutes to answer the questions.)

This method is the most high-tech; to use it you'll need to set aside this book and go on the Internet. When you're done, return to the book and fill in your Signature Strengths in the Retirement Circles on page 150.

The VIA survey was designed to be used online. No paper version of it is even available. It's the primary method for figuring out which of the twenty-four strengths are most characteristic of you. I strongly recommend that you take this online survey, if you can. Your time will be well spent. The online survey provides a much more accurate way of discovering your top five strengths than browsing the names and descriptions, and it produces a report showing your Signature Strengths.

The Third-Quickest Method for
Discovering Your Strengths

Find them in stories from your life. (Takes the longest of the three methods—several hours to do it well.)

This method is the most thorough, as it requires you to write down stories about your strengths or tell them to another person who will take notes for you. The danger of this method is that, with the best of intentions, you may set aside reading this book to pursue writing your stories. Then you may not get around to finishing the stories right away, so time passes, and before you know it, the whole process of creating a picture of your Ideal Retirement has come to a halt. I strongly recommend that you first complete one of the two quicker methods. If you can't resist the prospect of writing some stories, allow yourself a rough first draft, review it for your five Signature Strengths, then keep moving forward to finish this exercise, followed by the remaining chapters and your other Retirement Circles. You can always come back later for a deeper exploration and a final, more polished version.

Using this method, you'll identify at least three stories from your life. The stories that you choose are ones that fit a very specific description, first articulated by Bernard Haldane, which forms the core of what he called the *Dependable Strengths* process. Each must be a true story from your own life in which you actively participated in something. (Remember the baseball game distinction between being a spectator and playing on the team?) Also, it must be a specific event—not simply a type of event, or one of a series of events. (Not just "playing on a baseball team"; something more like "playing in that game on the Saturday before my birthday, two summers ago, when I hit a home run.")

Now that you know what can qualify as a story, here are the criteria for the stories that you want to pick out. They are all experiences of something that you:

- Enjoyed doing while you were doing it
- Feel that you did well
- Are proud of

Remember the three approaches to happiness or Three Levels of Retirement Happiness?

- Pleasure
- Engagement
- Meaning

Notice that the story criteria get you to identify experiences that cover all three types of happiness. If you enjoyed it while you were doing it, that obviously relates to pleasure. If the story was about something you did well, it was possible to *not* do it well, meaning that there was a challenge. You met that challenge successfully, which relates to engagement. Finally, if you're proud of what you did, it meant something to you— the definition of meaning.

Thus, each of these stories that you select represents quite an accomplishment. Essentially, a trifecta. So you're really going for the gold. At the same time, your stories don't have to be big life-changing events. And you may be the only one who was aware of how important they were. (That baseball game probably didn't change your life, and you're probably the only one who knows how important it was to you.)

Are you getting a good idea of the kind of stories that you're looking for? Remember the artist's palette? This exercise lines up the best scenes from your life so you can identify which colors you used to paint them. These three stories are some of your greatest artistic achievements. Aren't you curious which colors (strengths) you used? Think of these stories as though a gallery were showing a retrospective of your best paintings—your life's work. If possible, the gallery would want something from your early period, as well as your middle and later periods. It would also want your works of art from different contexts. Not just from your job, or hobbies, or social life, but ideally all three. So the stories you choose will be most helpful to you if they're from different times, and different contexts, of your life.

You may be thinking that finding such particular types of stories will be a difficult search. But trust me—you have tons of these stories in your memory banks. An entire collection. True, these positive experiences are sometimes pushed farther back in the memory warehouse, whereas experiences of disappointment and defeat are much more readily at hand. So as you start your internal inventory system running and let these stories come to your mind over the next twenty minutes or twenty hours, realize that it's perfectly normal to bring up all kinds of stories—not just those that meet the three criteria. Then you get to choose.

Now let's begin with one of your stories. What do you do with it for this exercise? You can write it longhand or type it into your word processor and print it out to work with. If you love to write, you may tell it with perfect spelling, grammar and syntax—but you can also just note phrases, fragments, and key words, as long as you use plenty of them. Remember, you'll be trolling your stories for your strengths.

If you're telling the story to someone else who is kind enough to take notes, there is one rule that they absolutely, positively must follow. They don't have to write down every word that comes out of your mouth, but every word they do write down must be one that *did* come out of your mouth. The words that end up on the paper need to be your actual, exact words, from your own vocabulary. Your friend must not translate your words into other words, or try to summarize your story. This is your story in *your words*. Ask your friend to take down as many of your important words as possible. You need enough material to comb through to look for your strengths.

Whether writing it yourself or telling the story to a "reporter," what matters is that you record the parts of your story that answer the following questions:

1. What, specifically, were you doing?

2. What was fun about it? (Remember, you enjoyed it at the time.)

3. More important, what was the challenge, and how did you meet that challenge? (Remember, this is something you did well.)

4. What is meaningful to you about this, now, as you look back on it? (Remember, you're proud of it.)

And one more question:

5. What did you bring to that experience that was unique? (That is, no one else would have brought quite the same thing that you did.)

After you have your story down on paper, you can look for your strengths—the colors that you've used over and over—through two basic methods: *color-by-numbers* and *freehand*.

Color-by-numbers. Start with a small box of markers, color pencils, or crayons. Assign the six basic colors (red, orange, yellow, green, blue, violet) to the six Strengths Themes. Make enough photocopies of the twenty-four strengths list to take notes on one for each story.

First, go back through your first story and underline the words that describe, or closely relate to, a Strength Theme.

Don't expect to find many examples of each; you may have just one or two of the Strengths Themes showing up.

Second, go back to the underlined words and think about what you were really doing in the context of the story. Which of the Signature Strengths within that Strength Theme is the best descriptor of what you were doing? Make relevant notes on one copy of the strengths list.

Do the same for each of your other stories. By the time you get to the second and third stories, you'll be much better at spotting the Strengths Themes and the Signature Strengths within them. Whichever colors seem to you to be the ones you've colored with the most in the scenes of your life, those are the clues to your strengths. Write them down in the Retirement Circle on page 150.

Freehand. This method starts with the same markers, color pencils, or crayons, but doesn't use the Strengths Themes. Instead, you simply comb through your stories for your own words that describe your strengths. After reading this chapter and familiarizing yourself with the concept of strengths from the lists on pages 140 through 142, you're completely qualified to select your own labels for these inner qualities that we've been calling strengths. Choose the words that you used frequently and that describe the best parts of you, assign and mark each with its own color (your choice). Whatever language you use to capture those parts of you—your ways of thinking, feeling, or acting that make you feel engaged when you use them—is fine. When you think you've found the five colors from your palette that are most common in the masterpieces of your life's experiences, those are your Signature Strengths. Write them in the Retirement Circle on page 150.

By the way—regardless of the quality of these scenes from your life, keep in mind that some of your best artistic achievements are still ahead of you.

Using one of the three methods to discover your retirement strengths, you should now have a list of five strengths. Enter these in the Retirement Circle to use for your One Piece of Paper in chapter 10.

**My Ideal Retirement
includes developing
these psychological
Strengths:**

1. _____

2. _____

3. _____

4. _____

5. _____

Meaning:
The Third Level of Retirement Happiness

In addition to a pleasant and engaged retirement, some people imagine having a *meaningful* retirement. Of course, they still want to be secure and comfortable and to enjoy themselves. And they want to be actively involved in life, using their strengths in a personally rewarding way. But they also want a sense of meaning and purpose. This usually comes from feeling that you are part of something larger than yourself—something that makes you proud of the personal contribution you're making. Which brings us to the third level of retirement happiness.

If pleasure is most closely related to your interests, and engagement is most closely related to your strengths, then meaning is most closely related to your values. You may well find that the third level of retirement happiness has a connection to your chosen Ways to Live from chapter 4.

If you already know, in the second box of life, what gives you a sense of meaning—perhaps you've found a fulfilling career—congratulations! If your sense of meaning comes from something outside of your work, that's even better, because you won't leave it behind when you move from the second to the third box. On the other hand, if you're not sure whether you really have a sense of meaning in your life, retirement just might be your best chance to look for it. It could be your golden opportunity! In fact, discovering your purpose in life could be one of the most important parts of your retirement. (More on this in chapter 10.)

Of course, you don't need to decide in advance how far up the levels of retirement happiness you want to go. But the clearer your vision of retirement and, especially, the clearer your vision of *yourself* in retirement, the more likely you will be to get there. And frankly, when it comes to developing a vision, sooner is better than later. You may even start to have a vision of yourself in retirement before you've finished reading this book.

So keep your mind wide open. In the picture of your Ideal Retirement, see yourself using your strengths in the service of something you believe in and really enjoying doing it. And if you see yourself not alone in these scenes but connecting with others, sharing the experience with people you hold dear, so much the better! You're envisioning both elements of the happiness dimension: the psychological, which you've learned about in this chapter, and the social, the subject of the next chapter. The three levels apply to relationships, too—and in retirement, we generally need to make a more active effort to build relationships that bring us happiness and fulfillment on all three levels. That's what we'll be delving into in chapter 7.

Who Are You to Be So Happy?

Does all this sound like you're hoping for too much happiness from retirement? After all, many retirees—some of them your friends and coworkers—will be relieved to simply not drag themselves back and forth to work every day. They will be content just resting their duffs, like on that old three-legged stool. They will wonder why you're putting so much thought and energy into planning for your happiness in retirement. Isn't discovering your strengths a lot of work? And just who do you think you are, taking off on a journey to adventure? Who are you to climb beyond pleasure to engagement, and beyond engagement to meaning? Why do *you* deserve to have all three levels of retirement happiness?

The answer, of course, is that we *all* deserve to have them. Retirement Well-Being isn't an exclusive commodity—everyone's entitled to it. And both your planning and the happiness you reap from it can serve as inspiration to your skeptical friends. Don't keep a good thing to yourself. Spread the word about the New Retirement, and invite them along on the journey.

Resources on Strengths and Happiness

Donald Clifton was the father of strengths psychology and chairman of the Gallup organization. After many years of rigorously studying strengths, he coauthored, with Paula Nelson, an introduction to focusing on strengths instead of weaknesses: *Soar with Your Strengths* (Dell, 1995).

Donald Clifton's follow-up with Marcus Buckingham, *Now, Discover Your Strengths* (Free Press, 2001), is both a general introduction and a detailed description of Gallup's proprietary StrengthsFinder Profile. This classification of strengths themes was developed for the workplace, but it can also be useful for identifying retirement strengths.

Rather than taking a workplace orientation, Martin Seligman offers the broadest possible perspective in his book *Authentic Happiness: Using the New Positive Psychology to Realize Your Potential for Lasting Fulfillment* (Free Press, 2004). This book introduced the VIA Classification of Strengths outlined in this chapter's exercise. Don't mistake this book for a pop psychology self-help guide—it is not in that category at all. Based on heavy-duty empirical research, it's closer to being a college textbook—but infinitely more personal and relevant.

If you want to go deeper into this subject, I recommend one book that actually *is* a textbook. Christopher Peterson's *A Primer in Positive Psychology* (Oxford University Press, 2006) doesn't read like the boring books we trudged through in school. Not only is it the most thorough introduction to Positive Psychology available, it's actually interesting to read.

Finally, if you'd like to understand flow and engagement, immerse yourself in the work of Mihaly Csikszentmihalyi. His original book is *Flow: The Psychology of Optimal Experience* (Harper Perennial, 1991); the shorter and somewhat more accessible sequel is *Finding Flow: The Psychology of Engagement with Everyday Life* (Basic Books, 1998).

"Call it a clan, call it a network, call it a tribe, call it a family:
Whatever you call it, whoever you are, you need one."

—Jane Howard

CHAPTER SEVEN

Who's in Your Social Circle?

M ost of our social relationships are based on *convenience.* Certainly, they're not *all* based on convenience; we maintain some very close relationships even when they're decidedly *inconvenient.* But most of our relationships with others along the journey of life grow out of our daily activities. While we're in the second box, our activities usually relate to work, so our relationships do, too. They're convenient, and there's nothing wrong with that. Relationships that sprout from convenience sometimes grow into strong connections that can last a lifetime. (A wonderful thing, when it happens!) Yet there is something you ought to know about this convenience aspect of social behavior: *when you retire, your relationships with people from your work life will typically wither and die.* This can leave you feeling socially isolated. But it doesn't have to be that way.

A note about terminology: If you don't spend much time reading or thinking about "relationships," then substitute any of the following:

- Connections
- Social networks
- Circle of people that you know
- Family, friends, and acquaintances

The Automatic Relationship Generator

In the first box of life, otherwise known as the world of education, you could say that there's an *Automatic Relationship Generator* in operation. Like many of us, you may have found that your time in the world of education, which you inhabited when you were in school, was a very tough time, socially. Social acceptance was probably the most important thing in the world to you then, yet you felt socially insecure. Some of us were in the popular crowd (probably you) and some of us were in the geeky crowd (definitely me), but most of us had *some* relationships with other people. Some little part of a crowd to call our own. Because you were thrown together with many others into similar circumstances and shared daily activities (classes, lunch, clubs, and so on), the Automatic Relationship Generator went to work for you. It was convenient to connect with other people, and so you did, and relationships developed.

Then you changed to another school or left the world of education altogether, and what happened? How many of those relationships kept going? How many withered and died? Dig out your school yearbooks and leaf through them—how many of the friends who wrote those long, heartfelt notes are still friends? I hope that a few relationships from that formative time of life are still alive, and may even have grown and developed. But chances are most of them are only a distant memory. Perhaps they're not truly dead, but merely dormant—look what happens at class reunions!

From the first box of life, you moved on to the second box, otherwise known as the world of work. Luckily, there's usually an Automatic Relationship Generator whirring away in that world, too. Again, you're thrown together into similar circumstances with other people, sharing daily activities, so the Automatic Relationship Generator connects you with new friends.

In this stage of life, you often have other responsibilities, outside of work, that operate in a similar way. Children (if you have them) tend to pull their parents into environments with their own Automatic Relationship Generators: the neighborhood, sports teams, school events, a religious community, and so on. Again, when you're thrown together into similar circumstances, sharing these activities with other people, the Automatic Relationship Generator connects you up with other people. Conveniently.

Often, as you progress through the second box of life, you move around. New jobs, new neighborhoods, new towns, new states. Your kids get older, change schools, find new interests; they drop old friends (and their parents, who may be *your* friends) and take up with new ones. How many of *those* relationships keep going? How many wither and die? Again, you are fortunate (or a very dedicated and loyal friend) if more than a few of those friendships stay active.

Can you see a pattern emerging?

There Is No Automatic Relationship Generator in Retirement

When you think about moving on from the second box of life to the third box, you may not give much thought to your relationships. After all, you've made life transitions before, haven't you? And you've always made new friends before, haven't you? You don't realize that although the first and second boxes of life have Automatic Relationship Generators, the third box typically doesn't.

You have, of course, been building deep, long-term relationships with friends and family members that will continue with you into retirement. And, depending on how your life is arranged in retirement, you may have some of those shared similar circumstances and daily activities that will get the Automatic Relationship Generator up and running again. Or you may not. (For some retirees, the television becomes an Automatic Relationship Generator. They build relationships with the people on TV. Except those relationships aren't *real*.) Since most of us consider our personal relationships to be the most rewarding part of our lives, it's worth a little planning to have plenty of good ones in it, wouldn't you say?

What Is a Relationship, Anyway?

To plan for a retirement that includes the rewarding relationships you want, you need to look at the *structure* of relationships—not so much from an emotional perspective as from a social science perspective. First of all, the potential variety of relationships is endless. It could take lifetimes to truly experience them all: parent, child, sibling, friend, lover, confidante, mentor, cheerleader, partner, caregiver—you could go on and on. You could compile another list of less *personal,* more *instrumental* relationships, too: colleague, teammate, coworker, client, vendor, supervisor, collaborator, neighbor, and so on. You could even compile a list of contentious relationships that are mostly based on friction—but let's focus instead on what goes into the kind of relationships that will provide you with the sharing and support you'll want in retirement.

TRUST AND RECIPROCITY

Robert Putnam, a sociologist at Harvard, has an idea about what all strong and healthy relationships share. Even though they're endlessly different, they're all the same in one basic respect: they're based on *trust and reciprocity*. Those two factors, together, are the basis for the kinds of relationships that most of us are interested in for retirement.

The first factor, *trust*, is a familiar concept. It's almost impossible to have a positive relationship with someone you don't trust. The word *trust* is frequently used in an adjective form to describe a relationship; that is, *a trusted friend, a trusted source, a trusted teacher or counselor.* You want relationships with people you feel are trustworthy. But you have different levels of trust for different relationships. You may trust the paperboy to have your paper on the doorstep at 7:00 A.M.; you may also trust your adult child to make medical decisions for you if you're in a coma and on life support. Those are two very different levels of trust. Also, trust can have different qualities, even at the same level. Trusting your lover with your heart and trusting your cardiac surgeon with your heart are both very high levels of trust. But they each have a different quality.

What about the second factor, *reciprocity?* That's not as familiar a word. But we all know what it means when it comes to relationships. If you do something for someone and they don't reciprocate, you may not do something for them again. You don't build a relationship, in that case. Or perhaps you've had a relationship that *was* reciprocal and then one of you stopped reciprocating and the relationship changed. Reciprocation could be emotional support, money, information, food, communication, back rubs, understanding, or whatever. And it doesn't have to be like for like; it can be mix and match.

The bottom line is this: you know it when you're getting it, and you know it when you *ain't* getting it. That's reciprocity.

BONDING AND BRIDGING

There's another important thing to know about relationships, and it relates even more particularly to retirement planning. Putnam also suggests that there are two broad types: *bonding* relationships and *bridging* relationships. This is a bit of a simplification, as relationships can exist somewhere along a continuum between them, rather than at just one end or the other. But it's a good way to start thinking about your relationships for retirement (and in the meantime, too.)

Bonding relationships are the ones you have with *people who are like you.* You can make anything you want of "people who are like you." You're the only judge of which people in your social network are "like you." However you identify this, you feel that these people are more like you, and you bond with them. Bonding means that they are a source of *support* for you. (There are lots of different kinds of support: emotional, financial, logistical, informational—think of all the kinds you've given and received.) These people also provide what is sometimes called your *strong ties.*

What about the people in your social network who are *not like you?* Those are the people with whom you're more likely to have a *bridging* relationship—that is, you are, in effect, crossing over your differences to have the relationship. You rely on these people for *information* rather than support. The very fact that they're not like you means that they probably have different sources of information than you have. People who are more like you are more likely to have the same sources of information that you do—which isn't that helpful! By bridging out, you tap into additional sources of information. These people provide what are sometimes called your *weak ties.*

A strong social network for retirement planning, and for retirement itself, includes both types: bonding relationships for support, and bridging relationships for information. Without your social network, you'd be all alone and in the dark. You can easily think of times when you've drawn on your social network for support—be it emotional, financial, or logistical. And you can easily think of times when you've drawn on your social network for information about getting a job, deciding where to live, or which products or services to buy. You'll need to do this in retirement, too. Totally aside from preventing loneliness, having a strong social network—relationships—helps you *get along in the world*. That's why you need to do some planning, well in advance, to ensure that you'll have a network you can count on in your retirement.

Build Third Box Relationships in the Second Box

At the beginning of the second box, we start to build relationships related to our work. The more of these relationships we develop, the more successful we're likely to be in our career. In fact, a good predictor of our productivity on the job is whether we have a best friend at work—for support or information or both. And by the same token, the more successful we are in our career, the more our relationships can end up being concentrated among people we know *through* work, if not exclusively *at* work. That's the way it is for most of the years we spend in the second box, and it's a good thing.

But when we approach the end of the second box, if a big part of our social network is still concentrated among people we know through work (rather than outside of work), we may be headed for trouble. Most of those work-related relationships will fade away. So as you get closer to the later stages of the second box, it makes sense to do two things:

1. Consciously build social networks that are *not related to your job*. Those relationships won't be affected when you retire the way that work relationships will be. If anything, they may be affected in a positive way, because you'll have more time and energy to devote to them after you retire.

2. Consciously build deeper relationships with some of the people in your job-related social network. Some of these folks have the potential for being your lifelong friends. But if you wait until after you retire, you may have lost your chance.

It's easier to build lasting relationships with these potential lifelong friends while you're still working with them—particularly if you make the effort to share time outside of work. By putting in the time and energy to establish relationships that extend beyond the work environment, you increase the likelihood that the relationships will survive when you leave the workplace.

THE THREE LEVELS OF RETIREMENT RELATIONSHIPS

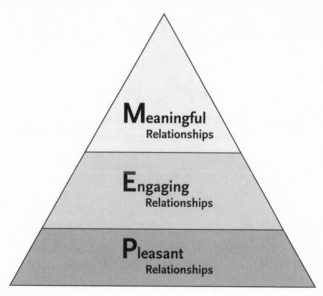

Meaningful
Relationships

Engaging
Relationships

Pleasant
Relationships

Relationships and the Three Levels of Happiness

Now that you know about the Three Levels of Retirement Happiness, introduced in chapter 6, you can apply the same thinking to the happiness that you get from your relationships. When you think back on the relationships in your life that have brought you the most happiness, you can even see which types of happiness they brought you. Some were mostly fun, some were mostly engaging, and some were mostly meaningful. And it stands to reason that some of your best relationships embraced all three approaches to happiness.

Even though these relationships may have originated through the Automatic Relationship Generators in the worlds of education or work, they went on to become rewarding and valued because they incorporated your approaches to happiness. Since this process has been operating in your life already, imagine how it might operate in retirement, too. After all, there is no Automatic Relationship Generator in retirement.

If you can, you'd probably like to preserve your relationships from the second box and also build new relationships in the third box. How might that happen? Let's apply the Three Levels of Retirement Happiness:

- **First Level.** This level is about *pleasant*, lighthearted fun—and some of your work relationships are built on just having a good time. Especially if you work in a low-pressure environment. These are people that you like hanging out with, and you may have common interests in undemanding activities outside of work. Work relationships based on pleasure may be more likely to survive if they expand to the second level (engagement) or the third level (meaning); for example, if you both take up a challenging hobby together (for shared engagement), or join a community project or political organization (for a shared sense of meaning). These activities open up deeper levels and offer the opportunity to discover whether you have compatible values, identity, and priorities (VIPs).

- **Second Level.** Because this level is about *engagement*, or using your skills and strengths for a well-matched challenge, these relationships are based on *shared* flow experiences—which can definitely happen in some jobs. Especially in high-intensity environments. When you're really in sync with coworkers on a project, you can develop this kind of strong relationship. But when you retire, that shared flow generally disappears along with the shared challenge. These work relationships are more likely to continue if you have a chance to discover that, away from the challenge of work, you can just have fun together.

- **Third Level.** This level is about *meaning*, or feeling that you're in the service of something larger than yourself. If you and your coworkers really care about the greater purpose of your work, that creates a bond. This could be especially true if you consider your work to be a type of calling. Of course, retirement changes that; it takes you out of the context in which you're sharing that sense of meaning. What might these relationships be based on after you retire? By adding activities that are either engaging or pleasant, you can broaden the relationship beyond the shared sense of meaning from work.

When you create the picture of your Ideal Retirement, the surest way to make such relationships a part of it is to include relationships based on the Three Levels of Retirement Happiness. The following exercise will help you identify three examples of involvement for building such retirement relationships based on the three levels.

BUILDING MY SOCIAL RELATIONSHIPS

The worlds of education and work usually function as Automatic Relationship Generators, creating social relationships through shared daily activities with other people. These relationships bring happiness in the form of pleasure, engagement, meaning, or some combination of these.

Because the world of retirement doesn't have an Automatic Relationship Generator, to have the social relationships that you want in retirement you need to identify your own relationship generators: retirement activities, memberships, or environments that perform a social function similar to education or work. Getting involved in these creates the shared activities from which relationships grow.

For each of the Three Levels of Retirement Happiness, you can identify examples that would be likely to create and build

---

social relationships. When you think about building these relationships from the perspective of the three levels, you're thinking about involvement in activities, memberships, and environments based on your values, strengths, and interests.

Involvement in activities, memberships, or environments based on your *values* is more likely to create meaningful relationships. Involvement that's based on using or developing your *strengths* is more likely to create engaged relationships. Involvement based on pursuing your *interests* is more likely to create pleasant relationships. Of course, all forms of involvement, and all social relationships, can develop on all three levels.

Beginning with the general list that follows, think of specific examples that could provide opportunities for social involvement for your retirement. Try to think of three or four opportunities for each of the levels. You will then choose one from each level as an example of the kind of involvement you'd like to explore for retirement and write those in your Retirement Circle.

Examples of Relationship-Building Opportunities

Alumni organizations
Athletic teams
Charitable organizations
Educational opportunities
Employment
Environmental groups
Extended family
Faith communities
Performing arts organizations
Political organizations
Service clubs

Meaningful Relationships

What types of involvement would I like to explore for retirement based on my *values?* These are social activities, memberships, or environments that would offer an opportunity to serve something larger than myself and could create a shared sense of *purpose* with other people.

_____   _____

_____   _____

Engaging Relationships

What types of involvement would I like to explore for retirement based on using or developing my *strengths?* These are social activities, memberships, or environments that would present a challenge and could create a shared sense of *flow* with other people.

_____   _____

_____   _____

Pleasant Relationships

What types of involvement would I like to explore for retirement based on just having *fun?* These are social activities, memberships, or environments that allow me to pursue my *interests* and could create a shared sense of enjoyment with other people.

_____   _____

_____   _____

Now choose one specific example from each of the levels—meaningful (M), engaging (E), and pleasant (P)—and write it on your Retirement Circle to use for your One Piece of Paper in chapter 10.

**My Ideal Retirement
includes building
these social
Relationships:**

M _____

E _____

P _____

You Can Choose Your Friends,
but You Can't Choose Your Family

For some, it may feel weird to contemplate building retirement relationships. They may wonder if deliberately taking this action means they're being insincere or manipulative. Is it like being a social climber or using other people? The answer is ABSOLUTELY NOT. On the contrary! Building genuine relationships based on shared pleasures, shared engagement, or shared meaning is a very sincere and respectful way to connect with fellow human beings. It's at least as sincere and respectful as convenience, wouldn't you say?

As is the case with any friendship, the underlying requirement for building and maintaining relationships this way is *genuine connection*. Aside from the shared experience of happiness, if the genuine connection is there, then it's there. If it's not, it's not. By using the three levels as a starting point, at least we know where to look.

What about people who just happen to have DNA that's very similar to our own? The old saying "You can choose your friends, but you can't choose your family" implies that we like our friends better. After all, we build those relationships from scratch. If our friendships don't operate on at least one of the levels of happiness, they don't endure.

But that may be true of our families, as well. We all know that family relationships can become estranged—between parents and children, or among siblings. Perhaps the family relationships that endure are operating on the three levels, too. Many people use the greater time and freedom of retirement to reconnect with family. The three levels can even be a guide for connecting with family, and with old friends, too.

Marriage on Steroids

In retirement, there's one family relationship that's in a category all its own. It sometimes even seems to transcend the requirements of trust and reciprocity. Ideally, it anchors the bonding end of the bonding and bridging continuum. And it has probably operated, at various times, on each of the three levels. This is, of course, your relationship with your *significant other*. There are many variations on this type of relationship, but for simplicity we'll use the terms *marriage* and *spouse*, as they are the most common. (Even if you don't have a significant other at the moment, keep reading. Who knows what the future may bring?)

The pithiest description of what retirement does to our relationship with our significant other is *marriage on steroids*. It becomes a bigger version of itself. (If you tend toward mathematics or literature, you might term it *marriage squared* or *marriage writ large*. You get the idea.) Whatever a marriage is like before retirement, it tends to become *more that way* in retirement. A marriage that's harmonious and loving, if allowed to evolve naturally, tends to become more harmonious and loving. A marriage that's discordant and intolerant, if allowed to evolve naturally, tends to become more discordant and intolerant.

Why? It's a simple matter of *space* and *time*. The laws of physics, applied to marriage. Let's assume that at least one marriage partner works outside the home—and these days, often both do. When the partners are still in the second box, they each have a space at work and a space at home. On a daily basis, the two partners occupy two or three distinct locations in space. Also, because of the time allocated to work, the time that they spend interacting with each other is limited.

How are space and time altered in the third box? First, *space is compressed*. Instead of having two or three spaces to occupy, both partners occupy the same space—home. Second, *time is expanded*. Instead of time being allocated to work, it's spent interacting with each other. So what happens when these two highly energized particles come together in retirement? They're either attracted to one another or repelled by one another. Marriage is like physics—or maybe more like rocket science. (*To the moon, Alice!*) Anticipating both partners' shifts in space and time is an element of good retirement planning.

You've probably heard of at least one couple who were together for many years until one or both partners retired; then not long afterward, to everyone's surprise, they filed for divorce. In some cases this isn't due to the simple physics of space and time. It runs deeper. Once the two got to know each other again, they may have discovered that their VIPs had evolved in such diverging directions that they were no longer in sync. They decided that life was too short—or the third box was too long—to stay together.

From a retirement planning perspective, what should you do about this possibility? If you're in a bad marriage in the second box, should you accept the inevitable and jettison your partner before you get to the third box? Or should you try to repair that troubled relationship in advance, so it has a better chance of surviving the concentrated conditions of retirement? Each marriage is unique, and you could be happily surprised. There are marriages that limp along during the couple's work life, languishing from inattention, and then become *revitalized* through conscious application of the more abundant time and energy of the third box. Retirement was just what the marriage needed!

When it comes to building a strong marriage for retirement, the stakes are high. Across many years, as we age, our social circles inevitable become smaller. Our worlds shrink; our activity levels decline; we spend more and more time at home and in the company of our spouse. This tends to happen in our advanced years even for those of us who are healthy and active. Our relationship with our spouse becomes a larger and larger part of our lives.

With age comes infirmity. Often, at the far end of retirement, one marriage partner needs some type of care and the other partner provides it. The burden on the caregiver is great (and there we can be thankful for the many books, groups, and other supportive resources now being devoted to the special needs of caregivers). Across the life course, many relationships are based on convenience. Becoming a caregiver is just the opposite. Nothing is more inconvenient than caring for another person. At the same time, needing care from another is very inconvenient, too. Our society values and promotes independence, and the loss of independence isn't an easy adjustment.

For a moment, think about your relationships—especially your marriage—at the far end of retirement. Imagine the inconvenience (and burden) of being the caregiver, and also the inconvenience (and loss) of being the one who needs care.

Now, stop for a moment to recognize your spouse as the person most willing to care for you, should that need arise. (This could apply to a caregiver who is not a spouse, too.) Pause to consider what that means, and to reflect on your relationship with that person in the following way:

1. Reconnect with what made the two of you fall in love with each other in the first place. What special chemistry brought you together so strongly? That's what grew into this willingness to care for you.

2. Think of all of the times that your spouse has supported you, comforted you, and seen the best in you over the years. Remember that your spouse has already been your caregiver, in many other ways.

3. Imagine how grateful you would feel in the future, knowing that your spouse has truly come to your aid.

Of course, you don't need to wait to feel this gratitude. You can begin feeling it today, and every day that the two of you are together. Ideally, you have a spouse who is your truest and closest companion on your journey.

One of the biggest decisions that the two of you will make together is where to spend the third box of life. The geography of your retirement is our next focus. The chapter that follows brings us back to the prosperity dimension of Retirement Well-Being—the Geo-Financial dimension. We took a good long look at the financial side in chapter 5; in chapter 8, you will add the geographical element to your planning—and to your One Piece of Paper in chapter 10.

Resources on Social Engagement and Relationships

For the really big picture of what's happening to our social connections, take a look at Robert Putnam's eye-opening *Bowling Alone: The Collapse and Revival of American Community* (Simon & Schuster, 2001). Putnam extensively documents the decline of "social capital," a resource that people have traditionally drawn upon in retirement.

Putnam's follow-up book is *Better Together: Restoring the American Community* (Simon & Schuster, 2003). Here he takes a hopeful view of the future by exploring specific programs and environments that successfully promote social engagement. One example is the Experience Corps, a volunteer organization for retirees.

A more personalized view of social engagement can be found in *Prime Time: How Baby Boomers Will Revolutionize Retirement and Transform America* (PublicAffairs, 2002). Marc Freedman also cofounded the nonprofit organization Civic Ventures to promote exactly this kind of positive revolution. Take a peek at www.civicventures.org.

On an even more personal level, see the books of John Gottman, one of the few researchers scientifically studying what keeps couples together. Two that could be relevant for your retirement relationships are *The Relationship Cure: A 5 Step Guide to Strengthening Your Marriage, Family, and Friendships* (Three Rivers Press, 2002) and *The 7 Principles for Making Marriage Work* (Orion, 2004).

You or your spouse could eventually take on the role of caregiver for the other—you may well get some advance practice with your parents. Hugh Delehanty and Elinor Ginzler's *Caring for Your Parents: The Complete AARP Guide* (Sterling, 2006) will help you not only cope with a parent's needs today, but also gain insight into your own needs in the future.

"We shall not cease from exploration
And the end of all our exploring
Will be to arrive where we started
And know the place for the first time."
—T. S. Eliot

CHAPTER EIGHT

Where in the World Will You Retire?

D o you imagine moving to a new place when you retire? That place could be just across town or across the country. Either way, letting go of the place where you live and making a new home somewhere else is one of the most adventurous things you can do. Even the old-fashioned, leisure-oriented approach to retirement was exciting when it included a move to a new location. Any change in geography is an adventure, after all.

It's easy to imagine moving for retirement, but it's not easy to actually make the move in a way that supports your Retirement Well-Being, because where you live affects almost every aspect of your life. Your geography and finances are linked, not only by the cost of your residence itself, but also by the general cost of living that goes with a particular location. Your location affects your social relationships, because you tend to spend more or less time with friends and family based on how easy it is to get together.

Geography can affect your health, too, through factors such as climate and the accessibility of medical care. Equally important, where you live can either support or inhibit healthy living habits—such as being physically active—that have a long-term effect on your health as you age.

Even if you decide to stay right where you are when you retire, that decision has all of the same effects on your well-being. Whether your preretirement abode has been *home sweet home* for a lifetime or just a few years, you can still evaluate it from a fresh perspective. Will it support the kind of life you really want to live? Would a few changes make your current place into your dream place? How do you know what your dream place is, anyway? Your life changes so much when you retire that the dream place you envision in the second box could turn into a bad dream in the third box.

Not only is your choice of where to live a profound decision, it's a high-stakes one, too. It's profound because it affects so many other areas of life. And it's high-stakes because making a move is such a major undertaking that you are unlikely to undo it if you get it wrong. Even if you discover you made the wrong choice, you may settle for just settling in, because it's too difficult (and too expensive) to move again. Another move would likely be to *another* new place. You surely know the expression "You can't go home again." (That's because someone else is probably living there now.)

On the other hand, if you make plans for retirement based on *not* moving and then design a life around your existing place, it can be difficult to reconsider later. There are, in life, certain windows of opportunity. Retirement (going from the second box of life to the third box) is a major life transition that may open the window to living in a new place. If you don't make your move during that transition, the window may close. It may be stuck—and you may be stuck, too.

The Geography of the Three Boxes of Life

The Three Boxes of Life provide a way to describe the life transitions that have been typical in modern society. Even though we're breaking down the boxes these days, education, work, and retirement are still dominant stages of life in the modern world. As you move through the boxes, you may notice that your degree of freedom tends to increase—and that means more geographic freedom as well.

In the first box, you lived wherever your family lived—through high school, and perhaps college too. You typically didn't have any choice about where you lived. It was just a given. Unless your family moved, you probably didn't think about moving. (There are those of us, though, who dreamt of faraway places from a very early age.) If you had a chance to go away to college, that may well have been your first glimmer of geographic freedom. And for most of us, even that was quite limited freedom.

The second box of life opened up new horizons. You had the power to choose where to live. But the need to support yourself meant getting a job, which put limitations on your geographic freedom. You may have also been limited by a desire to be close to friends and family. Over the years, your work may have been a deciding factor, keeping you in place or moving you around. Having children may have kept you close to family for support. Getting your children into the schools you wanted for them may have shaped your geographic choices, too.

Yes, the second box of life is filled with responsibilities, and many of those have geographic requirements. But the later part of the second box typically has fewer requirements. And the third box usually offers the greatest freedom of place you'll ever experience—at least at the beginning (more on that later). Here are five reasons why the third box offers you the greatest geographic freedom:

1. Your income isn't tied to living in a particular location. Unless you've been a telecommuter or a freelancer or you've done some other your-presence-is-optional type of work, your income and your geography have always been joined at the hip. But not anymore! The Social Security administration (and your pension plan, IRA account, bank, and so on) will send your monthly check wherever you tell them to.

2. If you want to work in retirement, you may be more geographically flexible in your search for work than you could be in the job that you retire from. Whether you work for the income, or to use your strengths, or to be socially connected with other people, you can probably find work in a variety of places. There are even more options when you're open to— or even prefer—temporary or part-time work.

3. Your residence may have appreciated in value, allowing you to sell it at a hefty profit when you retire. In particular, if you live in a region or a metropolitan area with a thriving economy,

with plenty of jobs and moneymaking opportunities, people still in the second box will be eager to buy your residence. They need to live somewhere convenient for their work. But once you're in the third box, you don't. Many great places to live have poor job opportunities—which doesn't matter to you, not one bit!

4. Family responsibilities typically lessen in the third box, so geographical constraints loosen. As your brood left the nest (or flew the coop), they may have stayed nearby or moved across the country. But either way, you're not as responsible for them. Staying connected with your family and being an important part of their life—these are affected by your geography, to be sure. But *connection* requires less proximity than *responsibility* did. In retirement, you may use your increased abundance of time to visit them, or you may stay in touch in other ways.

5. People you already know are blazing new trails for you. You have family, friends, and acquaintances who have moved to other places already, and they can provide you with opportunities to try out a different geography. You may have had less communication with them since they moved, but planning your retirement is the perfect opportunity to reconnect with them, and possibly connect with the place that they've moved to.

It's great to have more geographic freedom, isn't it? Now what you need is a simple way to consider all the places you could live and compare them to where you live now.

It's useful to think about retirement geography in four layers, forming the acronym SALE. On the opposite page is an image that makes the acronym easy to remember.

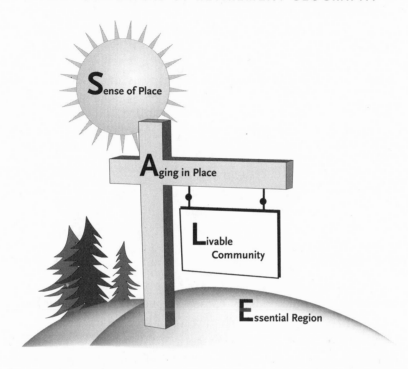

S is for *sense of place*. The innermost layer, it's the meaning that you derive from a geographic location.

A is for *aging in place*. The micro layer, it's what most people hope to do in their retirement residence.

L is for *livable community*. The middle layer, it's a supportive environment for retirement and aging.

E is for *essential region*. The macro layer, it's the part of the country that you absolutely must live in.

Does this acronym mean you should sell your place and move? Not at all. But you *should* at least evaluate your current place according to these four layers. That way, if you decide to stay there, it will be the result of a conscious decision. Consider the four layers in any order that makes sense for you. We'll explore them one at a time, starting with the big picture.

Your Essential Region:
The Macro Layer of Geography

Assuming that you really could pick up and move to another part of the country (or another country altogether), where might that be? You may have visited other regions for business, or on vacation, or to visit friends or family. Certainly there are other regions that you are curious about, or even attracted to deep down, but have never been to. Retirement may be just the opportunity you've needed to visit those places or hang out in them for a while—for weeks, months, or even years. But although retirement can have a vacation quality, it's important to make a distinction between the places you plan to sample and the one or two places that you may really want to call home. You know that expression "It's a nice place to visit, but I wouldn't want to live there"? It's not just a cliché—it holds a deeper wisdom than we give it credit for.

Whether a region is just nice to visit or is one where you'd happily live out your days depends, of course, on whether that region holds what you need to truly live. When you think about the life you want in retirement, there are probably certain things you can't imagine living without; you view those as essential. If some of your essentials are tied to a geographic region of the country, that makes it an *essential region* for you.

Now, you may not have an essential region. Your essential requirements may be the kind that can be found in many geographic locations—say, a first-rate symphony, year-round golf, a professional sports team, or a regional outlet mall. But a good way to explore the possibility is to consider what you *absolutely couldn't live without*, then see whether those things are connected to a particular area.

To identify your essential region, ask yourself these questions:

1. Is there a region that supports your most important *relationships*? Where are the people who are most important in your life (possibly children, grandchildren, lifelong friends, elderly parents)? You may not need to be right next door, but within easy traveling distance, perhaps? Consider, too, that these loved ones may relocate someday.

2. Is there a region that offers compelling opportunities to use your *strengths* in a way that's both engaging and meaningful for you? This could be a particular retirement job, an unusual volunteer opportunity, a chance to go back to school, or a once-in-a-lifetime special project, such as working to help protect the flora or fauna of a threatened ecosystem.

3. Is there a region that would allow you to pursue your *interests* or passions in a way that you could nowhere else? This could be physical geography like mountains or water, or cultural offerings such as the arts or entertainment.

4. Is there a region that could be particularly supportive to your *health*, especially if that's a challenge for you? You may need a climate that's beneficial to a physical condition, or proximity to uncommon medical specialists or alternative practitioners. Even basic access to medical care, such as a Veteran's Administration hospital, HMO, or PPO, could be a factor.

5. Is there a region that would make it easier to make ends meet *financially*, if that's an issue for you? This means not only a lower cost of housing, but a lower cost of living in general, or the chance to pool resources with family or others as a way to cut costs.

6. Is there a region that relates to your *values, identity, and priorities* (VIPs)? This means the area holds some special significance for you beyond the essentials of relationships, fulfilling opportunities, health, or finances. It could be the center of your religious tradition, cultural heritage, or family roots.

7. Is there a region that would uniquely support your chosen *Ways to Live?*

As you answer these, keep in mind that retirement changes over time. What's important at the beginning of the third box of life may not be what's important at the end. At the beginning, you're usually young and healthy enough to be very active in the world, so amenities and opportunities are at the top of your checklist for evaluating regions. Toward the end, you'll likely want and need more help and support from others, and you may need significant medical care. This evolution may necessitate two migrations during your retirement. A first migration could be made so you can do the things you want to do—an *amenity migration*. A later migration could be to get some help from your supportive relationships—an *assistance migration*. And that could be to a new place altogether, or back to the region where you lived before—a *reverse migration*.

Keep these migration types in mind as you think about what's important to you and where that's located. Your essential region for retirement may be a place that's very different from your essential region for your working years. And if your essential region has anything to do with people (and I hope it does!), your essential region could change if those people migrate. After all, you may be looking at thirty years of retirement.

Of all the changes in geography that you may consider, migrating to another region is the most expensive, labor-intensive, and logistically complex, and it has the greatest effect on your relationships. It's also the least common. You may already be living in your essential region and just haven't thought of it that way! All this adds up to the obvious conclusion that migrating to another part of the country is a level of geographic change that you need to research and consider most carefully. With a fresh perspective and a bit of ingenuity, you may be able to create your Ideal Retirement in the region where you already live. Perhaps you could instead make changes at another level—your community or residence. (In which case you might decide that another region that had beckoned you is a nice place to visit, but you wouldn't want to live there!)

Your Livable Community: The Middle Layer of Geography

What exactly is a community? For purposes of your retirement geography, think of a community in the broad and varied sense of the term. It's simply an area that you live in during your retirement—and it usually has little in common with that specialized planned development called a *retirement community*. Livable community, as the middle layer of your retirement geography, is the area around your home that you typically travel within to fulfill your daily needs and desires.

Think about your current community. How far do you need to travel to the coffee shop, the grocery store, your faith community, the pharmacy, the post office, the doctor, the library, or dinner and a movie? How much farther, if at all, do you to travel to see friends and family? How much farther for something a bit out of the ordinary, like an airport, a major sporting event, or a top-notch regional hospital? (Although in the later years of retirement, having a hospital close to home could well become more essential.) Whatever area you travel within to fill those daily needs is probably what you think of as your community. At some distance from home, you know the feeling that you have left your community behind.

If you think you might even consider looking around for a new community for retirement, it's worthwhile to think about all the different kinds that exist. In looking at types of communities, you might even redefine what you think of as the boundaries of your own community. A community can be described in a number of ways:

- It could be a political entity with easily identifiable borders, like a city or county (such as Santa Fe, New Mexico, or Door County, Wisconsin).

- It could be a political entity that is contiguous with others but still retains its own character (like Sarasota, Florida).

- It could be an area bounded by certain landforms or by water (like Cape Cod, Massachusetts, or Bainbridge Island, Washington).

- It could be a well-known urban area in a large city (like Buckhead in Atlanta or Wrigleyville in Chicago).

- It could be an area shaped by the presence of a university or other institution (as Clayton, Missouri, is by Washington University).

- It could be a real estate development organized by a corporation (like Sun City, Arizona).

It could even be what was once called a *neighborhood*, even if it doesn't have a specific name (but these are getting harder to find).

Many large cities have these enclaves, but knowledge of what makes each neighborhood special may be jealously guarded by locals.

Communities are wonderful things; more wonderful still is a *livable community*. This concept is a fairly recent one, but developing rapidly. Livable communities are good for everyone—whether they're in the first, second, or third box of life. In fact, one of the features that can make a community particularly livable is that it integrates people from all three boxes. Rather than separating age groups—young singles, families with children, retirees—from each other, all are included. People have lived in these kinds of age-integrated communities for most of human history, and there is a deep wisdom in it. You may even have spent your childhood in an environment like this, and you probably benefited greatly from your interaction with retired folks. They probably benefited from their interaction with you, too!

At the same time, there certainly are livable communities composed mostly of retirement-age people. Where these arise organically through the maturing of a neighborhood, they're called *naturally occurring retirement communities*, or NORCs. On the other hand, where these are created synthetically through land development, we might call them *developer-organized retirement communities*, or DORCs. Not all DORCs are created equal, and a few are even shining examples of livable communities. But please recognize that although DORCs always look very nice, looks can be deceiving. They may be more "lookable" than livable.

You can start thinking now about your current community and how livable it may be through your retirement years. After you retire, your awareness of the community may be heightened. For example, you could become more aware of how rich and varied the available activities are. In looking for activities, memberships, and environments to invest yourself in, you'll be able to explore your community at a deeper level. One part of that exploration will be getting to know other people in your community to build fun, engaging, and meaningful relationships with (since you'll be seeing less of your old friends from work). The more interesting and vibrant the activities are in your community, the more rewarding your explorations can be. The good news is that those activities attract interesting and vibrant people (like you!).

Is your community up to the task of being a livable community for your retirement? Or is it a dud? And you may want to gaze into your crystal ball. Not only will your own life change over the coming years, the life of your community will, too. Is it the kind of town that relies too heavily on just one or two industries, with a Main Street that's been abandoned as strip malls sprout just outside the municipal limits? Or is your town too appealing for its own good—attracting newcomers from pricier areas, so longtime residents' children can no longer afford a starter home (if they can find one)? As your community develops, do you see yourself wanting to live there *more* than you do now, or *less*? Is there another community, or are there several (right in your own backyard) that would be a better fit? Only by making a comparison will you know. You may discover that yours stacks up very well and you didn't even realize it. Lucky you!

THE SELF-CONTAINED COMMUNITY

Another facet of your community is more mundane: how self-contained is it? For many, retiring from work also means retiring from commuting. Commuting is an activity that automatically routes you near many services that you need. In fact, you've probably become a loyal customer of some retailers just because they're on your commute route. Or you may have gotten into the habit of shopping or running errands near your workplace. At lunch and along the way from home to work and back again, you may often fit in the side trips needed to keep the household functioning. They're just stops along the way. But once you don't need to commute, if those services aren't available in your community you'll need to make specific trips to obtain them.

You might think that's a good thing in retirement—it will get you out of the house and into the world. That may be true for some folks. But because you're reading this book, I suspect you're not looking for meaningless time fillers just to keep yourself busy in retirement. You'd prefer to take care of as many of your needs as easily and close to home as possible. Sure, you want to get out of the house—but for meaningful, engaging activities. If your retirement has the potential to be the high point of your life's journey, it would be a shame to spend it running errands, don't you think?

Some communities are called by a single name and thought of as a single entity, but are actually composed of several self-contained neighborhoods. Their lucky residents can fulfill their daily needs within just a few blocks from where they live. If they walk those blocks (in decent weather) instead of driving a car or taking public transit, they tend to stay more physically fit. The more activities they can participate in within walking distance, the more likely they are to know their neighbors, shopkeepers, librarians, pharmacists, and other nice folks. As people make their way further and further into the third box of life, these relationships become more valuable.

These self-contained neighborhoods exist in every region, in most cities, and in both low-rent and high-rent districts. Many smaller towns still operate on this principle. If you've never lived this way before, you owe it to yourself to experience it. Go stay a while with a friend who's fortunate enough to live in one. For a vacation, sublet an apartment or a house in an area that appears to operate this way (even though you may not get to know many residents in that short a time). There are no advertisements or marketing brochures (let alone salespeople) for these neighborhoods. They aren't trying to entice anyone, so you need to seek them out.

CALLING IT A COMMUNITY DOESN'T MAKE IT ONE

On the other hand, there are also places that are *called* "communities" but are communities in name only. You've seen the signs at the gates of developments: "A Community for Those 55 and Better," "A Community of 38 Distinctive Homes," "A Community for Active Living!" These places, whatever you call them, put their residents at a disadvantage. because they don't offer what people actually need to live, day to day. (Unless all you need to do is play golf or tennis, or swim.) These "communities" are isolated enclaves that force residents to rely on a car or public transportation, which can be an inconvenience or a hardship, depending on the situation. (Strangely, both gated communities and ghettos can share this limitation.) Because residents don't walk to the services they need, healthy exercise isn't as naturally integrated with their daily lives. Because they don't walk outside as much, they are less likely to know their neighbors, and others outside the gates.

As you move through the third box of life, in this kind of "community" you can easily become more socially isolated. Although the architecture and landscaping may be pleasing to the eye, the residents may or may not interact very much. This isn't something you can normally spot from photographs or even on a tour. But a little feet-on-the-ground research should reveal how residents get around, and how well they know each other.

The social life of a community is often revealed in its physical configuration. There is a saying in the field of geography: "The spatial is social, and the social is spatial." The idea is that the configuration of a neighborhood affects the social relationships of the residents. The flip side is that the social relationships of the residents will in turn affect how they create and modify the spatial configuration of the neighborhood. Every community offers clues. For example:

- Are there sidewalks? Are there people walking on them?
- Are there courtyards or parks with benches? Are residents gathering and visiting there?
- Are there commercial establishments where people linger and socialize? Or do they just hurry in and out?

Such distinctions may not be a big deal for you in the early part of retirement, when you're healthy, active, out and about in the world, and reveling in your new free time. But much later, when you may not be as active and may prefer to spend more time closer to home, this distinction could mean the difference between inconvenience and hardship, between a community that is livable and one that is not.

Your Aging-In-Place Residence: The Micro Layer of Geography

When the time comes, as it may, that you need assistance with the activities of daily living, would you prefer to continue living in your own home or move to a nursing home?

Although this question deals with the *end* of the third box of life, you should consider it as early as possible—right now, when you're thinking about the *beginning* of the third box. The decisions you make at this point will determine, far down the road, how long you can live in your own home. Will the home in which you choose to spend your retirement be one that allows you to live out your days there? (Hand in hand with choosing that home, of course, goes making every effort to preserve your health and physical self-sufficiency—the focus of chapter 9.)

At the middle layer of retirement geography—your community—the key concept is livability. At the micro layer—your residence—livability is the key concept, too. Just as you'll spend more time in your community in retirement, you'll also spend a lot more time in your residence than you ever have before. The question is not simply "How livable is it?" but also "How *long* will it be livable?" Based on what happens to you as you age, how easy or difficult might it be to live there? As you're planning your retirement and then transitioning into the third box of life, you need to take the long view.

Of course, even though many people claim that they want to "age in place" as it's being called, not *everyone* wants to. Perhaps you imagine living in one residence at first when you're vigorous and active, then moving to another residence when you can't get around as well. That's a perfectly good plan, if you really *do* that kind of two-phase planning. Just don't ignore the second phase—the later part of the third box—because you find it unpleasant to think about. A little long-range planning now can save you (and your loved ones) a lot of frustration, and work, and money, and heartache down the road.

You may have been thinking of moving to a new home for your retirement, or not. Perhaps you're definitely moving, because you want to downsize and get equity out of your home for retirement income. Perhaps you're definitely *not*, because you have so many memories and friends (and so much stuff) associated with your home that you can't imagine moving. In that case, if you need to draw equity out of your home for retirement income, you'll look into a reverse mortgage or a home equity line of credit.

Perhaps you've hedged your bets by buying a vacation home that you plan to make into your retirement home—this will eventually lead to a sort of hybrid move, as you bring the remainder of your belongings to join those you've been keeping in the second home, and adjust to *living* there as opposed to limited vacation visits. Perhaps you're open to moving but aren't sure yet what exactly you would be looking for, or whether a new home would be worth all the trouble. Whatever possibilities you're considering, remember this: Think both near-term and long-term. When you evaluate a residence—existing or contemplated—ask yourself two questions:

1. How well would that residence support your active early retirement life?

2. How well would that residence support your aging in place, later in retirement?

SIX USES FOR YOUR HOME IN RETIREMENT

Let's look at some examples of the active early part of retirement. Think of people you know who have recently retired; you've probably noticed that they use their homes in variations on the following six basic approaches. As you read each description, consider it in light of your Ways to Live and your VIPs. Have you been using your home somewhat like that in your working life? Is that how you'd really like to use it in retirement?

1. **Home as a Job.** These folks retire from their regular job and, in effect, take on a new job as the caretaker, handyperson, and housekeeper of their own residence. They take personal responsibility for just about every aspect of maintenance. These hardworking folks throw themselves into duties for which they might previously have hired a professional (or a local teenager). Some retirees may find this truly rewarding; others may just be trying to keep busy, because they really don't know what else to do with their time. Either way, handling physical and technical responsibilities helps keep us sharp as we age, so *some* of it may be a good thing for everyone. *How about you?*

2. **Home as a Project.** These folks use their newfound freedom (and sometimes, their retirement money) to finally get to the major home improvements they've contemplated for years. Whether they use the do-it-yourself or have-it-done approach, it's the focus of their interest and attention. If they're not careful, the remodeling ideas can be leftovers, fitting their old life more than their new one. But ideally the ideas are fresh and relevant to the way they want to live in retirement. The improvements really increase quality of life. At some point, though, the home improvement phase must come to an end. That's when these folks discover whether just living in their home is enough for their Retirement Well-Being. *How about you?*

3. **Home as a Museum.** These folks have accumulated a lot of physical possessions during their time in the second box, and their home is the place they display and store everything. Retirement is an opportunity to seek out and find even more of just the right stuff. Some people are true connoisseurs; others are true pack rats. For both, though, the thrill of acquiring more things or the sense of security in keeping them may be more important than the residence itself. Some may get involved as buyers or sellers at flea markets or in online auctions. The home may be just a warehouse or the ultimate display case, showing the entire collection. They may hope that their prized possessions will one day become family heirlooms. (If you're such a collector, one of the best ways to test that hope against reality is to talk with your family about it. Really, really talk with them. You may find that they treasure the time spent with you more than they would treasure having your treasure.) *How about you?*

4. **Home as a Community Center.** These folks turn their residence into a setting for finally spending more time with other people. In Western society, life in the second box is typically time deprived, and social relationships often suffer. Some people use their additional free time in retirement to entertain—seriously entertain. They get friends and family

into their home for large and small gatherings, and they encourage overnight guests whenever possible. Unlike the first two uses of a residence, this approach is focused less on the physical structure itself and more on its usefulness as a venue. Of course, if these folks have let their relationships slip away during the second box, they may be beyond reviving in the third box, regardless of the venue. *How about you?*

5. **Home as a Base of Operations.** These folks may not really be interested in their residence at all. They yearn to be somewhere else, traveling hither and yon. Whatever form their travels take, their home becomes more or less the base camp. These folks feel that they've been tied down long enough in the second box, and as long as they've got health and money, they'll seek their happiness on the road. But consider this: Sooner or later we all must stop to rest, and rest becomes a bigger issue the further we progress in the third box. At some point these folks will need to decide whether the residence they have is the one that they want to spend time in as their travels wind down. *How about you?*

6. **Home as a Retreat.** These folks may or may not be interested in their home per se, but they are interested in the privacy and serenity that it can provide. They may have found the requirements of the second box tiring, forcing them into more contact with the world than they really liked. Now they want to be left alone in peace and quiet and interact with the world on their own terms. Although home is a refuge even during the working years, it's usually only for a few hours each day. The long, unbroken time structure of retirement certainly allows home owners to retreat if that's what they want to do. However, later in the third box, a social support network will be an essential resource. The danger of residence as retreat is that unless the residents also emerge to keep relationships alive, those may not be there when they need them. *How about you?*

It all comes back to the essential message of this book: making plans for the life you want to live in retirement, then considering how your residence can *support* that life. Life planning comes first; residence planning comes second. This is really the foundation of your micro layer geographical decision. Only after you're clear about your own Retirement Well-Being can you think clearly about whether you should stay put or go looking for your retirement dream home.

Thinking about what you'll need in your residence in the later, aging-in-place phase of retirement is more straightforward than planning for the active early retirement years, because your options are narrower. The natural process of aging, even healthy aging, means that sooner or later it can become a challenge for you to live independently. However, you probably can't foresee what your own specific challenges will be, when and if that time comes for you. There is a broad range of infirmities that become more common as you age, and you don't get to choose them—they choose you. It may be a loss of strength or balance, physical dexterity, eyesight or hearing, cardio or respiratory capacity. If you knew in advance what infirmities might eventually force you to leave your home for some type of assisted living, you could plan better. You could make sure that the home you settle on, early in the third box, would be hospitable to the infirmities you expect to have later on. Your family genetics, your health history, any existing conditions, and your health habits are all factors, but these are far outweighed by the unpredictable. Seeing as you can't accurately predict, it's a good idea to consider some general ideas from the new concept of *universal design* (see the box on page 191).

A Sense of Place:
The Inner Layer of Your Geography

Your *inner* experience of your retirement geography is as important as the outer layers that we've already explored. *Sense of place* is that connection you feel to a particular place, your emotional reaction to it, the symbolic meaning that it has for you. Sense of place is not easy to pin down, because it is something different for each of us. It has to do with how unique or generic a place is, how personal or impersonal.

This idea has arisen in the context of sweeping changes in the way we live in Western society. Many people are uncomfortably aware of

Principles from Universal Design

Universal design offers great guidance for planning the micro layer of your retirement geography. To look at your home with a universal design perspective means asking, "If someone with [*fill in the limiting health condition*] were going to live in this residence, what would allow them to be self-sufficient—what would make it a lifetime home?" *Lifetime home* is a new term to describe the residence that we hope will support us in both the early and later parts of our retirement. It has a nice ring to it, don't you think?

So what makes a home a lifetime home? Mostly, that it can accommodate your changing needs. That can be as simple and easy as adding sturdy handrails in bathrooms, or more complex and expensive, like installing lower counters and cabinets or a chair lift on a stairway. But some livability fixes can be almost impossible to implement in the layout of many homes. For example, if rooms are on multiple levels—even if they're separated by just one or two stairs—there may not be space for a wheelchair-accessible ramp.

Thinking about your physical needs as you age may be something you'd prefer to put off. And even when you do address the issue, you don't have a crystal ball. But evaluating your residence now with these ideas in mind could eventually make the difference between continuing to live there and being forced to leave.

the sameness, the lack of authenticity, the *placelessness* that has proliferated across the country. Subdivisions filled with look-alike houses, business parks filled with work-alike offices—interspersed with standard-issue strip malls. National chains driving out local retailers, and franchises replacing family-owned restaurants. Places that once had a distinctive local character are being made over to fit into the same mold. There are parts of many cities that look just like parts of any other city. And they don't just look the same—they *feel* the same. It's difficult, if not impossible, to have a sense of place in such environments. Of course, many jobs are geographically connected to them, and in your working years you may need to live there. However, retirement offers your greatest geographic freedom. Are you curious where you might discover a sense of place?

UNIVERSAL OR PERSONAL?

Sense of place ranges from the universal to the personal. Certain landscapes evoke a strong sense of place for just about everyone. You have surely visited some unfamiliar places that you felt an immediate connection with—the mountains, the seashore, a deep forest, green rolling hills, the desert in bloom. You could say that those locations have a *universal* sense of place, and most humans would probably agree.

You have surely visited other places to which you felt a *culturally based* connection; for example, a classic Main Street in a small town—a setting that resonates with your childhood and the image presented in your schoolbooks and in magazines. Many people who share your upbringing would experience the same sense of place.

Finally, there are places that you connect with because of your own *personal* life experience; you would not expect others necessarily to experience the same sense of place that you do. You may have lived there in the past or dreamed about living there in the future. You may have gone to school there, or vacationed, or visited relatives there. Or you may have *never set eyes* on the place before, but once you do, you say, "This is the place." For your retirement geography, your own personal sense of place is the one that matters most.

You can't predict what will create that sense of place for you. You can't tell from pictures or descriptions alone. You can't tell from what other people say about it. You certainly can't tell from the statistics about it. No, sense of place comes from *direct experience*. It could be the evident features of a place—its climate, topography, vegetation, or architecture. It could be the people you interact with there. It could be what you know about its history or its importance in the larger scheme of things. It could be your own personal memories, distinct from your current experience of the place. You may even get the sense that a particular place will support your chosen Ways to Live.

The only way to really know if a location has a sense of place for you is to become an explorer; you need to be there and experience it. You may need to move to a new place, or you may instead need to see the place you live now as if for the first time. Only you can explore the geography of your Ideal Retirement. But it's worth exploring, because your retirement will last a very long time, if all goes as you hope.

Two factors that are critical to just how long it will last are the biology and medicine elements that make up the health dimension of your Retirement Well-Being—the focus of the next chapter. In this chapter, as we've explored where you might spend your retirement, we have frequently touched on the need to plan for both the natural aging process and the unpredictable infirmities that may arise. It's wise to choose a livable community and a home that incorporates universal design to support your aging in place. Having done that, you'll want to do all you can to preserve your physical vigor and independence for as long as possible. Chapter 9 is all about helping you do so.

But first, you get to brainstorm the geography of your Retirement Well-Being.

WHERE IN THE WORLD MIGHT YOU RETIRE?

Let's look again at the four layers of retirement geography introduced at the beginning of this chapter:

- *Sense of Place*—the meaning that you derive from a geographic location.
- *Aging in Place*—what most people hope to do in their retirement residence.
- *Livable Community*—a supportive environment for retirement and aging.
- *Essential Region*—a part of the country that has what you absolutely must have to live a fulfilling life.

Copy the following blank form or use a sheet of paper with the headings for four checklists. On each, brainstorm all the things you want from that layer of geography. Brainstorming means you don't hold back or censor yourself: if it comes to

---

mind, write it down. Then see if your existing place, or another place you've been considering, meets those requirements. As you list them, it's OK if some of them seem to belong in more than one list—in fact, you should pay *particular* attention to those that meet the needs of multiple layers of your Ideal Retirement geography. To get you started, take a look at the filled-in example that comes after the blank form.

BRAINSTORMING YOUR REQUIREMENTS OR EXPERIENCES

Inner Layer: Sense of Place

_____

_____

_____

Micro Layer: Aging in Place

_____

_____

_____

Middle Layer: Livable Community

_____

_____

_____

Macro Layer: Essential Region

_____

_____

_____

Here's a filled-in example of requirements:

Inner Layer: **Sense of Place**

- Close to nature
- Scenic beauty
- Wildlife friendly
- Seasonal changes, but not extremes
- Mature trees
- Feels like a small or larger town; not a city
- Peace and quiet

Micro Layer: **Aging in Place**

- Stand-alone house with attached garage
- One-level living
- Manageable garden space
- Neighbors looking out for each other
- Good health care resources nearby
- Good options for independent-living and assisted-living communities if necessary

Middle Layer: **Livable Community**

- Self-contained community
- Good library system
- Variety of restaurants
- Movie theater
- Live classical music performances
- Residents of all ages
- Civic involvement opportunities
- Public transportation
- Natural foods store
- Good health care options nearby
- Neighborhood feel; people looking out for each other

Macro Layer: **Essential Region**

- Temperate climate
- Seasonal changes, but not extremes
- Within a half-hour drive of a small city
- Within a two-hour drive of a big city
- Progressive, tolerant political climate
- Near family (at least in same state)

There's another way to use the four layers of retirement geography—one that is more intuitive. Instead of listing the things you want from each layer, list the *experiences* you want to have. You can begin with your Ways to Live exercise from chapter 4 and think about how your geographical location can support the ways you want to live in retirement.

1. Imagine that you are really living in those ways. Do you experience the inner layer—a positive sense of place?

2. Shift to the micro layer—aging in place—and imagine how your residence could support your chosen Ways to Live.

3. Shift to the middle layer—livable community—and consider how your community could support your chosen Ways to Live.

4. Shift to the macro layer—region—and ask how your essential region could support your chosen Ways to Live.

When you bring all the layers of your retirement geography into alignment this way, you may get different answers than you do with checklists of individual requirements for the layers.

Instead of using *requirements*, here are three examples using *experiences*, based on specific Ways to Live:

Example #1: Living in a NORC in an Established Neighborhood in the Southeast

Way to Live
Altruism (sharing sympathetic concern and affection for others)

Inner Layer: **Sense of Place**
Living in an established community of retirees who are growing older and need the help of younger, active retirees

Micro Layer: **Aging in Place**
Living in a home adapted for ease and efficiency, which allows me to devote time to service volunteering

Middle Layer: **Livable Community**
Being able to walk around town from home to run errands and make deliveries for my volunteer clients

Macro Layer: **Essential Region**

Living in a temperate climate and a connected, accessible community that attracts residents who could use my attention and assistance

Example #2: Living in a DORC in Arizona

Way to Live

Enjoyment (immersing myself in sensuous pleasures and festivities)

Inner Layer: **Sense of Place**

Living the leisurely resort lifestyle, with lots of desert sunshine but lush irrigated landscaping

Micro Layer: **Aging in Place**

Living on one level with all the amenities: built-in vacuum; home theater; kitchen, great room for easy entertaining

Middle Layer: **Livable Community**

The sports I love (golf, tennis, swimming); joining friends at the clubhouse for social events; spa treatments right where I live

Macro Layer: **Essential Region**

Living in the warm, dry desert; lots of leisure activities; year-round outdoor activities

Example #3: Living in a Small, Age-Integrated Town on Puget Sound

Way to Live

Receptivity (patiently opening to joy and peace through nature)

Inner Layer: **Sense of Place**

Taking a walk in nature every day; lying in my backyard on a summer night and looking up at the Milky Way; enjoying the birds and other wildlife that find a home in my native plant garden

Micro Layer: **Aging in Place**

Living close to nature (no need to drive to it); establishing a natural garden that's easy to maintain

Middle Layer: **Livable Community**

Living in a community where nature is valued and preserved; enjoying a slower pace of life without heavy traffic; building relationships with people of all ages who enjoy the outdoors

Macro Layer: **Essential Region**

Seeing trees blazing with fall color, bare in winter, leafing out in spring; exploring tide pools at low tide; hearing frogs chorus in a marsh on spring evenings

LIVING IN MY GEOGRAPHICAL PLACE

You've used the Four Layers of Retirement Geography to imagine the kinds of places that could best support all the other elements of your Retirement Well-Being. You should now have plenty of raw material for your final geography exercise: identifying the geographical element of your Ideal Retirement. That place could be the one you're living in now or someplace new.

You can approach the four layers in any order that makes sense for you. The acronym SALE doesn't mean you need to sell your home; it's just a way to help remember the layers. Again, these are

S for *sense of place*

A for your *aging-in-place* residence

L for *livable community*

E for *essential region*

If it's earlier in your career, you can note just the broad or general features of each layer. If it's later in your career, you should be more specific. If you're approaching retirement, you may have all the particulars completely worked out. The questions for each layer relate most directly to that layer, but you can apply them to the other layers, too.

My Sense of Place: The Inner Layer

What places could create a particular feeling or a sense of connection for you in retirement? These might have a sense of place on a universal, cultural, or personal level, or be especially symbolic or meaningful for you. Think of places you've already experienced and ones you would like to explore. Write the names of several types of places, or specific places, for this layer; for example, "Ocean shore; Colorado Rockies; Taos, New Mexico."

_____

_____

_____

My Aging-in-Place Residence: The Micro Layer

What role will your residence play in your retirement? Is it likely to become a job, a project, a museum, a community center, a base of operations, a retreat, or something else? To fill that role, what physical features would your home need? Financially, would your home be a significant expense, a low-cost place to live, or a source of income? Would your residence accommodate aging in place, or do you plan to move as you get older? If it's early in your career, identify a general type of residence (such as a city apartment, resort-style condo, or country house). If it's later in your career, try to identify a specific type of residence, or even a specific house (say, in your town, seen on vacation, or found on the Internet).

_____

_____

_____

My Livable Community: The Middle Layer
Considering how far into retirement you plan to live there, how supportive does your community need to be at different stages? Which livability issues are most crucial to you? A walkable neighborhood? Access to medical care and other services? Transportation? Social interaction? Activities? A retirement-age population or one that's age-integrated? What other features or amenities are most important for you? Financially, will your community provide opportunities to upscale or to economize?

_____

_____

_____

My Essential Region: The Macro Layer
Which part of the country offers what's most important to you? Could it involve the people you have relationships with? The opportunity to connect with your interests, strengths, or values? A supportive environment for your health or health care? A lower cost of living? Where are the things that you absolutely wouldn't want to live without? Is it likely your essential region will change during your retirement years?

_____

_____

RETIREMENT CIRCLES EXERCISE

Now go back to your responses for all four layers and, based on your current thinking, choose the one to three most appealing or significant responses for each layer. (These aren't set in stone; you can revisit and revise your choices later as your planning evolves.) Enter these on the appropriate lines of your Retirement Circle to use for your One Piece of Paper in chapter 10.

My Ideal Retirement includes inhabiting this geographical Place:

S _____

A _____

L _____

E _____

Resources on Where to Live

Starting at the macro layer, you'll find a number of books that rate and rank geographic places as regions and communities. However, for the third box of life, the most complete is from the famous wanderer David Savageau. *Retirement Places Rated: What You Need to Know to Plan the Retirement You Deserve* (Frommer's, 2004) evaluates 203 cities across the United States based on six criteria relevant for retirement.

Taking a narrower and deeper approach, Warren Bland uses twelve criteria to identify just the cream of the crop for *Retire in Style: 60 Outstanding Places Across the USA and Canada* (Next Decade, 2005). Who knows if the place you're interested in would be one of Bland's 60 or even Savageau's 203? A key benefit of these guides is learning how the experts evaluate places so that you can bring some of their expertise to your own investigations.

There's an even deeper kind of guide for rolling up your own sleeves and considering how livable your existing or prospective community might be. It's not a book, but a research report from AARP: *Beyond 50.05: A Report to the Nation on Livable Communities: Creating Environments for Successful Aging* (2005). It explains what a livable community is and the positive effects of living in one for retirement, and also touches on home design and other issues. Exhaustively researched, but not exhausting to read! The publication ID is 18316. Find it on the Web at www.aarp.org; choose "Policy & Research," then "Housing, Mobility and Care Options," then "Independent Living." Or get a print copy (for free) by requesting the report by both name and publication number from AARP Fulfillment, EE01681, 601 E St., NW, Washington, DC 20049.

Finally, at the micro layer of retirement geography, one of the very few books that addresses the residence and the community is Tom Kelly's *Real Estate for Boomers and Beyond: Exploring the Costs, Choices, and Changes for Your Next Move* (Kaplan Business, 2006). It looks at the physical, financial, and social aspects of planning your retirement residence.

"If I'd known I was going to live this long,
I would have taken better care of myself."
—Eubie Blake

CHAPTER 9

Your Health Is a Matter of Life and Death

D o you worry about staying healthy on your retirement journey?

As average human longevity has increased and more people have been living into their eighties and nineties, the issue is becoming less and less whether we'll live *long* enough. We may know people who've lived longer than they expected to, or even wanted to. No, more and more the issue is staying healthy as we spend decades in old age—and having access to the medical care we need. What we really want is a *health span* that matches our life span. However long our journey lasts, we want to be healthy along the way.

Health isn't just a personal retirement planning issue, though. We all know that our society is in turmoil around this subject. Medical care is becoming more and more expensive. Insurance is now the standard way to pay for care, so the premiums have been rising accordingly. Unless it's provided through an employer, many people simply can't afford insurance. But even for those insured through a job, employers are changing benefit structures and seeking new ways to reduce costs or shift them to employees.

The situation is simpler for those over age sixty-five, because they have access to Medicare for paying some medical costs. However, Medicare funding is similar to Social Security—and in chapter 2 we touched on the demographic challenges facing Social Security. Some projections for individual out-of-pocket medical costs in retirement run into hundreds of thousands of dollars, even with access to

Medicare.[1] It seems imperative that fundamental changes be made over the coming decades—but in the meantime, individually, we need to plan for health care in retirement.

Health is one of the three fundamental dimensions of Retirement Well-Being, along with prosperity and happiness. It's certainly a challenge to plan for a healthy retirement when you don't know what society is going to do about medical care, long-term. But in creating the picture of your Ideal Retirement, at least you can do your best to determine what health looks like to *you*.

Yes, planning for your health is like planning for the other dimensions of your well-being: rather than starting with the outside world, you start with yourself. That's why this chapter isn't about the latest strategies for paying medical expenses, like health savings accounts. (There are plenty of information sources already, and the details will change with the whims of Congress.) Nor is this chapter about the latest medical breakthroughs or self-care strategies. (It seems like a new book on those subjects is published every week!) No, this chapter has a different focus. It helps you identify your own unique approach to creating the health that you want for your retirement.

Don't Forget Your Biology

In the Retirement Well-Being Model, health is also called the Bio-Medical dimension. No one ever forgets the medical element, but the biological element is sometimes overlooked. Biology reminds us that, before we even consider medical care, we're first and foremost living biological organisms. We're in charge of our own bodies, and the way we live affects our health—our level of physical vitality. We either support that vitality or we deplete it. We may even consciously

1. In the July 2006 *EBRI Issue Brief*, the highly regarded Employee Benefit Research Institute published a study by Paul Fronstin on medical costs in retirement. For a couple aged sixty-five who lived to average life expectancy, the estimated total costs for Medicare Part B and D premiums, Medigap coverage, and out-of-pocket prescription drug expenses was $154,000. However, for couples paying premiums on an employment-based retiree health benefits plan, or with higher-than-average prescription drug use, or with a longer-than-average life expectancy, the estimated total costs approached $300,000. That will put a dent in your retirement savings!

decide to build it up so it can support us in retirement, like building up our personal savings or building up our social networks. We can even think of these as *unique forms of capital* that we can draw on in different ways, for different purposes, during retirement.

But biology also reminds us that retirement is a time of life when we get older. Even if we do remain healthy, we don't remain *young*. Aging is a biological process that affects us in so many ways that we must factor it into all the other elements of our retirement planning. And the last biological fact, of course, is that we die. Some people don't like thinking about the third box of life because it's the *last box*. They avoid planning for retirement because, biologically, it's a stage of life that eventually leads to sickness (for all but a fortunate few) and death. But that's where medicine comes in.

Medicine Is for When You're Not Feeling Up to Par

Here is a key distinction between biology and medicine: biology is mandatory, but medicine is optional. As long as humans have had bodies, we've had biology—but medicine, we invented. (And we keep reinventing it, too.) When our biology is working perfectly, we don't really need medicine. Medicine is for when we're not feeling up to *par*.

If all goes as planned and hoped, our retirement health equation is biology + medicine = health. Why make this distinction? Because our biology is inside of us; it's the part we have the most control over. (And it's actually the second part of this chapter.) In contrast, medicine (which we'll focus on first) is outside of us. It's a *system* that's out there in the world. We don't have the same level of control. We decide to access a medical system, or systems, for treatment. And as we age, we typically find that we need to access them more and more. You probably know some older people whose lives seem to *revolve* around accessing medical systems.

Our society is also in turmoil about defining what is and is not legitimate health care that should be covered by insurers. Medical choices are becoming more complex. There's the conventional

Western medical system—composed of medical schools, M.D.s, hospitals, and drug companies—which is completely connected to and supported by state licensing laws, insurance plans, and even federal tax laws. And there is also the enormous, unconventional *alternative* medical system that has not been connected or supported in the same way until fairly recently.

When you walk into a pharmacy to fill your prescription from the conventional medical system, you walk by an entire aisle of alternative treatments. Everything from herbs to vitamin and mineral supplements to homeopathic remedies. Huge quantities of these are sold at the pharmacy (and in natural foods stores), but because they don't require a prescription, few pharmacists have any in-depth knowledge of them.

Similarly, an entire section of the bookstore is devoted to alternative treatments, but because the topic is generally avoided in medical training, chances are you won't find many medical doctors browsing there. And even though offices of alternative practitioners like acupuncturists and chiropractors are often right next door to offices of M.D.s, there is generally little acknowledgment of them by the M.D.s or interaction between them. It's as though they're from different planets. More accurately, they're from different *paradigms*. Yet a large proportion of Americans—40 percent or more—may be using alternative approaches that are not recognized by conventional medicine.[2] The fact that many people use treatments that their medical doctors don't approve of or refer them to is a barrier to frank and complete communication between doctors and patients. Patients may simply not bring up the subject.

Have you ever used complementary and alternative medicine (CAM)? Would you consider it as you age? After all, you can't know

2. See the study by David Eisenberg and others, published November 11, 1998 in the *Journal of the American Medical Association*. From 1990 to 1997, the percentage of Americans using alternative therapies increased from 34 percent to 42 percent. Using a different methodology, Patricia Barnes and others published a study through the National Center for Health Statistics in 2004. They came up with 36 percent; if prayer specifically for health reasons was included, the number was a whopping 62 percent. But this is somewhat confidential—according to the Eisenberg study, less than 40 percent of alternative medicine users told their conventional doctors.

what health conditions you'll develop in retirement, so you can't know for sure which medical paradigms offer the treatments that will most appeal to you then. If you're interested in exploring CAM, there are many ways to do that, such as the resources at the end of this chapter. But right now, take a moment to complete the following exercise to jog your memory and stimulate your thinking.

YOUR COMPLEMENTARY AND ALTERNATIVE MEDICAL HISTORY

Many people have used some form of complementary or alternative medicine at one time or another. A good way to anticipate whether you might use CAM therapies in retirement is to consider which ones, if any, you've used in the past. You may have had direct experience with some of the approaches listed in the following table; you may have heard about others; still others may be new to you.

CAM approaches	Have you ever used this ?	Would you consider using it?
Ayurveda	No / Yes / Not Sure	No / Yes / Not Sure
Biofeedback	No / Yes / Not Sure	No / Yes / Not Sure
Botanical medicines or herbs	No / Yes / Not Sure	No / Yes / Not Sure
Chiropractic	No / Yes / Not Sure	No / Yes / Not Sure
Energy therapies like Reiki or Healing Touch	No / Yes / Not Sure	No / Yes / Not Sure
Homeopathy	No / Yes / Not Sure	No / Yes / Not Sure
Mind-body approaches like hypnosis or visualization	No / Yes / Not Sure	No / Yes / Not Sure
Movement practices like yoga or tai chi	No / Yes / Not Sure	No / Yes / Not Sure
Prayer or meditation for healing	No / Yes / Not Sure	No / Yes / Not Sure
Nutritional supplements or vitamin therapy	No / Yes / Not Sure	No / Yes / Not Sure

Therapeutic massage	No / Yes / Not Sure	No / Yes / Not Sure
Traditional Chinese medicine or acupuncture/acupressure	No / Yes / Not Sure	No / Yes / Not Sure
Unconventional or unproven science	No / Yes / Not Sure	No / Yes / Not Sure
Other: _____	No / Yes / Not Sure	No / Yes / Not Sure

Now read down the answer columns. Do you notice a pattern or theme in your use—or nonuse—of CAM? Even if you haven't discovered anything new, it is worthwhile to document your past and consider your future. Now let's see how this fits into your retirement planning.

The Retirement Medicine Cycle

What's your *medical philosophy?* You've probably never been asked that question. Instead of asking what your philosophy is, most books and practitioners tell you what it *should* be. If they're based in conventional medicine, they offer the truths from that paradigm as though they were the *only* truths. If they're from one of the alternative systems (like the approaches in the history exercise), they offer the truths from that particular paradigm as though *they* were the only truths. However, the *real truth* is that you're stuck in the middle, all by yourself, and you need to make up your own mind. If you wait until you're not feeling up to par, you won't be at your best. You'll be more likely to just accept a philosophy that's thrust on you, because you may not realize you have a choice. It's better to figure this out now, while you're of sound body and sound mind.

The *Retirement Medicine Cycle* is a model that helps you plan for the kind of medicine you want. It has three components: your medical philosophy, your access to medicine, and your medical relationships. You can think of it as *philosophy*, *access*, and *relationships*, which creates an easy-to-remember acronym: PAR.

THE RETIREMENT MEDICINE CYCLE

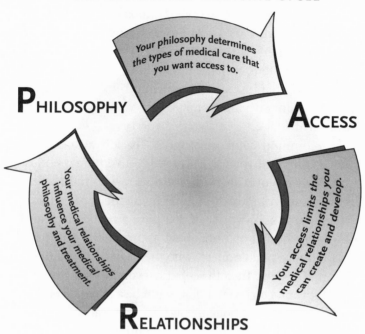

Your philosophy determines the types of medical care that you want access to.

PHILOSOPHY

ACCESS

Your access limits the medical relationships you can create and develop.

Your medical relationships influence your medical philosophy and treatment.

RELATIONSHIPS

- *Philosophy* includes your preference for conventional or alternative approaches, as well as your preference for greater or lesser medical intervention in general. Your philosophy determines what type of medical services you want access to. (Conventional or alternative? High-tech or low-tech?)

- *Access* includes your methods for getting treatment. (Insurance? Out-of-pocket cash? Government plans?) Your methods of access determine which practitioners you can use and thus limit the medical relationships you can create and develop.

- *Relationships* with practitioners are your sources of both treatment and information. The information you get from those practitioners will be limited by the paradigm they operate within—their own truths—which in turn influences your medical philosophy. That's what makes it a cycle rather than a linear process.

You can see that, if you're not careful, the Retirement Medicine Cycle can be a *closed loop* system. If your philosophy leads you to seek out access to one particular system and you develop relationships with those practitioners, they will tend to give you only information from inside that system or paradigm. That's where they live and practice. However, that just serves to further reinforce your original philosophy. You can have blind spots about your medical treatment and not even realize it.

Let's take a common symptom of aging—back pain and stiffness—as a simple example. If you have a purely conventional philosophy, you may seek access only to medical doctors, who then offer treatment options only within conventional medicine (drugs, traditional physical therapy, or surgery). Or if you have a particular alternative philosophy—say, herbal or nutritional approaches—you may seek access only to those practitioners, who then offer treatment options only within that system. In both scenarios, you probably wouldn't be referred to a chiropractor, even if that might be a beneficial treatment. (Although alternative practitioners may be more aware of and supportive of other alternative practices than conventional practitioners are.)

That's why it's so important to enter into your Retirement Medicine Cycle consciously, rather than just getting swept along unconsciously. You need to be the one who's in charge! The following section will help you to clarify your philosophy, identify your likely methods of access, and determine what relationships you'll need to support your health and well-being in your Ideal Retirement.

Identify Your Philosophy of Medicine for Retirement

Your medical philosophy combines two ingredients: your perspective on conventional versus alternative medicine and your tendency toward medical intervention in general.

First, where do you stand along the conventional versus alternative continuum? Do you see medicine from the narrower, more orthodox perspective or from the broader, more unorthodox perspective? Those are the two ends of the continuum, and your outlook may be somewhere in between. You already have one good indicator in your history of using—or not using—CAM approaches. However, that's a measure of your past actions, not your current perspective. To find out where you stand, consider the sets of paired statements below. For each pair, decide where your perspective is on the continuum from conventional to alternative and mark one of the boxes accordingly. Marking the far right or left box means you strongly agree with that philosophy; marking the next box in means you agree some-

Conventional Philosophy			Alternative Philosophy	
Medicine should be based on modern and rigorous research methods.			Medicine can be based on forms of knowledge other than modern science.	
❑	❑	❑	❑	❑
Treatments outside of conventional medicine should be avoided.			Conventional medicine treatments should be avoided.	
❑	❑	❑	❑	❑
All treatments must meet the same standards for safety and effectiveness.			Treatments that pose little risk and could be beneficial are worth trying.	
❑	❑	❑	❑	❑
High-tech is almost always more effective than low-tech.			High-tech or low-tech has little bearing on effectiveness.	
❑	❑	❑	❑	❑
Medicine is the weapon of choice in the fight against disease.			The body seeks to heal itself; medicine plays a supporting role.	
❑	❑	❑	❑	❑
As the expert, the doctor's role is to diagnose and prescribe; the patient's role is to comply with treatment.			The practitioner and patient both have knowledge and must actively share the role of promoting the patient's health.	
❑	❑	❑	❑	❑

what more with that philosophy than with the other; marking the center box means you're neutral or unsure. This topic is enormous and very complex, so it can't *really* be reduced to just this set of paired statements. But this exercise can be an important step toward clarifying your philosophy.

Second, consider your tendency to seek medical intervention distinct from how sick or healthy you are. The amount of medical care that you've sought out during your relatively healthier time in the second box of life may be an indicator of how much medical care you'll seek out in the (statistically) less healthy third box. Or not. You can't know for sure if your history of getting a little or a lot of help for small aches and pains is a predictor of how you'll react to major health crises in old age. (Or you may have already had major health

High-Intervention Philosophy			**Low-Intervention Philosophy**	
Too much treatment is usually better than too little.			Too little treatment is usually better than too much.	
❑	❑	❑	❑	❑
It's better to seek care sooner rather than later.			It's better to wait; conditions often resolve themselves.	
❑	❑	❑	❑	❑
Relying on a range of specialists provides better care.			Relying on a single trusted practitioner provides better care.	
❑	❑	❑	❑	❑
Multiple treatments for multiple conditions all at the same time makes sense.			Receiving multiple treatments at the same time can cause problems in and of itself.	
❑	❑	❑	❑	❑
Medical treatment is the most important thing, even when it may be inconvenient.			Medical treatment that is difficult or disruptive must be considered within the context of day-to-day life.	
❑	❑	❑	❑	❑

issues earlier in your life.) To the extent you think about this consciously, though, you may develop a certain consistency in your tendency to seek intervention.

Again, for each of the following pairs of statements on the previous page, decide where your perspective is on the continuum from high intervention to low intervention, and mark one of the boxes accordingly. Marking the far right or left box means you strongly agree with that philosophy; marking the next box in means you agree somewhat more with that philosophy than with the other; marking the center box means you're neutral or unsure.

Now we'll put these two aspects together to illustrate an overall way of thinking about your medical philosophy. In the following figure, you'll see that conventional is on the left side and alternative on the right, high intervention on the top and low intervention on the bottom. For each of these two aspects, mark the point that indicates where your philosophy lies on the continuum (the line with two arrows).

To identify your philosophy, mark the point where a line drawn across from your spot on the High Intervention–Low Intervention (vertical) continuum would intersect with a line drawn up from your spot on the Conventional–Alternative (horizontal) continuum.

THE FIVE MEDICAL PHILOSOPHIES

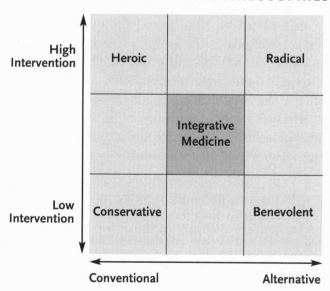

The figure combines these two different aspects of your medical philosophy and provides a simplified way to think about them in the practical world. The four corners each crystallize a particular perspective. If you tend toward a high level of intervention using conventional treatments (upper left), that's a *heroic* philosophy. A low level of conventional intervention (lower left) is a *conservative* philosophy. That same tendency for low intervention, but using alternative treatments (lower right), is a *benevolent* philosophy. And if you use alternative treatments and also tend toward a high level of intervention (upper right), that's *radical*, dude.

AN INTEGRATIVE APPROACH

What if you're somewhere in the middle? You should be delighted to learn that there is actually a fifth perspective, and you can see it right in the middle of the shaded area. *Integrative medicine* is a fast-growing movement that integrates these different perspectives.

Integrative medicine is midway between conventional and alternative, and high and low intervention. Of course, even without integrative medicine, it's possible to use both conventional and alternative treatments in an eclectic way. You know—some of *this*, and some of *that*. However, that's definitely *not* what integrative medicine does. At its core, it's based on adherence to the scientific method that is the foundation of conventional medicine.[3] For treatment options, it accesses both conventional and alternative approaches. It uses a rigorous approach to explore alternative treatments that are less dangerous and disruptive to the body than many conventional treatments but often just as effective. It looks for the best of both worlds.

The scientific approach that integrative medicine takes is somewhat different from that of conventional medicine, however. Conven-

3. Integrative medicine isn't storming the Bastille of conventional medicine from the outside. Rather, it's planting seeds inside the medical establishment—there are programs within many prestigious university medical centers. It should become easier and easier to find M.D.s who've been introduced to an integrative medicine perspective. Read about integrative medicine and find links to dozens of university programs at www.imconsortium.org.

tional medical science is sometimes skeptical toward phenomena that it should be curious about. Or dogmatic about assumptions that it should be questioning. In terms of the Retirement Medicine Cycle, conventional medicine can act like a *closed loop* system that isn't open to some types of new information. In contrast, integrative medicine is open to information from more sources. Specifically, it studies treatments from alternative medicine that may be beneficial—yet because it does adhere to the scientific method, it's rigorous about which alternative medicine treatments to use.

As for a low or high level of intervention, integrative medicine assumes that the lowest level that supports the body's own healing is the place to start. (Often the best intervention is a healthier lifestyle!) If a condition doesn't respond to the lower-level intervention, then it's time to move up the ladder. Sometimes a high level really is necessary.

Specific to retirement, integrative medicine suggests that biological aging is a natural part of life. Technically speaking, there is no such thing as "antiaging" treatment. No one has figured out yet how to reverse the natural aging process that inevitably ends in death. But it's possible to optimize your health at any age. And it's definitely possible to *optimize how healthy you feel and act in your daily life.* Often, ironically, when you focus on the symptoms and diseases that you *don't* want, they expand to assume a bigger role in your life. When you instead focus on how to support your body's own self-healing process, *that's* what expands. Which would you prefer?

Integrative medicine helps you to (1) build habits that support your biology and (2) use any natural treatments that are effective for your condition (with fewer adverse side effects). This helps you to focus on (and expand) your awareness of health and healing, rather than focus on diseases or treatments. This issue becomes more and more important as you age. In the first and second boxes of life, health conditions are often *cured*—they go away. But in the third box, most conditions related to aging *can't* be cured. Even if you need to gracefully accept those conditions, do you want them to be the focus of your life? Or would you prefer to focus on the health and healing that *are* operating in your life? The goal of integrative medicine is healthy aging—even though you may have chronic health conditions.

Now that you've had a chance to identify the fundamentals of these five medical perspectives, you'll have an easy way to identify them in the real world. If you read a book or magazine, talk to a practitioner, or get a recommendation for treatment, you'll have an idea which perspective it's coming from. Before you consider the specific information, you can consider your compatibility with the source. How does that perspective relate to your medical philosophy?

Of course, there's another level of evaluation that entire books are devoted to, so it's way beyond this little chapter. You need to ask "How valid is that perspective, or approach, or paradigm, in general?" And if it's valid, you can ask "How knowledgeable is that practitioner within the scope of that perspective or approach?" Even after you determine that your perspective and their perspective are compatible, there's always the question of whether the individual practitioner is experienced or inexperienced, competent or incompetent.

So, for the first stage of the Retirement Medicine Cycle, would you describe yourself as heroic, conservative, benevolent, radical, or integrative? Is there yet another term that better describes you? The answer is an important part of planning your Ideal Retirement.

How Will You Access the Type of Care You Want?

Now that you know your medical philosophy, you can plan how to gain access to the types of medical care that you want.

First, will conventional treatments be enough for you? If not, which alternative approaches do you plan to use? How will you gain access financially? One of the first observations we made about these two systems is that conventional medicine is supported by insurance companies, the Medicare system, and the tax laws. Much alternative medicine is not supported (although that's been changing in recent decades), which leads to higher out-of-pocket costs. Another part of access can be geographical—what will it cost to live near the treatments you want or to travel to gain access to them?

Second, what level of intervention do you expect? Do you tend toward more intervention rather than less? Are you more likely to pay a visit to your practitioner? More likely to pursue advanced treatments? This isn't about how sick or healthy you'll be (although that is another important question). Rather, the question is, for a given level of sickness or health, do you tend to seek out a lot of care or just a little? Do you tend to be lured by those prescription-drug commercials that coax you to "Ask your doctor if this New Miracle Drug is right for you"? Even when you have insurance, if you tend toward high intervention, you'll have higher out-of-pocket costs.

Let's repurpose our medical philosophy table to reveal your perspective on cost. In the figure, *total cost* means the actual true cost, ignoring subsidies like insurance plans or tax breaks. *Out-of-pocket cost* means what you might typically pay, taking into account subsidies like insurance plans or tax breaks. Based on the costs associated with your philosophy, you'll want to plan for adequate financial access.

RELATIVE COSTS OF EACH MEDICAL PHILOSOPHY

	Conventional		Alternative
High Intervention	High Total Cost/ Medium Out-of-Pocket		Medium Total Cost/ High Out-of-Pocket
		Medium Total Cost/ Medium Out-of-Pocket	
Low Intervention	Medium Total Cost/ Low Out-of-Pocket		Low Total Cost/ Medium Out-of-Pocket

Now, consider the most common methods for accessing medicine in retirement:

- *Social programs*, such as Medicare A and B, the Prescription Drug Plan (Medicare D), or your state's "Senior Care" type plan

- *Insurance plans*, such as a working spouse's group insurance, your own retiree medical coverage, a former employer plan through COBRA, or an individual medical policy
- *Membership rights*, such as access to the Veteran's Administration for those who served in the armed forces, or facilities that serve members of religious or fraternal organizations
- *Out-of-pocket expenditure*, such as earmarked funds like health savings accounts, or general funds—any of your PERKS (see chapter 5) that you would draw on to pay for out-of-pocket medical costs

Based on your philosophy, which one of these is likely to provide your primary method of access? Which one will take some advance planning to make it available? Where should your focus be?

What Medical Relationships Will You Develop?

Now that you know your medical philosophy, you can also identify the practitioners who will help you implement it. Although you'll probably be looking for good individual practitioners as long as you live and breathe, this is about identifying *types* of practitioners. Is your family practice M.D.'s expertise enough? Do you already have a condition that will make a medical specialist important? If you want to use alternative medicine, which approaches will you use the most? What two or three types of practitioners will provide the most treatment and be your greatest sources of information and advice? To stay healthy, this is an important part of the picture you're creating for your Ideal Retirement.

It's time for a reality check. Look back over your conclusions about your Retirement Medicine Cycle. Do the three stages all fit together as a whole? For example, does your philosophy fit your method of access? Will your access pay for the types of treatments and relationships that you want? Will your relationships provide treatment and advice that fit with your philosophy?

Looking back over the Retirement Medicine Cycle sections, consider the three components: philosophy, access, relationships. In your Retirement Circle, write the name of your medical philosophy next to the "P." Next to the "A," write your primary method of access, or the method that you most need to focus on in your planning. Next to the "R," write the medical relationships that will be most important for you to develop. All together, these help you create a vision of how medicine will support your Ideal Retirement to use when you fill in your One Piece of Paper in chapter 10.

**My Ideal Retirement
includes accessing this
Medicine:**

P _____

A _____

R _____

Biology + Medicine = Retirement Health

Now that we've covered medicine, let's turn to the other part of the retirement health dimension: biology. Biology has to do with your essential life force, or vitality. Remember, medicine is *out there*, a system in the world. But biology is *in here*, and part of you. It's much more under your control. So if you're the one who's in charge of your biology, the question is, how are you doing?

We each have our own measures of how we're doing biologically, of course. The most basic one is purely subjective: it's simply how good you feel. (Which is actually a good measuring instrument, when you take the time to calibrate it and use it.) You may have other, more objective measures, too: your clothing size, or weight measured on a scale; how many days of work you've missed; whether you're meeting the goals of your exercise program. These are probably all good measures, but on occasion you want something more official. You go for a checkup.

In the olden days, a checkup with a medical doctor involved a lot more poking and prodding than it usually does now. For example, physicians needed to palpate and gently thump different points on the patient's abdomen—sort of like testing a watermelon or a cantaloupe for ripeness. Each organ has a certain sound when it's healthy. If the organ doesn't sound right, that's a reason to investigate.

These days, doctors don't spend as much time listening to their patients. They gather data using much more high-tech methods. They take biological samples from us and run laboratory tests. Our body chemistry supplies the raw data, which is then analyzed using sophisticated statistical methods. How do we measure up compared to thousands of other people? For most tests, the goal is simply to be in the normal range. But for others (like cholesterol) the goal is actually to be better than normal. Gathering raw data and doing a statistical analysis is much less personalized than thumping on our organs, it's true. But it does provide a different, and extremely helpful, kind of analysis. New technologies made it possible.

There's an even newer technology that is making another kind of checkup possible. It's called a *health risk assessment* (often available through hospitals and medical insurance plans). Instead of collecting data about your bodily fluids, it collects data about your life. Then it does what you'd expect: it statistically analyzes your data against that of thousands of other people. But a health risk assessment is completely different from a lab report. Instead of telling you that you may have a particular health condition in the present, it tells you if you're likely to have a particular health condition in the future. A health risk assessment is like a crystal ball powered by statistics.

You may wonder why someone would want to know what diseases they're more likely to get. You may even feel that you wouldn't want to know. Wouldn't it just be better to live a healthy lifestyle and forget the crystal ball? After all, many of your health risks are inherited from your parents—and it's too late to choose different ones.

Some people find health risk assessments useful, because they really put the information to good use. Let's take an example: Say that a person—based on her heredity, her health history, her current data, and her lifestyle—discovers that the area she should be most concerned about is heart disease. One possibility is that she wasn't aware of her elevated risk for heart disease. But now that she has this new information, she'll adjust her behavior accordingly, make lifestyle changes, and reduce her risk.

However, another possibility is that she already suspected she had an elevated risk of heart disease. She knows her family history. She knows she's overweight and that her cholesterol is too high. She just hasn't been motivated to exercise more control over her biology. But seeing the health risk assessment changes how she feels. It's right there in black and white. It motivates her to finally make the changes that she already knew she should make.

In modern society, the big problem isn't a lack of information about what a healthy lifestyle is. No, the big problem is actually *making* those healthy lifestyle changes. And an even bigger problem is how to really stick with them over the long term and make them a part of our lives.

How Old Are You, for Real?

So, back to our biological question: How are you doing? Well, there's a new way for you to answer that question. It's an entirely new form of measurement. This form of measurement is beyond your subjective feelings, beyond being thumped like a melon, beyond giving up bodily fluids, and even beyond a health risk assessment. From a technical standpoint, in relation to a health risk assessment, it's just a small step forward. But from a conceptual standpoint, it's a giant leap. It's a form of measurement that uses statistics to tell you how old you are. Not your *chronological* age, but your *biological* age.

Let's review this whole idea of age. For most of human history, people didn't have a record of when they were born. The concept of how old they were didn't require mathematical precision; it was functional and biological, not chronological. Then record-keeping improved, and in the industrial era a worker's chronological age became the standard for when to retire. Industrialists standardized everything, including people. That kind of thinking still drives the *timing* of retirement, all these years later.

Now imagine for a moment that you're fifty-seven years old. That's what it says on your driver's license. However, your "age" of fifty-seven is only a tally of how many times the earth has traveled around the sun since you've been in residence. That tally determined when your school allowed you to attend first grade and when the state allowed you to take a driver's test. It will determine when the Social Security Administration allows you to apply for retirement benefits. Other than satisfying that kind of legal, operational red tape, your chronological age has never done that much for you. (Although the birthday parties were nice.) But what if you also knew your biological age? How would that affect your retirement planning?

Imagine again that you're looking at your driver's license, and it says you're fifty-seven years old. You plan to retire in five years, when you turn sixty-two and first become eligible for Social Security. By then, you'll have enough PERKS to afford the retirement that you want. Now, imagine that you take this new form of assessment that measures your biological age. Much to your horror, you discover that your biological age is *already* sixty-two. You do the math in your head and realize that in five years, when your driver's license says you're sixty-two, your biological age could possibly be . . . (gulp) . . . *sixty-seven!* You realize that your retirement may not be as physically active as you had hoped. You realize that it may not last as long as you had hoped. You realize that you won't be retiring on the *early* side (you were going by your driver's license), but you will actually be retiring a bit on the *late* side, biologically speaking. What should you do?

A. Pay attention to your driver's license age, ignore your biological age, and retire in five years as planned. If your retirement is short and sedentary, so be it. At least you won't run out of money. And maybe you'll beat the statistics and have a long and healthy retirement anyway.

B. Pay attention to your biological age and retire as soon as you can possibly afford to. If you need to reduce your cost of living to make ends meet, so be it. You want to make sure you have as healthy and active a retirement as possible. If it turns out you beat the statistics, that will be a bonus.

C. First, find out what lifestyle changes you can make that would reduce your biological age. Make those changes in your life. Continue to monitor your biological age. Second, reduce your cost of living. Increase your retirement savings dramatically. Continue to monitor your financial ability to retire. Third, put together a new plan for when to retire.

There is, of course, no right answer to this question. But the scenario demonstrates the potential power of knowing your biological age. The scenario is equally interesting if you change just one of the details. Imagine that instead of your biological age being five years *older* than your driver's license, it's five years *younger.* What effect would that have on your planning? Would you work to a later chronological age, anticipating that you'd need more savings for a longer retirement? Or retire on schedule, but live more modestly to make your savings last longer?

There's no question that your biological age should be factored into your retirement planning somehow. And although the stakes are

Aging: A Reality Check

- Remember that aging is a basic biological process for humans.

- There is currently no science or technology that can stop or reverse aging.

- The most useful way to think about biological aging is to focus on *healthy* aging.

- The measurement of biological age is an incredibly powerful tool for education, motivation, and planning.

- If you were to make lifestyle changes that reduced your statistically calculated biological age, you wouldn't really reverse the aging process—you would just get healthier. Sound good?

much higher in the years close to retirement, knowing your biological age at every stage of your career is useful information. Like any health risk assessment, it can provide you with information on the changes you should make to become healthier. And probably more than any other type of health risk assessment, it can *motivate* you to make those changes. Any way you look at it, knowing your biological age is a good thing.

The only widely available method for calculating your biological age can be found at www.RealAge.com. It's even free, although it may be priceless to you. You'll also find a related book in the resources at the end of this chapter.

Creating Your Dream Body for Retirement

When you decide to exercise more control over your biology, perhaps you'll go to your doctor for a checkup, or take a health risk assessment, or calculate your biological age. Or perhaps you won't. Maybe you feel that you don't need additional information from experts, suggesting changes you should make in your lifestyle. You may feel that you already know what you should do to become healthier. If you feel strongly about this, then you should trust your feelings and begin to make those healthy changes. After all, advice from experts that you *don't* follow isn't nearly as valuable as your own best instincts that you *do* follow, especially if you stay with it over time.

You completed your Retirement Circles exercise for the medicine element of your health earlier in this chapter; now let's turn to your Retirement Circles exercise for the biological element. You support your biology by making healthy lifestyle decisions. You've certainly tried out various healthy changes in the past; some were likely short-lived, while others became a part of your life. Obviously, the ones that become a part of your life are the ones that help the most.

This section will help you identify three biological practices that you'd like to include in the picture of your Ideal Retirement to support your health for the journey. These are three practices to do on an ongoing basis to increase your vitality from the inside out. There are three categories of practices for this purpose: *relaxation, eating,* and *movement*. By making sure you address all three, you're taking a comprehensive approach to supporting your vitality. You can remember them by the acronym REM (for your dream body).

THE THREE TYPES OF BIOLOGICAL PRACTICES

RELAXATION   **E**ATING   **M**OVEMENT

The word *practice* in this case has a fairly specific meaning. It's an activity that is complex and challenging enough to invite years of involvement. It could be an activity that you can learn quickly but probably never completely master. Or it could be an activity that you can master more readily but still find so completely engaging that you are drawn to it again and again.

Here's an example from the third category, movement. Martial arts could easily fit the definition of a practice; jumping jacks probably could not. Martial arts (a category that encompasses many schools and varieties) have the capacity to keep people involved for years, or even a lifetime. But how long could anyone keep up a practice of just jumping jacks? For each of these three categories, you're the best judge of whether an activity offers the depth to sustain you over years of practice.

These practices may be things that you currently do and want to make absolutely sure that you keep doing. Or they may be things that you tried in the past, and they worked for you, but for one reason or another you stopped; now you'd like to incorporate them in your life again, going forward. Or they may even be things that you've never done but you're almost positive would work for you.

NOW, JUST RELAX

Relaxation is the first category. Some people may think of it as stress reduction. We're not talking about sitting in front of the television or having a few cocktails. Far from it. A relaxation practice is a specific activity that elicits what Herbert Benson identified as the *relaxation response* in the famous book of the same name.

The relaxation response is the biological opposite of the fight-or-flight response. The fight-or-flight response triggers the release of chemicals that put us on edge, to better deal with danger. In our society, that response is often triggered many times every day, from obvious stressors like driving in traffic or dealing with work deadlines to seemingly passive and innocuous activities like watching TV or listening to the radio. We can expect to keep experiencing this response even in retirement. Being subjected to the fight-or-flight response so frequently has a strong negative effect on our biology. The best anti-dote is to intentionally evoke its opposite: the relaxation response.

A relaxation practice is a specific activity that you engage in to elicit the relaxation response. Benson originally focused on meditation but later identified many additional ways. Prayer, especially repetitive prayer—like with a rosary—is another way. So is visualization or self-hypnosis. There are also physical ways to elicit the relaxation response, like tai chi, yoga, or even some types of walking. You can even make up your own relaxation practice, or perhaps you already have. What would you call the relaxation practice that you can imagine as a part of your Ideal Retirement?

YOU ARE WHAT YOU EAT

Eating is the second category. Of course, we all have to eat. And to a greater or lesser degree, at different times, we all try to eat "healthier," whatever that means for us. There is no shortage of official recommendations for healthy eating, and no shortage of diet books. (No shortage of fast-food commercials, either!) But the idea of an eating practice has nothing to do with following a diet or trying to eat more healthily for a particular time period.

To follow an eating practice means adopting a way of buying and preparing food and of choosing food when you eat out that you could realistically imagine sticking with for the rest of your life. An eating practice is an approach that you've seen real people adopt in their lives, consciously or unconsciously, and then stick with for years. Some fairly strict, easy-to-identify examples are veganism, raw food diets, and macrobiotics. But less extreme (and thus harder to identify) examples abound.

Think about people you've known who seem to have some internal guidance system for healthy eating habits. Can you identify what their internal standards might be? For example, you may know someone who simply doesn't eat fast food when eating out and doesn't use prepared foods when cooking at home. These folks have an internal standard for only eating food that someone cooks in the way that we traditionally think of cooking. Or you may know someone who has an internal standard for eating at least one salad every day. Others may have a standard for what size portions they eat, regardless of what they're eating.

The casual observer wouldn't even be aware that each of these people has particular standards, and you probably couldn't fit their standards into any official approach. These people, intentionally or intuitively, came up with healthy practices for eating. You yourself may already be doing exactly that—if so, congratulations. If not, consider what your most natural inclinations would be for establishing your own internal standards. Rather than trying to adopt some system created by others, is there some healthy homegrown system already inside you, just waiting for you to give it a try? If so, how would you describe this eating practice?

YOU GOT TO MOVE

Movement is the third category. This means some type of full-body movement, although it doesn't have to be what you normally think of as exercising. What's more important than meeting specific guidelines for aerobic activities, or for strength and flexibility activities, is meeting your own internal standards for sustainability. It's about finding something that can become nearly automatic and a lifelong practice. For most people, this will be a specific activity, like swimming, or bicycling, or golfing (without a golf cart, please).

The lifelong part is what can make finding a movement practice trickier than finding a relaxation or eating practice. Most of those other practices are not affected by aging. In contrast, depending on what happens to you as you age, you could find yourself unable to continue some movement practices—for example, running. What do you do then? Ideally, you would find another practice. But a surer way is to explore and experiment with practices that can be done at higher intensity while you're younger and lower intensity when you're older.

One opportunity you may want to consider is combining or pairing your relaxation and movement practices in some way. Again, the point is not to identify the "best" type, according to the experts. It's to identify—based on your own body and your own experience—what's likely to work for you over the long term. What would you call this practice?

What Role Does Health Play in Your Journey?

Wanting to be healthy on your journey is completely natural. It's a basic human need. Some would even say that it's the most fundamental dimension of well-being. They would acknowledge that prosperity and happiness are wonderful, and the absence of either is terrible. But in contrast, health relates directly to existing or ceasing to exist. When your health deteriorates below a certain point, you're not sick—you're dead. You're no longer a human being. That's a different order of magnitude than being merely destitute or unhappy. Death trumps poverty and misery.

But from a higher perspective, establishing a hierarchy among the three dimensions of well-being isn't the point. As fundamental as health may be to existence, is it an end in itself? Is it enough for human beings simply to be healthy? Enough if they're also prosperous? Enough if they're also happy? Or is it possible that even the state of complete well-being exists for something more? What if prosperity, health, and happiness *are all just provisions for our journey?*

And so we have reached the final chapter in our journey through this book. Chapter 10 brings together all the elements of your Retirement Well-Being, invites you to create that One Piece of Paper that offers a picture of your Ideal Retirement, and asks the question: Do you have a Retirement Calling?

Looking back at the section on biological practices, consider the three categories: relaxation, eating, and movement. In the Retirement Circle, next to the "R," write the name of the relaxation practice that you can most easily imagine engaging in for your retirement. Next to the "E," write the name of the eating practice that you can most easily imagine following. Next to the "M," write the name of the form of movement that you think you could practice at a higher intensity first and at a lower intensity as you get older. Together, your REM practices support your biological vitality and help you create your Ideal Retirement. Use these responses in your One Piece of Paper in chapter 10.

**My Ideal Retirement
includes deepening
these biological
Practices:**

R _____

E _____

M _____

Resources on Increasing Your Health Span

Whether you're interested specifically in integrative medicine or not, Andrew Weil's *Healthy Aging: A Lifelong Guide to Your Well-Being* (Anchor, 2007) is a great introduction to biology and medicine for the third box of life. Because it's from an integrative medicine perspective, it suggests that aging should be seen not only as natural, but also as an opportunity for personal growth and development. Like Weil's other books, this contains many specific recommendations.

Michael Roizen comes from a more conventional medical perspective, although his creation of the RealAge test for measuring biological age is not conventional at all—it's a breakthrough. His book *The RealAge Makeover: Take Years Off Your Looks and Add Them to Your Life* (Collins, 2005) explains this measure. You'll find plenty of health recommendations as well.

If you're like most people, it's not a challenge to find plenty of health recommendations. But it is a challenge to follow them, especially for the long term. James Prochaska, John Norcross, and Carlo DiClemente have researched the process we all go through, and they guide us through it in *Changing for Good: A Revolutionary Six-Stage Program for Overcoming Bad Habits and Moving Your Life Positively Forward* (Collins, 1995). The surprising finding is that regardless of the behavior you're changing, the stages of long-term change are pretty much the same!

If staying healthy for the long term—the really, really long term—interests you, take a peek at *Living to 100: Lessons in Living to Your Maximum Potential at Any Age*, by Thomas Perls (Basic Books, 2000). You may not have inherited the same genes as the centenarians in this book, but their stories will change how you think about old age. Also, you can try Perls's thoroughly researched longevity calculator at www.LivingTo100 .com (registration is required as the last step). When you combine it with your biological age from www.RealAge.com, you'll know more about your biology than you may have wanted to.

"If you follow your bliss, you put yourself on a kind of track that has been there all the while, waiting for you, and the life that you ought to be living is the one you are living."

—Joseph Campbell

Retirement Calling

A nd so we reach the final chapter in your journey through this book. You've come a long way. To even pick up this book and begin to read it meant answering a call to adventure and crossing a threshold into a potential new world. Modern society keeps us so darned busy with day-to-day realities, it's as though we're *submerged* in them. It takes a heroic effort to step back from your everyday life and make an effort to see things clearly, as you have done. You are to be commended.

Now that you have emerged victorious from the tests and trials of the Retirement Circles (or at least survived them), it's time for your reward: the picture of your Ideal Retirement. This picture is composed of the seven Retirement Circles that you completed as you progressed along your journey. (At this point, I hope you really *have* completed them and aren't merely reading this book! If you haven't yet, before you continue with this chapter I urge you to go back and complete them. I'll wait for you.)

Let's review the elements: The outer circles represent six fields of scientific knowledge that correspond to six elements of your life. These element are paired up to create the Three Dimensions of Retirement Well-Being that we all want for retirement: prosperity, health, and happiness. The *icons* in the outer circles are there to remind you of an essential aspect of each element, which you explored through the exercises you completed in chapters 5 through 9. The exercises provided a *process* for you; the *content* you produced is completely your own. So your Retirement Circles are as much a picture of *you* as they are of your Ideal Retirement.

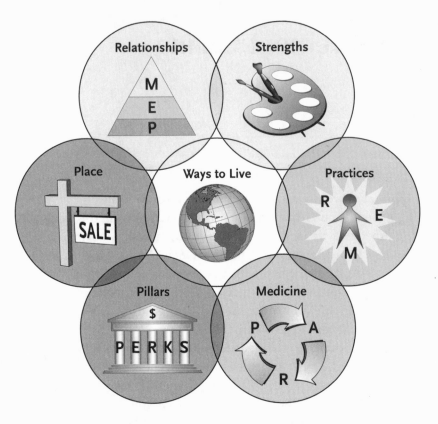

The icon for the central circle is a picture of the world, to remind you to bring your preferred Ways to Live into the everyday world. Your Ways to Live are the practical approaches to life that connect with your values, identity, and priorities (VIPS). These are at the center because they're at the center of your life. The exercises in chapter 4 gave you a taste of them. The more deeply you get to know your center, the more you can bring the other circles into alignment with it. You can use your Ways to Live and your VIPs as guides in making decisions for your Retirement Well-Being.

This guidance is crucial, because there aren't obvious, objective answers to all your retirement planning questions for all of your six outer circles. Based on the research and knowledge in each scientific field, some decisions are obviously the right ones. But for other decisions there is no objective standard, no right or wrong, no shining truth. Your answers will be subjective, personal. Ideally, they are based on your chosen Ways to Live. That's the part of retirement planning that you need to do from the inside out.

Putting Your Retirement Circles Together

You can choose from a variety of methods to assemble the picture of your Ideal Retirement. If you wrote your answers in the pages in this book, just flip back to each of those exercises to get your answers for the fill-in-the-blanks exercise that follows. If you wrote your answers on photocopies of the exercises, you can of course make a photocopy of the fill-in-the-blanks exercise and write on that. Or—and this is really more fun—you can assemble those Retirement Circle sheets onto a larger sheet of paper or poster board. Just paste or tape them on the appropriate spots. Being the resourceful and adaptable creature that you are, you may think of even more interesting ways to assemble your complete picture.

Whichever methods you use, the point is to create that One Piece of Paper that allows you to see the whole system at once. Seeing a *visual* representation of these connected elements helps to create a *compelling vision* of the retirement that you really want.

Retirement planning has traditionally focused on just one life dimension—financial. When it *has* included others, it's been arbitrary—there hasn't been a *natural* way to select, and then connect, the dimensions. They've typically been isolated from one another. And when you plan for each in isolation, it's easier for them to be out of sync with each other. When that happens, you may not be able to really see it, but at some level you'll probably feel it. Because well-being is fundamental to humans, being able to finally see it all interconnected on your One Piece of Paper is a real breakthrough.

For your retirement planning, some of the easiest connections to spot are between adjacent circles. You already know about the close connections between the two elements that make up each dimension of Retirement Well-Being: biological and medical, psychological and social, geographical and financial. But there are also close

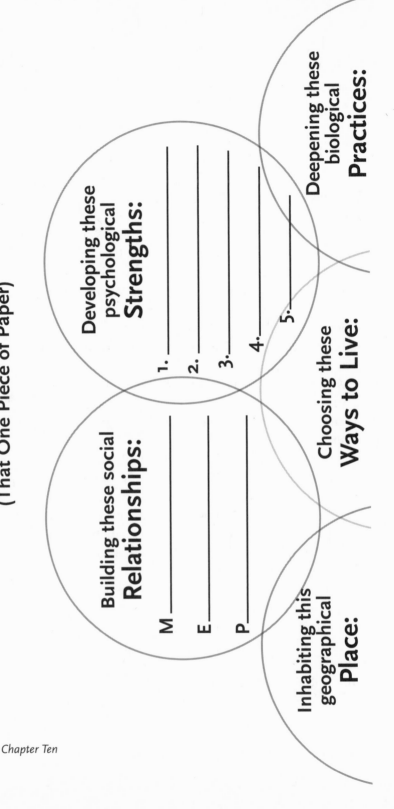

MY IDEAL RETIREMENT
(That One Piece of Paper)

Developing these
psychological
Strengths:

1. _____
2. _____
3. _____
4. _____
5. _____

Deepening these
biological
Practices:

Building these social
Relationships:

M _____
E _____
P _____

Choosing these
Ways to Live:

Inhabiting this
geographical
Place:

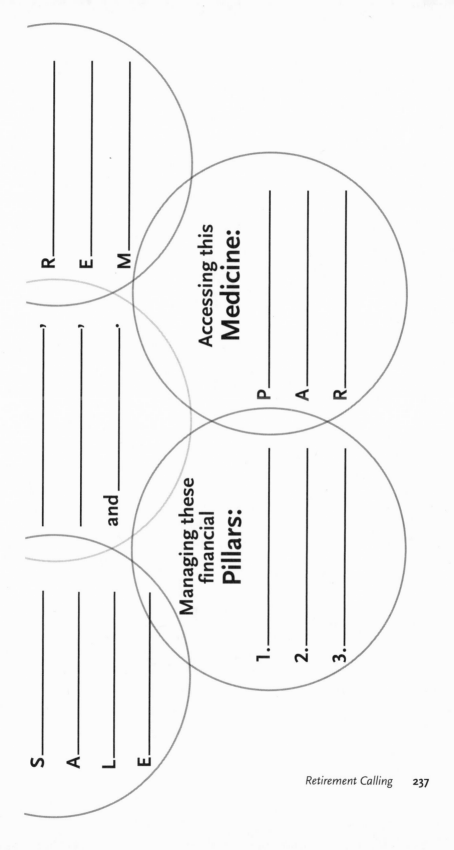

S _____

A _____

L _____ and

E _____

R _____

E _____

M _____

Accessing this
Medicine:

P _____

A _____

R _____

Managing these
financial
Pillars:

1. _____

2. _____

3. _____

connections between the other adjacent elements. For example, geographical and social are next to each other, because they have a strong connection. Remember "social is spatial, and spatial is social"? Also, you'll notice that financial and medical are next to each other, and you probably know why—much access to medical care is based on finances, and medical care can be one of our biggest expenses. Finally, psychology and biology are next to each other because psychology has a biological aspect. And on a practical level, we know that psychology has an effect on biology—research is starting to show that happier people tend to be healthier. So these connections between circles are easy to see, even when they're from different dimensions of well-being. But all the circles are connected *in our lives*, even if they're not next to each other in the Retirement Well-Being Model.

The assembled picture of your Ideal Retirement as seven interconnected circles is a unique and powerful planning tool. However, you can go beyond that to see it as an *integrated whole*, something complete in itself. A gestalt. The purpose of the seven Retirement Circles isn't to break your planning down into smaller parts—modern life does that already. No, the purpose is to help you put it all back together. As an integrated whole, you might think of your picture as:

- A retirement dream
- A strategic plan
- A treasure map
- A life plan

Or any other term that comes to mind and makes sense for you.

Your Retirement Calling

Could this picture of your Ideal Retirement offer something more? Might it offer a clue to your *calling* in retirement? If you think that you may have a calling, you should know that it's not always easy to find in the third box of life. Even though the third box can offer the greatest freedom, sometimes it's actually easier to find a calling in the first box. Life is generally simpler then. Things get much more complex as we get into the second box. We can be so strongly conditioned by society to follow the well-worn path that we sometimes mistake it for our own authentic journey. We can be so strongly influenced by marketers to consume a prefabricated lifestyle that we sometimes mistake it for our preferred Ways to Live. We can be so strongly pulled in by everyday reality and "the ten thousand things" to do that we sometimes mistake them for the reason we're here.

So . . . why *are* you here?

If you still want to be here for the third box of life, is it because there's still something important left for you to do? Depending how early or late it is in your career, when you're still in the second box you may not be able to get a sense of it. As you get closer to retirement, though, it may become easier to get a sense of your calling.

When you look at the picture of your Ideal Retirement, does it give you a hint about some contribution that you still want to make? That contribution could be connected to one of your circles. Or it could be *inspired by* your picture, rather than being *part of* your picture.

Does some special purpose call to you?

No, nothing calls to me. What should I do?

Maybe it's still too far away for you. Or maybe some of your circles are harboring bits of society's expectations, marketers' hogwash, or the low-level responsibilities of everyday life, instead of your heart's desire. They provide a picture for retirement planning, but they aren't the stuff that callings are made of.

To get closer, revisit your Ways to Live and your VIPs, in chapter 4. That's the core. As you home in on how you truly want to live in the world, it will help you put more of your authentic self into the other circles. (Your picture is a work in progress, always open to revision.) The most important thing is to appreciate the journey, give yourself credit for the work you've already done, and stay open to the possibility that you may have a Retirement Calling.

Maybe there's a calling in there somewhere, but it's faint. Is that enough?

Perhaps it represents only half of your heart. That's a step in the right direction—but you don't want to pursue your Retirement Calling halfheartedly. Perhaps you've chosen your preferred Ways to Live and identified your VIPs, but in the other circles you've settled for only half of your dreams. Be encouraged, because you're on the right track. Try revisiting some of those Retirement Circles exercises to find the missing half. Which circle does your heart tell you to look in first?

Yes, something calls to me, beckons me, draws me toward it. I'm willing to do whatever I need to, to get there. I can imagine following that calling in the third box of life. In fact, I'd like to start tomorrow!

Congratulations—you've found your heart's desire.

You can see that finding your Retirement Calling isn't a one-time, now-or-never deal. The ability to look for your heart's desire and hear a call improves with practice. In taking this journey, in doing these exercises, you may be tapping into parts of yourself you haven't been in touch with for awhile. As you continue to visualize your retirement, you'll get better and better at it, and you may discover that the picture of your Ideal Retirement may contain a calling.

Whether you've identified your calling yet or not, are there any changes you should make to your picture *right now*? Would you like to change or add something in any of your Retirement Circles? Is there a name, a title, or a label that you'd like to give this picture? A phrase, a sentence, or even a paragraph that you could add to your picture that would be meaningful to you? You can do any of these things any time you want. It's your picture!

Share Your Picture with Your Dream Team

Who's coming with you on the journey to your dream retirement? Some companions? Some helpers? Let's see who those folks might be.

Your companions are the people with whom you have relationships. If you have a spouse or significant other, that loved one is your closest traveling companion. It will help immensely if your partner is also creating a picture of his or her Ideal Retirement. Initially, it's better to do these exercises separately and create your own individual pictures. When some couples work together, one partner can end up driving the process, and the other doesn't get enough of a voice.

It's important for each of you to have your own authentic vision that comes from your own heart, then put your hearts (and minds) together. You'll want to get on the same page—or at least adjoining pages. Two compatible pictures can be even more powerful than one!

Beyond your spouse or significant other, who else might be your companions? Your children? Your parents, if they're alive? Your best friends? Who are the people you most want to spend time with in your retirement? You might do some of them a great service by inspiring them to create their own picture. But at the very least they'll gain a deeper understanding of you, what's most important to you, and where you're headed on your journey. When you become really clear about what you want and other people can see it too, they may even want to help you. (Although you may have some companions who tend to be jealous, or naysayers—you're the best judge of who will help and who might hinder you.) Who knows what wonderful things might happen when you share your picture?

In addition to your companions—your fellow adventurers—you have some helpers, too. These are folks who don't accompany you on the journey so much as they provide assistance along the way, especially at key points. Do you have, or can you imagine having, any of these helpers?

- Accountant
- Alternative medical practitioner
- Attorney
- Benefits counselor
- Career counselor
- Financial planner
- Human resource professional
- Life coach
- Medical doctor
- Personal trainer
- Realtor
- Religious or spiritual guide
- Therapist, counselor, or psychologist

With your helpers, you may choose to share the full picture of your Ideal Retirement or just a part of the picture that's relevant to them. Some of these will be true helpers who genuinely want to assist you on the journey *you* have mapped out. Of these well-meaning helpers, some are competent, others less so, but at least they have your best interests at heart. However, along the way you may discover others who appear in the guise of a helper but seek only to serve themselves. You need to sort out the help from the hogwash. Pay close attention, and use your Retirement Hogwash Detector!

Returning to the Everyday World

How do you bring this vision—the picture of your Ideal Retirement—back with you into the everyday world? Even when we gain clarity and can see what we really want, it's not always so easy to make that connection. But for retirement planning it is essential, because the everyday world is where you actually prepare for retirement. That's where you gain the knowledge and make the changes in your life that will put you on the path to your Ideal Retirement. The more clearly you hold on to that vision, the more your day-to-day planning and preparations will come into alignment with it.

There are three effective approaches to bringing the vision of your Ideal Retirement into your everyday life: the *no-brainer* approach, the *left-brain* approach, and the *right-brain* approach. Although quite different from one another, they share a common perspective that retirement planning is not a *problem to be solved* but an *opportunity to be created*. (A problem-solving and fixing perspective works well for things like machines. When a machine is working and then malfunctions, troubleshooting is the way to get it back up and running. But your Ideal Retirement isn't like that at all. You're not troubleshooting it; you're creating it.)

Brief descriptions of the three approaches follow, and you'll find instructions and worksheets for using each at the end of this chapter.

1. THE NO-BRAINER APPROACH

Is your brain tired after your long journey through this book? Rest assured, this approach doesn't take a lot of hard thinking. (Although it's actually very smart!) It's a no-brainer only because it's such an obviously good idea. This approach comes from the psychology of human performance, and it has been used by athletes for many years. It's based on the idea that we don't always need to think consciously about something we want to achieve—we can turn it over to our automatic, unconscious mind. This approach brings the vision of your Ideal Retirement into everyday life in three distinct ways: as pictures, words, and feelings. If you want to try just one approach right now, this is the one for you.

On the other hand, if you're up for a bit more thinking, try one of the other two approaches. They come from a very different source—organization management. Management is a discipline that coordinates a wide variety of disparate elements to reach a goal. That sounds a bit like retirement planning, doesn't it?

2. THE RIGHT-BRAIN APPROACH

Do you see yourself as a right-brain person? Are you intuitive, creative, and focused on the big picture? If so, this may be the approach for you. It's loosely based on *Appreciative Inquiry*, a revolutionary field of organizational development. Appreciative Inquiry looks for the best in people, searches for their highest values and abilities, and helps them to expand. Using this approach, you *discover* positive experiences grounded in the past, *dream* of an even better future, *design* conditions that make that future possible, and then *deliver* it through inspired action. The creator of Appreciative Inquiry, David Cooperrider of Case Western Reserve University, received the 2004 Distinguished Contribution Award from the American Society for Training and Development. If you want an approach that increases your energy and helps you see new options, try this one!

To learn more about how Appreciative Inquiry is used in organizations, check out Diana Whitney and Amanda Trosten-Bloom's book *The Power of Appreciative Inquiry* (Berrett-Koehler, 2003).

3. THE LEFT-BRAIN APPROACH

Do you think of yourself as a left-brain person? Are you logical, linear, and focused on the details? This could be your ideal approach. It's loosely based on a breakthrough approach for strategic planning and execution, the *Balanced Scorecard*. This system creates performance standards not only for financial assets but also for nonfinancial ones. By establishing objectives, measures, targets, and initiatives across multiple domains, it offers quantitative feedback from a balanced perspective.

The Balanced Scorecard was created by Robert Kaplan of Harvard University and David Norton, a management consultant. Their seminal book on this topic is *The Balanced Scorecard: Translating Strategy into Action* (Harvard Business School Press, 1996).

You're the sole judge of which of these three approaches is best for you. At different times you may even use all of them. But please try at least one as soon as you finish this chapter—before you get caught up in those day-to-day realities again. You wouldn't want all of your hard work to be lost!

Live Your Ideal Retirement Life
While You're Still Working

Here's one final intriguing idea: You can bring your life into alignment with your Ways to Live and achieve the states you identified for each of your Retirement Circles *while you're still in the world of work*. When you do that, you begin to live the life of your dreams now— you don't have to wait until retirement. Wouldn't that be grand? For you, creating your Ideal Retirement while you're still in the world of work will feel almost like retirement itself. Except for one small detail—your job.

Remember Margaret Mead's quote at the beginning of this book? Some people love their work so much that they can't even imagine retiring. Those lucky souls are free to create their Ideal Retirement while they're still working, because that one small detail—their job—

doesn't detract from their life at all. In fact, it enhances their life so much that they don't want to give it up.

There may or may not be a job out there in the world that you could love *that* much. But if you're curious about that possibility, there's another book you should read (if you haven't already): the original *What Color Is Your Parachute?* for job-hunters and career-changers. If you still have many years of work ahead of you, finding a job you love is especially important. But even if you're close to retirement, it's not too late to find work that you absolutely love. It could become a fulfilling part of your retirement.

In fact, it might even be an adventure.

And in that spirit, off you go—with all my fond farewell for your retirement adventure and with these fitting words from Joseph Campbell:

> *"What I think is that a good life is one hero journey after another. Over and over again, you are called to the realm of adventure, you are called to new horizons. Each time, there is the same problem: do I dare? And then if you do dare, the dangers are there, and the help also, and the fulfillment or the fiasco. There's always the possibility of a fiasco. But there's also the possibility of bliss."*
>
> —Joseph Campbell

BRINGING THE VISION OF YOUR
IDEAL RETIREMENT INTO THE EVERYDAY WORLD

The No-Brainer Approach:
Visualization and Affirmations

This approach brings the vision of your Ideal Retirement into everyday life in three distinct ways: as pictures, words, and feelings. Follow these three simple steps. *You may want to use a blank sheet of paper to record your answers and ideas.*

Pictures. Expand or embellish the Retirement Circles picture of your Ideal Retirement just as you please, with clippings from magazines, fine-art reproductions, or your own drawings. Then keep it where you can see it easily and refer back to it often. Where might that be? Your office wall? Your refrigerator? In front of your exercise equipment? Where you sit to pay the bills? Over time, you'll notice that the words and images have seeped into your subconscious, forming an *internal* image of your Ideal Retirement that is more portable—and powerful—than that One Piece of Paper. The goal is to keep visualizing your Ideal Retirement in as much detail as possible.

Words. Are you familiar with affirmations? These are statements in the present tense about conditions and accomplishments you would like to realize in your life. You can use the terms, phrases, and statements from all of your Retirement Circles to create your own affirmations—a set of statements about your future retirement. Be as specific and clear as possible, and state them in the *present tense*. Although there are all kinds of affirmations out there, in self-help books, magazine articles, websites, greeting cards, and so on, those that come from you will be a perfect fit. They will feel natural, easy for you to memorize and repeat to yourself every day, and they can have a significant positive effect. *Internalizing* those words makes them even more powerful than just displaying them on your picture. Repeat some of your affirmations several times every day—indeed, any time you think of them—until they become automatic.

Feelings. Positive feelings in your body about your Ideal Retirement are usually triggered by your pictures or words (whether external or internal). With a little practice, you can learn to cultivate those positive feelings and connect them strongly to your pictures and to your affirmations. The stronger your positive feelings, the more effective this approach will be. So when you use your visualizations and affirmations, remember to recognize and welcome these positive feelings. Your goal is to feel confident and excited when you think about your Ideal Retirement.

Practicing the no-brainer approach all by itself will bring you closer to your Ideal Retirement and also bring it closer to you. You'll find yourself acquiring knowledge and accumulating resources without consciously planning to do so. Before you know it, you'll catch yourself taking actions that move you in the direction of your Ideal Retirement.

BRINGING THE VISION OF YOUR IDEAL RETIREMENT INTO THE EVERYDAY WORLD

The Right-Brain Approach: Appreciative Inquiry

Appreciative Inquiry helps you to *discover* positive experiences grounded in the past, *dream* of an even better future, *design* conditions that make that future possible, and then *deliver* it through inspired action. You'll complete this process separately for each element of your Retirement Circles, beginning with the ones that give you the most pride in your accomplishments. *Use a blank sheet of paper to record your answers and ideas.*

Choose the first Retirement Circle that you'd like to learn about and explore. Regardless of how well you think your planning and preparations have been going for this circle, here you will focus on what *has worked*, not what hasn't. And no matter how much success you feel there has been already, you'll focus specifically and completely on *what you want more of*.

Discover. Think back to a specific time when things were going well in this element. Remember one of your high points or a peak experience. What were you grateful for or excited about? What did you do that was so successful? How did that make you feel? What made that success possible? What was the root cause of your success?

Dream. Now, based on your Retirement Circles exercise, consider the role this element plays in your Retirement Well-Being. What is the best possible future for this element? What would that future feel like?

Design. Now, keep in mind what has really worked in the past for this element when things have gone well. To bring about that best possible future, what values or principles would you need to act from? What conditions would you need to create?

Deliver. Now brainstorm a wide variety of actions that you could possibly take. Generate options that are exciting but also tangible. Which actions would be a stretch for you, but you would feel confident about taking? Which actions would be the most inspiring to take and follow through on? What structure could you put in place to support those actions? What could you celebrate as a result of taking those actions successfully?

You can expect the actions you take as a result of this exercise to lead to more experiences of success. You can make them part of another discover, dream, design, and deliver exercise. You can consciously create a *virtuous cycle* that repeats itself.

BRINGING THE VISION OF YOUR
IDEAL RETIREMENT INTO THE EVERYDAY WORLD

The Left-Brain Approach: The Balanced Scorecard

The Balanced Scorecard is an approach for strategic planning and execution, that creates performance measures not only for financial assets but also for nonfinancial ones. By establishing objectives, measures, and initiatives across multiple elements, it offers feedback on your progress from a balanced perspective.

For retirement planning, your strategy is represented by your chosen Ways to Live. This worksheet will help you implement your strategy across the six elements of your Retirement Circles.

First, as a reminder, list your three chosen Ways to Live:

_____,

_____,

and_____.

Second, consider (1) the objectives you can identify that will bring you closer to your Ideal Retirement, (2) how you might measure your progress toward the objectives, and (3) what initiatives you can take to get there.

Objectives. When you filled in each of your Retirement Circles, you identified a state that you want to achieve for your Ideal Retirement. You can probably identify many other *intermediate* objectives that could lead up to it. Some of your objectives will be about accomplishing something specific, but many could be about learning, investigating, or making future plans.

And for all six elements, a worthy interim objective is sharing your plans for your Ideal Retirement.

Here are examples for each Retirement Circle:

Geographic: Researching potential retirement places; evaluating your existing place; taking a vacation or visiting people you know; making lifetime home improvements; interviewing a realtor about trends and opportunities.

Financial: Checking your Social Security projections; calculating your Number; retaining a financial planner; setting up an autopilot for saving or investing; reaching an account balance goal.

Biological: Calculating your biological age; establishing a practice through a club or class, or tracking your frequency of participation; replacing an unhealthy habit with a healthy one; reaching a target weight, fitness measure, or lab result.

Medical: Researching the terms of your retirement medical plan; comparing Medicare Part D or other prescription plans; investigating your Veteran's Administration benefits; getting medical screenings or tests suggested for your age; completing a medical power of attorney; interviewing a new potential doctor or practitioner.

Psychological: Taking the VIA survey online; shifting job responsibilities to better use your skills; exploring opportunities to use strengths outside of work; trying a new hobby for enjoyment; exploring a potentially meaningful responsibility or opportunity; testing the waters for engaging retirement work.

Social: Meeting with coworkers outside of work; looking up old friends; investigating a club or other membership; volunteering for an organization to meet new people; joining an athletic team; making specific arrangements to help family or friends.

Measures. How can you measure your progress toward each objective? It could have a numerical measure, as for a financial account or a biological test. If it's a goal for participation in appealing groups or activities, it could be a simple count of memberships or dates (you're never too old for star stickers on a calendar!). You can't measure your progress toward some objectives numerically, but you should be able to identify milestones that show you're getting closer to your objective. It's good to set target dates for reaching numerical goals or milestones—then celebrate or treat yourself when you get there.

Initiatives. What specific actions can you take toward your objectives that fit your numerical or milestone measures? Better yet, what systems can you put in place to automatically reach your objectives? What can you put on autopilot?

Now use the following table to record your important objectives, measures, and initiatives for each element that will bring you closer to your Ideal Retirement. You may have one or many objectives for each element.

Element	Objective	Measure	Initiative

Resources on Why You're Still Here

In preindustrial society you wouldn't have had to create a picture of your Ideal Retirement; you would have naturally matured into the role of respected elder. Richard Leider and David Shapiro drew on this timeless wisdom for *Claiming Your Place at the Fire: Living the Second Half of Your Life on Purpose* (Berrett-Koehler, 2004). They suggest that, rather than retiring, you keep your fire alive by taking on the role of New Elder.

Whether it's called retirement or something else, the freedom of the third box provides an opportunity to integrate the outer life with the inner self. If you sense that the demands of the second box have forced you to lead a divided life, you'll want to read Parker Palmer's *A Hidden Wholeness: The Journey Toward an Undivided Life* (Jossey-Bass, 2004). Palmer suggests that the way to integrity is to enter into a community of trust while listening to one's inner teacher.

Listening is a prerequisite to hearing any kind of call, as described by Gregg Levoy in *Callings: Finding and Following an Authentic Life* (Three Rivers Press, 1998). The book offers a broad exploration of the phenomenon in history, myth, and religion, combined with very personal accounts from Levoy and others. In this down-to-earth book you'll discover the endlessly varied and fascinating experiences of those who hear and heed a call.

Harry R. Moody and David Carroll describe a very specific kind of call in *The Five Stages of the Soul: Charting the Spiritual Passages That Shape Our Lives* (Anchor, 1998). By the time we've reached midlife, many of us have begun to search for a deeper sense of meaning and a higher state of consciousness. Moody and Carroll have distilled thousands of years of spiritual wisdom—from many faiths—into this very readable book. Real-life stories illustrate the stages that you may find yourself traveling through on your own journey to your Ideal Retirement.

Acknowledgments

This book is the result of a journey that began in 2003. That's when I quit my job to go back to school for a Ph.D. in retirement education. However, there is no academic field called "retirement education." It doesn't exist.

It's true that the fields of economics and personal finance study the money part of retirement. And the career development field considers retirement the final career stage. There's even a multidisciplinary field—gerontology—that studies aging. But there isn't one that teaches people how to plan for the life they want to live in retirement. The knowledge and tools people need for the parts of life are scattered hither and yon. It's almost impossible to see the big picture, let alone plan how to integrate all the parts.

So I signed up for a degree in the boundary-spanning field of adult education. Betty Hayes and Alan Knox, my advisers at the University of Wisconsin, encouraged me to survey the landscape and follow the trail wherever it led. It led first to Bob Atchley, who fundamentally shifted my direction. It led to courses in ten different academic departments. It led to outside professors who profoundly influenced my thinking: Marty Seligman at the University of Pennsylvania and Dave Cooperrider at Case Western Reserve University. Ultimately it led to seeing the big picture, integrating the parts, and creating the Retirement Well-Being Model that is the foundation of this book. Thank you, learned teachers.

While creating and developing the model, I visited eighteen states and met others who are pursuing a new vision for retirement. Sally Hass and Andy Landis of Weyerhaeuser and Carol Anderson of Money Quotient made me feel completely at home in the epicenter of the life planning movement. Al Summers was among the first to understand the model, and he invited me to share it with the uniquely qualified employees of AARP. Marv Tuttle, Martin Siesta, Elizabeth Jetton, and Brad White of the Financial Planning Association have provided the opportunity to make the model available to personal financial planners. Serendipitously, some crystal ball gazers provided feedback precisely when it was most needed: Rick Moody, Bill Arnone, Jennifer Schramm, Anne Tergesen, and Marci LeFevre. Thank you, fellow retirement envisioners.

The model was chosen as the organizing structure of the retirement education program for the federal workforce: the Retirement Readiness project. As a result, I've been fortunate to work with colleagues from the International Foundation for Retirement Education and the Office of Personnel Management: Mary Willett, Betty Meredith, Kevin Seibert, Ray Kirk, and Irene Meader. Other valued coworkers have been Matt Greenwald, as well as Tom Holubik and Vickie Hampton of Texas Tech. Kathie Vaughn of CalPERS and Ed Derman of CalSTRS provided invaluable opportunities for feedback. Thank you, fellow Retirement Readiness explorers.

Phil Wood of Ten Speed Press gave this book the initial push, and George Young and Lorena Jones kept it rolling. Without my developmental editor, Kristi Hein, and project editor, Brie Mazurek, it never would have made it across the finish line. Friends who kept the faith include Lee Eisenberg, Tim Nuckles, and Rue Hass. Thank you, fellow believers.

Most of all, dear reader, you should know that my coauthor, Dick Bolles, is the one who made it possible for the seed of this idea to blossom into the pages you are now holding. Not only did he bless my humble proposal, but he provided the ideal map: more than thirty editions of *What Color Is Your Parachute?* Another of Dick's books offered many revelations, too, as it's the bible of life planning: *The Three Boxes of Life.* Thank you, Dick, and God bless.

Joseph Campbell observes that embarking on the journey to adventure invites both fulfillment and fiasco. This has been a journey to fulfillment, rather than fiasco, only because of my family. My deepest love and gratitude to Cheryl, Erik, Sean, Evan, Julia, Don, and Russ Nelson; and Gordie, Heidi, and Sharon Johnson. Thank you for helping me to follow my bliss.

—John E. Nelson

Index

Health *(continued)*
  as vitality, 55, 204–5
Home. *See also* Geography;
    Real estate
  equity, 113–14
  as retirement pillar, 93
  uses for, 187–90

I

Ideal Retirement
  bringing the vision of, into
      everyday world, 242–44,
      246–52
  creating picture of, 4,
      235–38
  living, while working,
      244–45
  well-being and, 48
Integrative medicine, 211–12,
    231
Integrity, 253
Investing
  automatic, 110–13, 114, 123
  diversification and, 107–8,
      109
  expenses and, 110
  five rules of, 109–10
  garden metaphor for, 106–9
  key decisions for, 115
  real estate, 113–14
  rebalancing portfolio, 108,
      110, 112
  risk and, 108, 109–10
  saving vs., 105, 106

L

Leisure, 12–13, 15–17, 19
Life
  as a journey, 4, 47
  stages of, 12–16, 20–21, 64,
      174–76
Lifecycle funds, 112
Life Cycle Hypothesis, 34–35
Life expectancy
  age and, 42
  life span vs., 42
Life planning, 20
Lifestyle funds, 112
Lifestyle marketing, 66–67
Location. *See* Geography

M

Marketing, 63–67, 73–75, 78,
    86, 133. *See also* Retire-
    ment Hogwash
Marriage, 167–70, 171
Meaning
  happiness and, 128, 130, 151
  relationships and, 163, 165
Medical care
  access to, 209, 216–18
  aging and, 43
  conventional vs. alternative,
      205–8, 209, 210–12
  cost of, 42–43, 204, 208
  high- vs. low-intervention,
      212–13
  insurance, 203
  philosophy of, 208, 209,
      210–16
  relationships and, 209, 218
Medicare, 203–4

Modern portfolio theory,
109–10
Money. *See also* Prosperity;
Retirement income
budgeting, 96–97
effect of additional, 49–50
enough, 48–49
enthusiasm spectrum,
89–90, 121–22
geography and, 179
history of, 23
relationship with, 123
three boxes of, 24–25
Movement, 225, 226, 228–29
Moving. *See* Geography

N

NORCs (naturally occurring
retirement communities),
182
Number, calculating your,
44–45, 101–5

O

One Piece of Paper, 235–38. *See also*
Retirement Circles exercise

P

Pensions. *See* Employer pensions
PERKS
on autopilot, 94–95
components of, 91–94
managing, 116–18
after retirement, 120–21
Personality traits, 137
Pleasure
happiness and, 127, 128–29,
131

planning for, 132–34
relationships and, 162, 165
Positive Psychology, 126–27,
129, 153
Productivity, 12–13, 15–17, 18
Prosperity
as dimension of well-being,
51, 53, 54, 55
happiness vs., 61
Psycho-Social dimension of
well-being, 52–55

R

Real estate. *See also* Home
amortization and, 113
appreciation and, 114
as retirement pillar, 93, 121
Reciprocity, 158–59
Relationships
automatic generators of,
155–57
bonding vs. bridging, 158
building, 160–61, 163–67
convenience and, 155
examples of, 157–58
family, 167
geography and, 178
importance of, 158–59
marriage, 167–70, 171
with medical practitioners,
209, 218
resources on, 171
three levels of, 161–65
trust and reciprocity in,
158–59
Relaxation, 225, 226–27
Replacement ratios, 27–28, 41

About the Authors

Richard N. Bolles is the author of the best-selling job-hunting book in the world, *What Color Is Your Parachute?* He has been a leader and the #1 celebrity in the career development field for more than thirty years.

Richard was trained in chemical engineering at MIT; in physics at Harvard University, where he graduated cum laude; and in New Testament studies at the General Theological (Episcopal) Seminary in New York City, where he earned a master's degree. He is the recipient of two honorary doctorates, is a member of MENSA, and is listed in *Who's Who in America* and *Who's Who in the World*. He lives in the San Francisco Bay Area with his wife, Marci.

Visit www.JobHuntersBible.com.

John E. Nelson is a retirement planning researcher, writer, and speaker. His calling is to be a catalyst in the positive transformation of retirement life planning.

For many years, he consulted with organizations on the technical aspects of employer-sponsored retirement plans. Recognizing that the responsibility for retirement planning and preparation was shifting to the individual, he shifted his own focus to employee education and communication.

John is the creator of the Retirement Well-Being Model, which is being used by government, nonprofit, and corporate employers to provide a structure for their retirement education programs.

He is currently completing a Ph.D. in adult education, focusing on retirement education, at the University of Wisconsin-Madison. He earned a master's degree in adult education from Northern Illinois University and a bachelor's degree in business administration from Rockford College. He holds the Certified Retirement Counselor designation from the International Foundation for Retirement Education. He lives in the Madison, Wisconsin, area with his wife, Cheryl, and their sons, Erik, Sean, and Evan.

Visit www.RetirementWellBeing.com.

This Book Is Only the Beginning!

Go to **www.ParachuteRetirement.com** for:

- A free newsletter
- Audio clips
- Book reviews
- Completed exercise samples
- Frequently asked questions
- Readers' visions of their Ideal Retirement
- Web links to recommended sites and resources

Also, special tools for human resources, benefits, and retirement professionals; counselors and coaches; financial planners; health practitioners; realtors; and trainers and instructors. You'll find articles, worksheets, and other resources customized for your profession.

NOTES

Also available from the Parachute Library

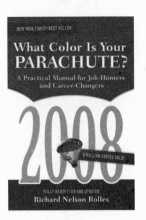
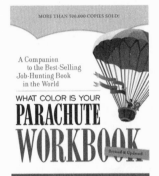